INSIGHTS

General Editor: Clive Bloom, Principal Lecturer in English, Middlesex University

Editorial Board: Clive Bloom, Brian Docherty, Gary Day, Lesley Bloom and Hazel Day

Insights brings to academics, students and general readers the very best contemporary criticism on neglected literary and cultural areas. It consists of anthologies, each containing original contributions by advanced scholars and experts. Each contribution concentrates on a study of a particular work, author or genre in its artistic, historical and cultural context.

Published titles

Clive Bloom (*editor*)
JACOBEAN POETRY AND PROSE: Rhetoric, Representation and the Popular Imagination
TWENTIETH-CENTURY SUSPENSE: The Thriller Comes of Age
SPY THRILLERS: From Buchan to le Carré

Clive Bloom, Brian Docherty, Jane Gibb and Keith Shand (*editors*)
NINETEENTH-CENTURY SUSPENSE: From Poe to Conan Doyle

Dennis Butts
STORIES AND SOCIETY: Children's Literature in a Social Context

Gary Day (*editor*)
READINGS IN POPULAR CULTURE: Trivial Pursuits?
THE BRITISH CRITICAL TRADITION: A Re-evaluation

Gary Day and Clive Bloom (*editors*)
PERSPECTIVES ON PORNOGRAPHY: Sexuality in Film and Literature

Brian Docherty (*editor*)
AMERICAN CRIME FICTION: Studies in the Genre
AMERICAN HORROR FICTION: From Brockden Brown to Stephen King
TWENTIETH-CENTURY EUROPEAN DRAMA

Rhys Garnett and R. J. Ellis (*editors*)
SCIENCE FICTION ROOTS AND BRANCHES: Contemporary Critical Approaches

Robert Giddings (*editor*)
LITERATURE AND IMPERIALISM

Robert Giddings, Keith Selby and Chris Wensley
SCREENING THE NOVEL: The Theory and Practice of Literary
  Dramatisation

Dorothy Goldman (*editor*)
WOMEN AND WORLD WAR 1: The Written Response

Paul Hyland and Neil Sammells (*editors*)
IRISH WRITING: Exile and Subversion

Maxim Jakubowski and Edward James (*editors*)
THE PROFESSION OF SCIENCE FICTION: Writers on their Craft
  and Ideas

Mark Lilly (*editor*)
LESBIAN AND GAY WRITING: An Anthology of Critical Essays

Christopher Mulvey and John Simons (*editors*)
NEW YORK: City as Text

Adrian Page (*editor*)
THE DEATH OF THE PLAYWRIGHT? Modern British Drama and
  Literary Theory

Frank Pearce and Michael Woodiwiss (*editors*)
GLOBAL CRIME CONNECTIONS: Dynamics and Control

John Simons
FROM MEDIEVAL TO MEDIEVALISM

Jeffrey Walsh and James Aulich (*editors*)
VIETNAM IMAGES: War and Representation

Gina Wisker (*editor*)
BLACK WOMEN'S WRITING

Twentieth-Century European Drama

Edited by

Brian Docherty

Tutor in Literature
Birkbeck College Centre for Extra-Mural Studies, London

First published 1994 by
THE MACMILLAN PRESS LTD
Houndmills, Basingstoke, Hampshire RG21 2XS
and London
Companies and representatives
throughout the world

ISBN 0–333–53284–8 hardcover
ISBN 0–333–53285–6 paperback

A catalogue record for this book is available
from the British Library.

Printed and bound in Great Britain by
Biddles Ltd, Guildford and King's Lynn

8   7   6   5   4   3
02 01 00 99 98

Series Standing Order

If you would like to receive future titles in this series as they are published, you can make use of our standing order facility. To place a standing order please contact your bookseller or, in case of difficulty,write to us at the address below with your name and address and the name of the series. Please state with which title you wish to begin your standing order. (If you live outside the United Kingdom we may not have the rights for your area, in which case we will forward your order to the publisher concerned.)

Customer Services Department, Macmillan Distribution Ltd
Houndmills, Basingstoke, Hampshire RG21 2XS, England

For Keith Shand
in memoriam

Contents

Notes on the Contributors

Alba Amoia was formerly Associate Professor of French and Italian, Hunter College of the City University of New York. She has written extensively on European drama, and her previous publications include *Jean Anouilh, Edmond Rostand, The Italian Theatre Today, Women on the Italian Literary Scene: A Panorama, Albert Camus* and *Thomas Mann's Fiorenza*.

Susan Bassnett is Professor of Comparative Literature, and Chairwoman of the Graduate School of Comparative Literary Theory and Literary Translation. Her publications include *Sylvia Plath* and *Shakespeare: The Elizabethan Plays*.

Lance St John Butler is a lecturer in English studies at the University of Stirling. His publications include *Samuel Beckett and the Meaning of Being* and *Rethinking Beckett* (editor, with Robin J. Davis).

Gary Day teaches English and drama in Brighton. He is editor of *Perspectives on Pornography* (with Clive Bloom), *Readings in Popular Culture* and *The British Critical Tradition*, all in the **Insights** series.

Brian Docherty is a tutor with the Birkbeck College Centre for Extra-Mural Studies. He is editor of *Nineteenth-Century Suspense* (with Clive Bloom, Jane Gibb and Keith Shand), *American Crime Fiction, American Horror Fiction, Twentieth-Century American Drama, American Modernist Poetry, Twentieth-Century British Poetry*, volumes 1 and 2, all in the **Insights** series, and *The Beat Writers*.

Michael J. Hayes is a lecturer at the University of Central Lancashire, and he has contributed to other titles in the **Insights** series.

Graham Holderness is Head of Drama, Roehampton Institute. He is editor of *Shakespeare's History Plays, The Politics of Theatre and Drama*, and has written *Shakespeare: The Play of History* and *Shakespeare: Out of Court* (both with Nick Potter and John Turner).

Roger Howard is a lecturer in drama at the University of Essex.

Bettina L. Knapp is Professor of Romance Languages and Comparative Literature at Hunter College, City University of New York. She has published many books including *Jean Genet: A Critical Study of his Writings, Antonin Artaud: Man of Vision, Paul Claudel, French Theatre 1918–39, Dream and Image, Offstage Voices, Women in Twentieth-Century Literature* and *Music, Archetype and the Writer*.

Peter Majer is a senior lecturer in theatre studies at Roehampton Institute and also works as an actor.

Angela Montgomery is a lecturer at Milan University in Italy.

Ronald Speirs is Professor of German at the University of Birmingham. He has published *Brecht's Early Plays, Bertolt Brecht* and *Thomas Mann: 'Mario und der Zauberer'*.

Claude Schumacher is Reader in Theatre Studies at the University of Glasgow, and editor of *Theatre Research International*.

Anna-Marie Taylor is a lecturer in drama at the University College of Wales, Aberystwyth.

1

Introduction: Thirteen Essays in Search of a Reader

BRIAN DOCHERTY

If we accept that modern drama in the broad sense began with the work of Ibsen, Strindberg and Chekhov, then we may equally say that twentieth-century drama begins with the work of Luigi Pirandello. To be over schematic about these matters and to reduce the history of theatre and drama across Europe for over one hundred years is of course absurd. This volume, however, does not pretend to be a survey of European drama but presents instead thirteen essays on some of the major figures having some claim to be significant or representative of the thousands of playwrights whose work has been performed or published this century. Europe has been taken to mean continental Europe, since Britain's relationship with 'the Continent' has been notoriously problematic, with cultural xenophobia being a popular sport with a large following. A companion volume in the *Insights* series, *The Death of the Playwright? Modern British Drama and Literary Theory*, edited by Adrian Page, discusses British drama from 1956 to the present, while *The Politics of Theatre and Drama*, edited by Graham Holderness, discusses a variety of British, European and Australian drama. Yet another volume in the *Insights* series, *Irish Writing: Exile and Subversion*, as the title suggests, covers various forms of writing in Ireland or by Irish writers.

Since Raymond Williams has discussed the work of Ibsen, Chekhov and Strindberg thoroughly in *Drama from Ibsen to Brecht*, to name only one major critic, there seems little need to rehearse the history of drama from Ibsen onwards.[1] Instead, we may move straight to Luigi Pirandello, a Sicilian born in 1867, who led the revolt against romantic drama in Italy, a movement with counter-

1

parts across Europe. According to Williams, this revolt was initiated in Italy by Luigi Chiarelli with his 1914 play *La Maschera e il
Volto* ('The Mask and the Face').[2] This play returns to the Italian
tradition of commedia dell'arte, which Pirandello also utilised,
particularly the emphasis on acting skills, and the potentially
subversive and chaotic technique of improvisation based on masks,
stock characters and stock phrases and gestures.

Pirandello's best-known work in Britain is probably *Six
Characters in Search of an Author*, the very title of which indicates the
extent of Pirandello's break with the past. However, Susan
Bassnett, in her essay on Pirandello, has chosen to focus on some of
his later work. She notes the narrowness of his reputation in the
English-speaking world, based on plays such as *Six Characters in
Search of an Author*, and *Henry IV*, written prior to 1925, and
Pirandello's brief period of international fame. The pre-1925 plays
offer strong roles for male actors, one reason at least perhaps for
their popularity with actors, directors and critics, while the women
in the plays tend to be passive, and portrayed in negative terms.
The later plays, by contrast, offer women the major roles, often
written specifically for Marta Abba. This essay offers a feminist
analysis of these plays without glossing over Pirandello's fascist
politics. Another Pirandello than the one that men in the theatrical
world have offered audiences is presented here.

Ronald Speirs's essay on Bertolt Brecht offers an outline of
Brecht's theory of theatre before examining the nature of the
relationship between theory and practice – always a crucial question for any Marxist. Although it is obviously not true simply to
claim that Marxism and fascism are mirror-images of each other,
both are contemptuous of bourgeois democracy and aim to trans-
form society by the most effective and thorough methods. (The
difference, I would argue in simple terms, is that socialism, of
which Marxism is only part, has an ethical base and a concept of
social responsibility while fascism is ethically deficient. The defi-
ciencies of Stalinism's perversion of Marxism need not be rehearsed
here.) The point at which we come nearly full circle is Brecht's
insistence that bourgeois society is rotten to the core and cannot be
reformed. Literary politicians of the Right, from Pirandello to Paul
Claudel, T. S. Eliot, Ezra Pound, D. H. Lawrence or W. B. Yeats,
would agree with the aim but not the means or the outcome. (I am
not claiming all of the writers named as fascists, especially
Lawrence and Yeats.) Fortunately, since these people were writers,

intellectuals, a species despised by Stalinists and fascists equally, practical politicians tended to laugh up their sleeve and then forget about them, as witnessed by the occasion Pound so misunderstood Mussolini's response to *The Cantos*.

Brecht sought in his writing and in his theatrical practice to bring about a fundamental change in his audience and in society as a whole – a revolutionary theatre in short. Some of the key terms in Brechtian theatre, such as 'epic theatre', *'Einfühlung'* (empathy), 'the theatre of the scientific age', and *'Verfremdungseffekt'* (the alienation effect), are defined by Ronald Speirs and related to specific moments in Brecht's plays. *Brecht on Theatre*, edited and translated by John Willett, should of course be read in conjunction with any discussion of Brecht, preferably *after* seeing the plays.

Roger Howard's essay on the Polish playwright Stanislaw Witkiewicz focuses on the work of a writer far less well known to the public than Brecht. Howard notes that Witkiewicz enjoyed comparatively little success in his lifetime, with only twelve out of forty plays enjoying productions in Poland. Most of his plays were written between 1918 and 1925, at the time of Pirandello's greatest popularity and when Brecht was writing his early works such as *Baal*. From 1928 to 1956, there was no professional productions in Poland, and the first foreign production was in San Francisco in 1967. The dates, of course, are significant, as a little thought will show. Howard notes that there are deep-seated problems of reception with the plays, and forecasts that Polish audiences of the 1990s, searching for an articulation of the search for alternatives to Stalinism, will be just as perplexed as audiences in 1956 after socialist realism was discredited. 'A theatre of death' is the term used to describe Witkiewicz's theatre, and Howard goes on to outline the political attitudes underlying the plays. Witkiewicz seems to have been hostile to almost every known ideology prevalent in the first half of this century. He is not, however, a prophet of doom; the catastrophe has already occurred. (He does, though, have a successor in Tadeusz Kantor.)

In his opposition to Realism and Naturalism, Witkiewicz is not such an isolated figure, since Artaud, Genet and Beckett, notably, share similar attitudes, however different the results may be in each case. Howard goes on to note that the theories underlying the plays may not have been fully implemented in all cases, since many features of realist drama appear to remain. From the audience's point of view, perhaps this is just as well. A restructuring or deformation of the dramatic text, with realistic elements retained for formal reasons, was his aim. Yet, in his own view, Witkiewicz was not avant-garde, a term he rejected. He was also quite clear what his fate would be under a totalitarian regime. In September 1939, the Nazis invaded Poland from the west, the Russians from the east. Caught between the two, he fled to the woods and committed suicide.

Another notable non- or anti-realist is discussed in Lance St John Butler's essay on Samuel Beckett. The theoretical perspective offered here is that of deconstruction, with Beckett positioned as an exemplary figure, the poet of the post-structuralist age. Beckett was James Joyce's amanuensis in Paris, and Butler reminds us that Beckett's early work of the late 1920s and 1930s is Modernist and formalist with a poetics derived from Joyce. He goes on to note that *Murphy* and *Watt*, the two novels written either side of the Second World War, go beyond Modernism, with the latter having resemblances to the work of William S. Burroughs (although Burroughs did not publish anything until *Junky* appeared, under the pseudonym of William Lee, in 1953 and was not well known before the publication of *Naked Lunch* and the subsequent 'obscenity trial'). Butler divides Beckett's writing career into two halves, with the 'classic' texts (such as *Waiting for Godot*) written between 1934 and 1961. He dates *Waiting for Godot* from 1948–9, contemporaneous with Book 1 of William Carlos Williams's *Paterson*, a bleak time when Europe was attempting to recover from the war but before the Cold War paranoia of the 1950s was fully manifested.

Beckett, of course, has been well served by Billie Whitelaw, who has made something of a speciality of interpreting his work on stage, and indeed it is difficult to imagine the plays, especially the later ones, without Whitelaw's persuasive and authoritative advocacy. Whether the late minimalist work such as *Quad* would even have been staged if submitted under another name than Samuel Beckett, we cannot tell, but it could be argued that seeing the later works staged is important, even essential, to an under-standing of *Waiting for Godot*. In some obvious senses Beckett's work is very far removed from the bourgeois realism of Ibsen, but watching Beckett or Ibsen today, or even the French circus, Archaos, provokes questions about the very meaning of terms such as 'dramatic' and 'theatrical'. Like Brecht, Beckett's work redefines these terms, and most others in the associated vocabulary: what do, say, *Hedda Gabler* and *Waiting for Godot* have in common?

Something more, or something different from mere entertainment, is offered, something more than a night out in the West End and a good dinner.

This sense of something other than entertainment is one of the first things on offer from Antonin Artaud, author of another widely known twentieth-century catchphrase, 'Theatre of Cruelty'. However much this expression may have been misunderstood, it seems clear that Artaud, like several of the other playwrights under discussion, was opposed to the practices of predecessors including Ibsen, Strindberg and Shaw, where recognisable characters spoke lines with a causal connection, where a well-made plot was played out in the usual three-walled living room. Like Brecht and Yeats in their very different ways, Artaud's interest was in ritual used for spiritual and religious reasons. (Although seeing communism as a species of substitute religion is perhaps being especially unfair to Brecht.) Artaud had no overt political aims, as did Brecht, but he did aim to give his audience a collective theatrical experience which would act as a catalyst on their thinking and alter their conception of 'reality'. Like Yeats, he reached back to some of the oldest theatrical resources, myths, symbols and precisely stylised gesture. His concept of the theatrical experience, however, was very different from that of Yeats, who used Irish legends and mythology, and the Japanese Noh theatre, to embody what he considered to be permanent or enduring personal and cultural values. Since Artaud was 'mad', the closeness of his interest in myth and in the irrational nature of our unconscious thoughts and drives, and his interest in Surrealism, similarly concerned with breaking the structures of rational bourgeois thought patterns, should not be surprising. Those of us able to pass ourselves off as 'normal' have no business being shocked or dismayed by the writing or acts of those whose inner (or outer) reality is 'different'. (It could be argued that the First World War made Breton's Surrealist Movement a redundant gesture, but Artaud broke with Breton after the Surrealists adopted Communism as their 'official' politics.) Artaud's *The Theatre and its Double*, along with the plays, defines his practices better than any brief paraphrase can.

Eugene Ionesco, countryman of Dadaist Tristan Tzara, employed similar strategies in his plays, dispensing controlled doses of the insanities and absurdities which surround us, as a sort of collective homeopathic medicine. His 'Theatre of the Absurd', like Artaud's 'Theatre of Cruelty', takes the opposite stance to Yeats's aestheticism. It is not a mimetic theatre, holding up the mirror to nature, or illustrating the belief of Ionesco, or of the philosopher of his choice, about the human condition. Instead, it is a series of provocations, shock therapy for a society which is a rotten and corrupt fraud. One thing Ionesco and Artaud have, with Nietzsche (the prophet of the irrational, but in general terms 'barking mad'), is a horror of psychological dishonesty. (As a term for attitudes which can produce two World Wars, dozens of 'minor' wars since, deliberately create and maintain mass unemployment, massive environmental destruction, and so on, this term seems too mild for the set of attitudes, beliefs and practices modern European playwrights have tried to deal with in their plays.)

Like Tzara, Ionesco uses seemingly irrational or non-rational types of language to shock us out of our complacencies and intellectual stupor. Expectations of 'meaning' are disrupted or parodied to show that the conventions regarding the social use of language are precisely that: conventions: Michael Hayes's essay employs linguistic theories to examine Ionesco's plays and their likely effects on an audience. As with any Surrealist project, the means are paradoxical but the aims are deadly serious. After we have laughed or been in shock, the next step is to ask '*Why?*' Asking questions is always the first step to social change.

Yet another sort of theatre is represented by the plays of Jean Anouilh, which are characterised by Alba Amoia as dominated by strong women, with men presented in fairly negative terms. This is not to say that Anouilh was a feminist; the concept of 'male feminists' is a notably dubious one. Indeed, any writing which idealises women, ascribing particular desirable or superior qualities to them, presumably would not be claimed by feminists as helpful to their projects. Nevertheless, Anouilh's plays make a change from the outright sexism and chauvinism exhibited by so many male writers. He uses subjects and well-known characters from history and mythology, such as Joan of Arc and Antigone, for his themes. Refusal of happiness and of mediocrity are characteristic gestures by his characters. Power games, money, codes of honour and accepted structures of society are rejected by his women. Most of his male characters are anti-heroes with few redeeming features, while the women remain true to themselves. He also makes a distinction Brecht would have approved of, the 'poor' race who produce heroines, and the 'rich' who are corrupt and decadent, with a family life that is rotten to the core. In this sense he is not too far away from a writer such as D. H. Lawrence, although Lawrence's views on the working classes are more ambivalent.

Questions of class relations and of real social relations between men and women, which occupied Brecht and Lawrence in different ways, also came to manifest themselves in the plays of Fernando Arrabal, the Moroccan born Spanish playwright whose relations with the Franco regime were difficult to the point of imprisonment in 1967. Arrabal is in some senses a successor to Beckett and Ionesco, although Claude Schumacher points out that Arrabal had never heard of these giants of the modern theatre when he started working as a dramatist. Direct influence must therefore be minimal, even allowing for the general influence of one generation on the next. One obvious difference is the question of traces of the author's presence in the work. Beckett's work is strikingly austere and impersonal, whereas Arrabal is very much present in his plays. Arrabal has rejected the label 'Absurdist', although in 1962 he created the 'panic movement' in conjunction with Alexander Jodorowsky and Topor, as a derisive gesture designed to attract maximum attention to his work at a time when the theatrical establishment in France was ignoring plays which were successful elsewhere. (It is curious how each generation of artists devises essentially the same strategies *pour épater le bourgeois*.)

Inevitably, Arrabal was jailed in Franco's Spain in 1967 (the 'Summer of Love' elsewhere) after inscribing a book proffered by an *agent provocateur*. After a campaign for his release, involving many well-known figures, he left Spain with a clearer and sharper political direction. He was involved in the Paris 'May Days' in 1968 and wrote overtly political dramas during and after this period. Another aspect of Arrabal's work which probably derives from the thinking of the Sixties is his willingness to allow directors to treat his plays as *pretexts* for theatrical performances. He does not stand over them to ensure that only the 'approved' text and setting, music and style of acting are presented to the audience.

Gary Day's essay considers the influence of Artaud on Jean Genet, and proceeds to an analysis of Genet's *The Maids*. He gives an account of Artaud's 'Theatre of Cruelty' as defined in *The Theatre and its Double*, pointing out some of the implicit contradictions in Artaud's writing. Day contends that Artaud's influence on Genet is less pervasive than is commonly thought, and that in fact *The Maids*, in particular, does not conform to Artaud's theories. *The Maids*, if described in terms of Artaud, turns out to be a typically

Western piece of theatre, dependent on a script being delivered accurately by the actors. The cruelties described and advocated by Solange and Claire have, according to Day, been misunderstood on a superficial level by critics who failed to realise that petty bourgeois violence was not what Artaud meant by 'Theatre of Cruelty'. Genet's interest in criminality has very little to do with Artaud's theories; although Artaud certainly wanted a theatre which would present everything, including love, crime, war and madness, Genet's aim would appear to be, at least in part, the offering of a cathartic experience to the audience. So this playwright, who still shocks many people by his modernity, offers the most traditional theatrical experience possible, a gesture which Greek writers and audiences would understand perfectly.

Graham Holderness, in his essay on Peter Weiss's play *Marat/ Sade*, as interpreted by Peter Brook and the Royal Shakespeare Company, makes the point that this one play by a major German dramatist is likely to be the only one at all familiar to potential theatre goers. Weiss produced major work for at least twenty years, and Holderness suggests that the sort of politically committed drama exemplified by Weiss is very different from the drama produced by British playwrights with a political interest or commitment. (These issues are explored in another volume in the Insights series, *The Politics of Theatre and Drama*, edited by Graham Holderness.) Weiss's Brechtian drama became something closer to Artaud in Peter Brook's hands, the sort of strategic appropriation which emphasises the importance of powerful directors in the modern theatre. In practice, this would tend to produce the opposite effect to that demanded by Brecht, and presumably expected by Weiss himself. Holderness points out that the conclusions drawn by the audience at the end of their experience could hardly have been those Weiss intended them to depart with. Whether Weiss will experience a revival of interest in his work in the post-Thatcher period is hard to tell.

If Peter Weiss has disappeared from public view, another playwright very much in the public eye is Václav Havel, now President of the Republic of Czechoslovakia. While Presidents have occasionally been pianists or poets, Havel is still sufficiently unusual for Shelley's well-known remark about poets being the unacknowledged legislators of their times to be capable of being read in various ironic ways. Havel, who sometimes seems uncomfortable in the role of President, nevertheless plays his part conscientiously. It will not be forgotten that Havel was in and out of prison, under house arrest and had his work banned by the Stalinist bureaucrats who formerly ran Czechoslovakia as a client state of the Soviet Union. (No prizes for suggesting that Boris Yeltsin would be better cast in Opera Buffo than as Russian President.) .

Peter Majer's essay places Havel, as both playwright and philosopher, in a native Czech tradition informed by the writing of T. G. Masaryk and Jan Patočka, among others. And of course, the ever present, if reticent, figure of Franz Kafka is never far away. Patočka, who died in 1977, was one of the main spokesmen of the Charter '77 movement, which Havel was also closely involved in. Patočka's interpretations of Heidegger were important as an element in the formation of Havel's thinking, especially the concept of Time. Havel, who in some senses is an Absurdist playwright, has a more concrete and less metaphysical understanding which manifests itself in his plays. If some of the practices of the Stalinist regime recall Kafka's work, Havel's plays show the ways in which individuals try to survive their encounters with a malignant and perverse bureaucracy where every home is a prison. Preservation of identity in a deformed social reality where repetition of meaningless banalities is the least dangerous procedure, is the concern of Havel's characters, stuck in a time capsule where there are no clocks. It is to be hoped that Havel's Czechoslovakia will flourish as a democratic state where people cannot be abused by the State or its agents, and that Havel as politician will carry out the promises inherent in his plays.

Anna-Marie Taylor's essay discusses the relationship between British drama and the German theatre, before going on to consider the reception of recent German drama in Britain. She points out that although Glasgow's Citizens Theatre, and Edinburgh's Traverse, have mounted productions of German playwrights such as Rolf Hochhuth, Manfred Karge, Franz Xavier Kroetz, and Fitzgerald Kusz, other British theatres have been less willing to put on German drama. This state of affairs is not peculiar to German drama, of course, since other contemporary European dramatists, with the exception of Dario Fo and Franca Rame, are similarly under-represented on our stages. Given the importance of Brecht for theatre in Britain since the Second World War, this lack of interest in either German drama as a whole or contemporary German work in particular is hard to account for. Taylor compares

Brecht, as a dominant influence on modern theatre, to Louis Armstrong or Charlie Parker in the world of Jazz, noting that, while these practitioners changed forever the way things are done, they are far enough in the past for current performers to underplay or even deny these influences. Taylor describes the possibility of seeing a contemporary German play as 'haphazard', although work by Lessing, Goethe, Hebbel and Schnitzler are staged. Why did theatres in the 1980s choose to produce eighteenth and nineteenth century German plays, rather than the work of, say, Durrermatt and Frisch?

Taylor notes that those dramatists who have been best received, such as Franz Xavier Kroetz, could be seen as having affinities with the work of Bond or Pinter, or even Osborne and Wesker. Whether the breakdown in cross-cultural relations between Britain and Germany in recent years is a peculiarity of the Thatcher era, a by-product of saturation by American mass culture, or due to hostility from metropolitan critics, is a complex question too large to be adequately debated here. The increased number of German plays in production recently is a belated response to changes in Eastern Europe, but it is too early to tell if this is mere opportunism or a positive development in literary–cultural relations with Germany. Perhaps a similar volume early next century will be able to answer these questions.

The work of Dario Fo and Franca Rame has met with more success in Britain over the last twenty years or so, although their plays were first performed in Italy in the 1950s. Angela Montgomery provides a short history of Dario Fo's and Franca Rame's respective backgrounds before going on to discuss the plays. As with Fernando Arrabal, there was a strong response to the 'May Days' in Paris, and to similar events in Italy in the autumn of 1969. Fo's and Rame's work can accordingly be divided into two periods, with 1968 as the watershed. As with Havel, Fo's theatre features the workings of a crippling and inhuman bureaucracy, although Fo and Rame are able to satirise Italian bureaucracy openly, since the farcical features of this bureaucracy are seen as a normal part of Italian life. Fortunately, although the Italian Communist Party (PCI) has enjoyed power in Italy on occasions, the distinctive style of Italian bureaucracy has not acquired the malevolent overtones of the various East European states now struggling to determine if there is life after Stalinism.

After 1969, Fo and Rame, in Italy at least, abandoned the commercial theatre, since they realised that bourgeois audiences could stand any amount of criticism or satire and still not be moved to change their lives or practices. Instead, Fo and Rame opted for an openly proletarian theatre, putting on performances in factories, town squares, schools, covered markets and other arenas where the working classes could be reached directly. Not so much theatre for the people as theatre from the people, since Fo and Rame developed new ways of presentation and audience involvement, along with public debate on the script, beforehand, as well as political debate of the general issues surrounding the play performed, afterwards. Perhaps inevitably, there was a split between their theatre company, Associazione Nuova Scena, and the PCI, after Fo and Rame criticised the PCI as insufficiently revolutionary. In 1970, another group was formed, opposed not only to bourgeois theatre, but also to what they saw as the revisionism of the PCI. British audiences will be familiar with productions of Fo's and Rame's work, including plays such as *Accidental Death of an Anarchist*, and *Can't Pay? Won't Pay!*, which have been used to support political campaigns over here. I would hope that they are also familiar with the populist feminism which informs Franca Rame's work, and with the later plays, which provide strong platforms for Rame to engage with her audience on those questions which are important to her as a feminist.

Montgomery's conclusion points out that, although society (and therefore audiences?) is increasingly consumerist and apathetic, their plays remain successful, and their commitment to the class struggle and to the process of radical social change remains undiminished. I have no doubt that Fo and Rame would argue that those who claim communism is dead, or socialism is finished, are liars and stupid reactionaries. They would probably point out that the need for their type of theatre, aimed at provoking ordinary people into action on behalf of their own objective class interests, is nowhere greater than in the various former client states of the Soviet Union, and in the various new republics run by Boris Yeltsin et al.

It would be presumptious to make generalisations about the state of the theatre, or its future; playwrights, actors, directors, critics, can do that for themselves if they wish. In a debate on the current state of poetry, Leo Aylen remarks: 'a theatre lawyer friend, continuing his father's business, claims that every year for two generations someone has pronounced "The theatre is dying"'.[3] Aylen's point, I think, is that poetry, like theatre, will survive despite mumblings of doom and gloom from some quarters. Some of us may not accept Aylen's dismissal of Freud and Marx as 'fashionable lunacies', but his general point that the avant-garde will always be a minority whose strategies may turn out to have been misguided may have some validity. However, 'popular' or 'mainstream' theatre will also change, perhaps by smuggling in elements of Brecht or Artaud by the stage door. According to the listings magazines in London, it is possible to see plays by Fo and Rame, Anouilh, Chekhov, Feydeau, Pirandello, Lorca, as well as Shaw, Ayckbourn, Brian Friel, Mamet, as well as *'Allo 'Allo*, and Lloyd Webber's *The Phantom of the Opera*. Whether Fo and Rame draw the audiences that *'Allo 'Allo* does, may or may not tell us something about either audience taste in the early 1990s or the 'state of the theatre', but at least in London, at any rate, a range of theatrical experience is available for those with the money and inclination to go to the theatre.

NOTES

1. See Raymond Williams's comments in *Politics and Letters* (London: New Left Books, 1979) pp. 189–234, for his later, and revised, views.
2. Raymond Williams, *Drama from Ibsen to Brecht* (Harmondsworth: Penguin, 1968) p. 176.
3. Leo Aylen, *Poetry Review*, vol. 81, no. 4 (Winter 1991/92) p. 47

2

Female Masks: Luigi Pirandello's Plays for Women

SUSAN BASSNETT

In *Six Characters in Search of an Author*, the Father protests that he is 'hanging in chains, fixed for all eternity' in the image that the Step-daughter has of him.[1] This notion of a person being 'fixed' by the gaze of another, forced to assume a mask and unable ever to be free of the roles that other people impose, was central to Pirandello's prose works and to his plays throughout his life. In his *Essay on Humour* (1908), that set out the basis of his vision of the world and of the relationship between art and life, Pirandello wrote that:

> The more difficult the struggle for life, and the more conscious we become of our own ineffectualness in the struggle, then the need for a universal stratagem of mutual deception becomes that much the greater. The feigning of strength, honesty, sympathy and prudence...of every virtue which seems to have a quality of greatness and truth about it, is merely our way of adjusting and adapting ourselves to the compromise of life...the humourist is quick to seize on these various pretences...he finds it amusing to tear off our masks.[2]

Pirandello would doubtless have found it both ironic and yet unavoidable that in the years since his death in 1936 he has come to be seen as the playwright of the twentieth century most renowned for the 'cerebral' quality of his drama. He is variously described as a'philosopher' or as an 'intellectual', and a great many critics and reviewers have found it convenient to use one or other of these labels in assessing his work, often accusing him of writing to a formula. He might also have smiled wryly at the fact that in the

English-speaking world he is even more narrowly defined and labelled, for most of the plays he wrote after the mid-1920s are barely known. His reputation seems to be based on *Six Characters in Search of an Author* and *Henry IV*, along with three or four others, all of which belong to the period prior to 1925, when Pirandello enjoyed a temporary phase of being a major international celebrity.

Another important point that is frequently overlooked, especially by the English-speaking world, is Pirandello's steady move into practical theatre. There have been very few studies of his work as director and founder of the Teatro d'Arte in Rome in the mid-twenties, and until very recently this crucial stage in his career was rarely discussed.[3] Pirandello was always regarded as a playwright, on the strength of statements he made about the central role of the writer and on those plays that entered the international repertoire. Yet the story of Pirandello's career as a dramatist is intimately linked to his increased interest in theatre practice, from the early experiments with Nino Martoglio and dialect theatre, in 1910, to the establishment of his own theatre, with his own company, in 1925. The collapse of that company in 1928, after three years of intensive touring, was a blow from which he never fully recovered, and his failure to break into the cinema and make a new career for himself in the late 1920s also added to his bitterness and sense of injustice.

For the purposes of this essay, I have divided Pirandello's plays into two groups – those written prior to the founding of his company in 1925 and those written afterwards. The hinge play, that marks the transition, is *The Festival of Our Lord of the Ship* (*La sagra del Signore della nave*), a one-act piece for a very large cast, that was written for the opening night of the new theatre and performed together with an Italian translation of Alfred, Lord Dunsany's *The Gods of the Mountain*.[4]

What characterises a substantial number of the plays written after 1925 is the stress on big roles for women, which was due to Pirandello's collaboration with the young actress Marta Abba. Leonardo Bragaglia has pointed out that Pirandello's female characters tended to be characterised by their passivity,[5] and even the most cursory glance through many of his plays prior to 1925 reveals a series of tormented, crushed, unhappy women, unable to fight back against the fate that has so cruelly condemned them to suffer. The Marta Abba plays, on the other hand, offer a different image of woman, and although the female protagonists do not avoid pain, they nevertheless fight against it. La Spera, central character of *The New Colony* (*La nouva colonia*, 1928), is, with her baby, the only person left alive after the final destruction, a symbol of hope and of new order; Cia, in *As You Desire Me* (*Come tu mi vuoi*, 1930), chooses the hard way forward in her demand for absolute honesty, as does Donata, in *Finding Oneself* (*Trovarsi*, 1932)[6] and Ilse, in *The Mountain Giants* (*I giganti della montagna*; posthumous production 1937), while Verroccia, in *When One is Somebody* (*Quando si è qualcuno*, 1933), is the symbol of youth, energy and integrity, the very opposite of the values that the writer ∗∗∗ finally espouses (this play is significantly autobiographical, and deals with the conflicting world vision of a famous, ageing author and a young, vital woman).

Pirandello had, of course, frequently written plays for specific actors, though usually for men. (It may be that one of the reasons why plays such as *The Rules of the Game* (*Il giuoco delle parti*, 1918) and *Henry IV* (1922) are so frequently revived in English by star actors is because such plays offer strong male roles.) He had also written parts for actresses, though interestingly, and for reasons never made quite clear, the greatest of them all, Eleonora Duse, refused to appear in the role he created for her in *The Life I Gave You* (*La vita che ti diedi*, 1923), her place being taken instead by Alda Borelli. There are various hypotheses as to why Duse refused the role of the bereaved mother who tries to delude herself that her son is still alive, and she herself professed to be scandalised by its intrusion into what she perceived as intimate feelings. It is likely that her reaction was due to an aspect of Pirandello's treatment of women in the early plays that has not been much discussed – an uneasiness that manifested itself in a variety of ways, from what, today, would be termed overt sexism to voyeuristic misogyny.

I have commented elsewhere on *Liolà* (1916), the play a number of eminent male critics have described as one of Pirandello's most joyous, celebratory comedies.[7] It seems to me to be distastefully misogynistic, and to demonstrate not so much a love of life as a hatred of women. Liolà, the Pan-figure who seduces women, makes them pregnant and then gives his children to his mother to be brought up, is a male fantasy figure who categorises women according to the narrowest of frameworks. Other critics have noted the emphasis on female infidelity in Pirandello's works, on women as deceitful, jealous or simply inadequate. The two women in *Six Characters in Search of an Author*, the Mother and the Stepdaughter, are examples of unsympathetic female characters, as are Matilde and her daughter Frida in *Henry IV*. The wretched Ersilia Drei, in *To Clothe the Naked* (*Vestire gl'ignudi*, 1922), is stripped bare of her pathetic illusions of love and dignity, in a play whose title plainly indicates the voyeuristic nature of the content.

Two almost unknown fragments of texts by Pirandello shed some light on his attitude to women, on his uneasiness and ambiguous feelings, that cannot simply be explained away, as some critics have tried, by arguing that he was typical of Sicilian males or that his unhappy marriage had soured his views. The first is a fragment that was published in 1934, possibly part of an unwritten novel and probably dating from before the Great War. It consists of a short description of a man going to Madame Pace's establishment, overwhelmed by a sense of shame and yet, 'contrary to the impression he must have given of being an ageing man, he could feel that grotesque, shameless desire shrieking within him'. Pirandello describes the man's feelings as he walks through the streets and then climbs the stairs to the brothel, and then abruptly breaks off the narrative, commenting in another voice:

> What is quite funny really is that they left me and started acting out the scenes of the novel amongst themselves, just as they ought to be acted. They performed in front of me, but as though I were not there, as though they did not depend on me, as though I could not stop them at all.
>
> The girl more than anyone. I see her come in…she is a perfect reality created by me, but who simply cannot involve me, even though I can feel the deep pity she arouses.[8]

This identification with the man, who then becomes the Father in *Six Characters*, is set in opposition to his alienation from the girl, (the Stepdaughter). Pirandello has created a scenario in which he has associated himself with the Father and disassociated himself with the female character, the girl who is paid to satisfy the man's sexual urges that he so despises in himself.

The second text is also a fragment, dating from 1909 and entitled 'Feminism'.[9] It is a bizarre piece, written in the form of a short story, which describes an encounter between the narrator and Dr. Paolo Post. The narrator declares his willingness to discuss contemporary issues, 'such as feminism, for example', at which point 'a guttural, masculine voice' speaks from behind a pile of papers and a hideously ugly woman, Dr Post's second daughter, appears.

She is a self-declared feminist, offended by her father's anti-feminism, but when Dr Post explains at length to the narrator that in his view 'the ideal structures of feminism will disintegrate' once a woman has the chance of marriage, the narrator realises that the age-old process of a man trying to find a husband for an ugly daughter is taking place, and runs away.

The piece is distasteful both in its attack on feminism (the old, 'all-feminists-are-too-ugly-to-get-themselves-a-man' line) and its attack on women in general. The father of the story is profoundly uneasy with his daughter, while the narrator is panic-stricken. Taken together, what these two fragments show is Pirandello's inability to relate to women, his admitted lack of empathy, his suspicion, distance and even hostility. What a woman wants, he seems to be saying, is a man – either one who will pay for her sexual favours, or one who will pay for her in marriage. It is a bleak vision, and one in which feminine virtues appear to be entirely absent, but it is also a vision that derives from a particular ideological position.

Writing about fascist concepts of womanhood, Maria-Antonietta Macciocchi says:

> The body of fascist discourse is rigorously chaste, pure, virginal. Its central aim is the death of sexuality: women are always called to the cemetery to honour the war dead, to come bearing them crowns, and they are exhorted to offer their sons to the fatherland. The language of Mussolini is overwhelming, but it succeeds in charming, in possessing the women who, at least for a moment, are caught between childbirth and the last supreme sacrifice.[10]

Pirandello's espousal of the fascist cause in the most public way in 1924 has presented subsequent generations of readers with a problem. He chose to declare his support for Mussolini just after the brutal murder of the Socialist deputy Matteotti in 1924, and, although he later left Italy for a time and moved to Germany, he returned in the 1930s and in 1935 gave a speech in Mussolini's presence appealing for world understanding of the Italian invasion of Ethiopia. However we look at it, Pirandello did publicly support the dictatorship, and, however disillusioned he may have felt later, that disillusionment seems to have had more to do with the failure of his theatre company than with his opposition to fascism. Moreover, in his treatment of women his ideological stance is clearly apparent: Mussolini called upon Italian women to contribute their gold wedding rings to the party cause, symbolically uniting them to him with replacement iron rings, thereby becoming what Macciocchi terms their Mystic Bridegroom, while Pirandello, the disillusioned husband, punishes women by depicting them as whores, adulteresses or mad, and invites us to join him in spying on their anguish through the two-way mirror of the stage.

The plays created for Marta Abba, however, appear to offer an alternative perspective to Pirandello's bleak vision, though two of his later pieces, *A Dream, But Perhaps It Isn't* (*Sogno, ma forse no*, 1931) and *You Don't Know How* (*Non si sa come*, 1934)[11] return to the older model and again depict women in very negative terms. Those letters that are available from him to her (and a larger collection will be appearing at some point in the 1990s) show that he cared a great deal about her negative opinions of some of his plays, and wanted to create parts for her that would go beyond the crushed, fallen women of so many of his works. Writing to her about *The Wives' Friend* (*L'amica delle mogli*, 1927) he says: 'What you really need is will power, will power, will power. I shall imbue you with it, through my own.'[12] Part of the process of creating new women for Marta Abba to play involved showing her in a favourable light against other, less favourably depicted women. In the three plays discussed here, *The Wives Friend*, *As You Desire Me*, and *Finding Oneself*, that feature is very apparent. The Abba role stands out, it is a big part and a part that enables her to appear as special, an exceptional, we might even say ideal, woman among her own kind.

The female protagonist of these three plays is, in common with the Pirandellian world-view, trapped by circumstances: Marta Tolosani, the protagonist of *The Wives' Friend* (and the name Marta is common both to the character and to the actress representing her) is trapped by social convention; The Unknown Woman in *As You Desire Me* is trapped by the past; while Donata Genzi, in *Finding Oneself*, is trapped by the life she has chosen to lead as an actress. None of the women escape to happiness, though all are granted a glimpse of it during the course of the play, and the contrast between what they know they might have had and what they are forced to accept allows ample scope for Pirandello's irony. The three figures take on the tragic status that he generally accords his male characters.

In 1926 Pirandello directed Ibsen's *Lady from the Sea*, with Marta Abba in the role of Ellida Wangel. This play was well-known in Italy, having been a vehicle for the talents of Eleonora Duse, who had chosen it for her return to the theatre in 1921 after more than a decade away. Marta Abba's portrayal of Ellida Wangel was a success, although her portrayal of Hedda Gabler two years later, in the only other Ibsen production directed by Pirandello, was not. In an essay that examines Pirandello's repertoire as director, Claudio Vicentini discusses his version of the *The Lady from the Sea*, noting the close parallels between this play and *Finding Oneself*, written in 1931–2. He points out that the choice of the play in which the great Duse had excelled served as a means of highlighting Marta Abba as a rising star, as the Duse of the new generation, and that when Pirandello came to write his own play, constructed around the figure of a great actress,

> that figure is in fact Marta Abba, to whom *Trovarsi* is dedicated, transformed into Eleonora Duse, that is, in her superb portrayal of the *Lady from the Sea*, from which *Trovarsi* borrows themes and other details. …Through a network of thematic echoes, *Trovarsi* recalls *The Lady from the Sea*, and through the leading character, the great actress, Donata Genzi, Pirandello endeavours to bestow upon Marta Abba all the theatrical gifts belonging to Duse…Donata Genzi is, quite simply, Marta Abba seen as Eleonora Duse.[13]

The Lady from the Sea was obviously a crucial production for both Marta Abba and Pirandello. A letter from him to her gives some hint of the conscious and unconscious processes at work:

> Yes, your probing into the part of Ellida is correct. There can be no doubt that her desire for liberty is desire for love. Her husband is old; the vast sea ever changing. The waves roll back upon themselves, break loudly and then flow back giddily, to turn over endlessly. I never understood the sea so well, I who carry so many of its vortex waves in my soul – ever changing! And I 'feel' poor Ellida in exactly the way you do. Make her live as though the roar of the sea were echoing through her.[14]

Later in the same letter he writes 'but now I have become completely absorbed in *L'amica delle mogli*'. Vicentini draws attention to the parallels between Ibsen's play and *Finding Oneself*, but there are also links with *The Wives' Friend*. It is speculation, but not without cause, that Pirandello was helped in his search for new female parts for Marta Abba, for a new, less degraded image of woman, by Ibsen – not the feminist Ibsen of *A Doll's House*, but the more lyrical Ibsen who spoke in a language that the ageing Pirandello (he was 58 when he began his directing career) could understand.

The Marta Abba plays all revolve around questions of idealism and femininity. In the first play he wrote for her, *Diana and Tuda* (1926), that ideal is physical – Tuda is the beautiful model of the sculptor Sirio Dossi, who proposes a loveless marriage so that he can possess her completely and prevent her from modelling for anyone else. When the man who genuinely loves her kills the artist in a fit of jealousy, Tuda declares that now he is dead, and so unable to complete the great work that would have immortalised her, she is reduced to nothing. In *The New Colony*, the ideal is motherhood that can triumph over all evil, and, in *When One is Somebody*, the ideal is youth and honesty, personified by Veroccia. The end of this play is an ironic reversal of the end of *Diana and Tuda*, for the great nameless writer *** becomes a statue of himself, turned to stone because he did not have the courage to seize the opportunity of a new, honest life offered by the young woman who loves him.

The Wives' Friend is a curious play, in that the story-line offers a character who is an ideal woman in every respect – she is an ideal daughter, an ideal image onto which men project their fantasies, and an ideal friend to other women. Marta Tolosani is the only single woman in a circle of married couples; she is friend to all the wives and has helped them all to come together, even though the men have all at one time been in love with her. The crisis in the play comes when the repressed feelings of two of the men begin to emerge – they are both in love with Marta, and she, it appears, is in love with one of them too. When Elena, the wife of Fausto dies, Francesco kills him and makes it look like suicide, because he cannot bear to think of Marta marrying anyone. The play ends with Marta, who knows the truth about the murder, screaming at everyone to leave her alone.

The play was well received when it was first performed, but has not been very frequently revived. There was one major revival, in 1968, by the Rosella Falk–Giorgio de Lullo company. A significant feature of that production was the way in which it brought out the patterns of repression running through the play. Pirandello's early plays may have focused more on the secret life of ageing men, but what Rosella Falk did with the role of Marta was to hint at a subtext that concerned the secret life of a woman. The character of Marta is problematic for an actress; she is supposedly so perfect, and yet that perfection is articulated in petit-bourgeois terms – Marta teaches other women how to do their hair, how to attract and keep their men, she is always beautifully dressed, she restrains herself and holds back from expressing her feelings. Yet those feelings exist – passion for Fausto, rage against Venzi, contempt for her female friends. What Rosella Falk did was to draw out a set of inferences from the role of Marta, interpreting her refusal to marry, her patronising female friendships and demand to be alone as evidence of suppressed lesbianism. This reading of the play, which worked well in performance, created a powerful set of tensions in what would otherwise have been a very bland piece, so bland, in fact, that some of the reviewers of the first production declared that Pirandello appeared to have lost his Pirandellian touch.

Rosella Falk's interpretation of Marta Tolosani becomes even more interesting when we consider the extraordinary use of lesbian sexuality in *As You Desire Me*. The character of Mop, daughter of The Unknown Woman's brutal German lover Salter, is described as having her hair cut short like a boy's and with a face that has 'something ambiguous and repulsive about it, together with a trace of something tragic which is deeply disturbing'.[15] Mop is also in love with the Unknown Woman, who throughout the first act keeps hinting at sexual perversions between herself, father and daughter. Lesbian sexuality, as a sign, is in this play representative of corruption and decay, but the way in which Pirandello presents it to us is more titillatory than condemnatory. In an unusual recent production, Susan Sontag directed the play in Turin in the 1980–1 season, and stressed the voyeuristic elements in Pirandello's text by making Mop appear more feminine, with long hair, and giving the Unknown Woman a shaven head under a wig. Sontag's production was very controversial, but significantly it chose to focus on the sign system of lesbianism running through the play, whereas the 1932 film version, with Greta Garbo, omitted the character of Mop altogether.

Another form of perversion runs as a subtext through *Finding Oneself*. Donata Genzi falls in love with the young Swedish sailor, Elj Nielsen, who loves her for herself, not for her fame. But the relationship founders when Donata returns to the stage, for Elj cannot cope with Donata being possessed by her audiences, he feels ashamed, as though their love were defiled by her representations of passion on a stage. Donata refuses to give up her life as an actress, and the play ends with her alone, reflecting that the only truth she will ever find is in her creativity. The play contains echoes of Eleonora Duse that are additional to the ones pointed out by Vicentini: the autobiographical novel, *Il fuoco*, by Duse's lover Gabriele D'Annunzio, dwells at length on the erotic stimulation that the herò gets from dwelling on the way in which his lover is 'possessed' by her audiences when she performs. There are long passages in the novel detailing how the hero is aroused by his fantasies about the actress, and in fact the novel was based on transcripts of intimate conversations between Duse and D'Annunzio, a betrayal of confidence that led to the disintegration of their relationship.[16] Again there is a voyeuristic element, and audiences who saw Marta Abba as a reincarnated Duse, in the role of Donata Genzi, may well have recalled D'Annunzio's depiction of the erotic relationship between public and performer.

There can be no doubt that Pirandello tried to rethink some of his assumptions about roles for women when writing for Marta Abba. Her roles are different; her characters are stronger, more combative, more lyrical than most other Pirandellian females, and they invite sympathy rather than pity or contempt. Of course Abba also played some of the roles he wrote before he met her, and the repertoire of the Teatro d'arte was very varied indeed, but, in creating parts especially for her, he seems to have started an exploration of aspects of the feminine that he had hitherto ignored.

Biographers will continue to speculate on whether the relationship between Marta Abba and Pirandello was purely professional, but that is of no concern here. What is important is that she provided him with the material excuse to explore new territory, and through his explorations he created some very good female roles that deserve to be much better known. Nevertheless, he did not undergo some kind of mystic conversion; his ambiguous sexual and social attitudes to women, his suspicion of feminism, his misogyny and his ideological stance continued to shape his plays. The voyeurism of the Father in *Six Characters in Search of an Author* continues in another form, through his superficial interest in lesbian sexuality, in relationships between women, in the possession of the actress by the crowd. In his last play, the unfinished *The Mountain*

Giants, that actress was torn to pieces by the audience for daring to challenge their demands and, although Marta Abba did not appear in the role of Ilse, the character is clearly related to the female figures he created especially for her.

A striking feature of Pirandello's career was his willingness to learn. He kept changing his ideas about the theatre, moving from the hostility expressed in an essay of 1899 to the celebratory in his address to the Volta Congress in 1934. He began as a writer and moved into theatre practice, learning about the craft of the actor and skills required of a director. He rewrote *Six Characters* after seeing Pitöeff's 1923, Paris production of the play; he constantly reshaped material used in short stories or novels into plays; he wrote parts for specific actors; he tried his hand at different forms of theatre; he revised and reutilised component parts of other texts (for example, *The Mountain Giants* is linked both to his own fable, *The Changeling*, and to the play by Dunsany that he chose for the opening night of the Teatro d'arte). When he began to work with Marta Abba, he seems to have struck a balance between using her as a vehicle for his world-view and trying his hand at writing a new kind of part for an actress. Their collaboration came at a crucial moment, at the point where Pirandello had the possibility and the means of both writing and realising his plays on a stage.

Pirandello's later plays deserve more recognition than they have received. The strong male roles of many of his earlier plays have ensured their more frequent revival, but the later plays are characterised by a growing interest in Expressionism, together with his experiments with female roles, and, perhaps for a combination of these and other reasons, have received less attention. A number of critics have dismissed many of the plays written after 1925 as inferior, suggesting that Pirandello was moving towards the creation of a mythic theatre, and they point to the lack of commercial success as evidence of impoverished writing. I would dispute such claims, for, on the contrary, it seems to me that many of those plays, particularly the ones written for Marta Abba, offer an outstanding range of challenging parts for women that deserve further exploration. To stress the strengths of his theatre-in-the-theatre trilogy, while neglecting *Finding Oneself* or *The New Colony*, is perverse. There is another Pirandello waiting for a new generation to go out and find him.

NOTES

1. Luigi Pirandello, *Six Characters in Search of an Author*, trans. John Linstrum (London: Methuen, 1979).
2. Luigi Pirandello, *Essay on Humour* (*L'umorismo*), trans. Jim O'Malley as *The Art of the Humorist*, *Atlantis*, nos 2 and 3 (1969).
3. See Richard Sogliuzzo, in *Luigi Pirandello, Director: The Playwright in the Theatre* (Metuchen, NJ: Scarecrow Press, 1982); also Alessandro d'Amico and Alessandro Tinterri, *Pirandello capocomico* (Palermo: Sellerio editore, 1988).
4. For a discussion of the two productions of the opening night, see Susan Bassnett, 'Pirandello's Debut as Director: The Opening of the Teatro d'Arte', *New Theatre Quarterly*, vol. III no. 12 (Nov. 1987) pp. 349–52, and Alessandro Tinterri, '*The Gods of the Mountain* at the Odescalchi Theatre', *New Theatre Quarterly*, vol. III, no. 12 (Nov. 1987) pp. 352–8.
5. See Leonardo Bragaglia, *Interpreti Pirandelliani* (Rome: Trevi, 1969).
6. *Trovarsi* is generally referred to as *Finding Oneself*, though the English-language première on BBC Radio 3, 30 June 1987, in a translation by Susan Bassnett and David Hirst, was entitled *A Woman in Search of Herself*.
7. See Susan Bassnett, *Luigi Pirandello* (London: Macmillan, 1983) and for the opposite position, see Eric Bentley, '*Liolà* and Other Plays', reprinted in Eric Bentley, *The Pirandello Commentaries* (Evanston, Ill.: Northwestern University Press, 1986).
8. Luigi Pirandello, 'Foglietti', first published in *Nuova antologia*, Jan. 1934, reprinted in Pirandello, *Saggi, poesie, e scritti varii*, ed. Manlio lo Vecchio-Musti (Milan: Mondadori, 1965).
9. Luigi Pirandello, 'Feminismo' appeared in *La Preparazione*, no. 12, 27–8 Feb. 1909. There is an English version, trans. Susan Bassnett, in *The Yearbook of the British Pirandello Society*, nos 8 and 9, 1988–9, pp. 102–7, and an essay on the fragment by Maggie Günsberg, 'Parla pure, Papà: non ti sento', pp. 91–102.
10. Maria-Antonietta Macciocchi, 'Female Sexuality in Fascist Ideology', *Feminist Review*, 1 (1979) pp. 57–83.
11. For a detailed discussion of *You Don't Know How* from a variety of perspectives, see Tim Fitzpatrick (ed.), *Altro Polo: Performance: From Product to Process* (Frederick May Foundation for Italian Studies, University of Sydney, 1989). In the Sydney production the English title was *A Fault Line*.
12. Luigi Pirandello, letter to Marta Abba, cited in her introduction to her translation of three plays, '*The Mountain Giants' and Other Plays* (New York: Crown, 1958).
13. Claudio Vicentini, 'Il repertorio di Pirandello capocomico e l'ultima stagione della sua drammaturgia', in *Pirandello e la drammaturgia tra le due guerre* (Agrigento: Centro nazionale di studi pirandelliani, 1985) pp. 79–98.
14. Pirandello, letter to Marta Abba, op. cit.

15. Luigi Pirandello, *As You Desire Me*, unpublished English version by Susan Bassnett and David Hirst.
16. English version of Gabriele D'Annunzio, *Il fuoco*, trans. Susan Bassnett (London: Quartet Books, 1992).

3

The Theatre of Bertolt Brecht: Theory and Practice

RONALD SPEIRS

Brecht's theory and practice of theatre changed considerably during his career. In particular, once he had adopted a Marxist view of society (towards the end of the 1920s) Brecht began to develop a conception of theatre that would propagate that view of society and thus help to bring about fundamental social change. This essay will first outline the main principles of Brecht's theory before going on to examine the relationship between his declared intentions and his practice as a writer and producer of plays.

Brecht argued for a completely new type of theatre on the grounds that this was demanded by certain large-scale historical changes:

> The old form of drama does not make it possible to represent the world as we see it today.
> What we nowadays regard as the typical course of a man's fate cannot be shown in the current dramatic form.[1]

By this Brecht meant both that the world had changed, and was still in the process of changing, objectively, and that this was accompanied by a process of subjective change in the way men looked at the world.

The 'objective' change Brecht had in mind was the historical transition from the age of bourgeois capitalism to a socialist, and ultimately communist, society in which ownership of the means of production would be in the hands of the working class. According to Marxist theory, such a change in the economic 'base' of society was necessarily accompanied by changes in its ideological 'superstructure', to which such institutions as the theatre belonged. Because the bourgeois-capitalist epoch was one founded on

26

individual enterprise, so Brecht argued,[2] the drama of that age had focused attention on the individual, particularly on the 'great' or problematic individual, and the theatre had presented the conduct of these individuals in such a way as to invite the spectator to identify with the experiences of the central character or characters in the play. This act of identification or 'empathy' was, in Brecht's view, primarily an emotional act; the German translation of 'empathy' as '*Einfühlung*' puts the emphasis where Brecht believed it ought to be put. The new historical age which was in the process of emerging was, by contrast, an age of the collective, one in which the individual would no longer have the social (that is to say, economic and political) importance he once had. The dramatic form suitable to the depiction of the new historical reality would have to be one which reflected the individual's loss of importance, a form which would be capable of giving theatrical expression to the collective and impersonal forces now shaping the course of history:

> Simply to comprehend the new areas of subject-matter imposes a new dramatic and theatrical form. Can we speak of money in the form of iambics? 'The Mark, first quoted yesterday at 50 dollars, now beyond 100, soon may rise etc.' – how about that? Petroleum resists the five-act form; today's catastrophes do not progress in a straight line but in cyclical crises. The 'heroes' change with the different phases, are interchangeable etc. ...Even to dramatize a simple press-report one needs something much more than the dramatic technique of a Hebbel or an Ibsen.[3]

The subjective historical change which, in Brecht's view, made the creation of a new type of theatre necessary was the advent of the 'age of science' – 'das wissenschaftliche Zeitalter'.[4] On the one hand, Brecht understood by this term the growing importance of the natural sciences for man's understanding and exploitation of the material world (as in the example of petroleum, cited above). He also meant by it the relatively recent application of scientific methods to the study of human behaviour and the historical development of society. In Brecht's view, the 'classic' examples of this new science of man were the writings of Marx and Engels. He believed that their historical–materialist analysis of society was in the process of becoming *the* modern way of looking at the world. Thus, the modern theatre, Brecht argued, must expect that the audience will view its representations of life with the 'cool investigative eye' of the scientific mind. The proper function of the theatre nowadays was not to invite the spectator to share the emotions of the historically no longer relevant 'great individual', but rather, to develop in the audience the ability to analyse general social phenomena rationally and in the light of the spectator's self-interest as a member of a particular class in society.

Brecht's conception of 'the theatre of the scientific age' meant relating both the subject-matter and the techniques of drama to a number of central tenets of Marxist theory. Human behaviour was to be presented not as the consequence of unchanging passions but as a 'variable of the milieu', following the Marxist axiom that 'social being determines thought' (*BT*, p. 37).[5] The social processes shaping the attitudes of individuals and groups were to be shown as arising from large-scale historical developments, and the contradictions in people's lives were to be related to the funda-mental contradictions in class society. To give but one striking illustration, the entire plot of *The Good Person of Szechwan*, in which the consequences of a good woman's natural impulses force her to adopt the social disguise of a hard-hearted 'cousin', is structured by the alternating appearance of Shen Te and 'Shui Ta', as the contradictions generated by the antagonistic organisation of capit-alist society tear the heroine apart.

In the area of dramatic and theatrical technique, the 'theatre of the scientific age' had to develop means of presentation which would promote an attitude of intellectual enquiry on the part of the new spectators. In place of the Aristotelian concept of 'empathy', Brecht's 'non-Aristotelian' theatre would, he claimed, allow the spectator to remain at a cool distance from the play by using the 'Verfremdungseffekt', a technique of 'alienation' or 'de-familiarisation' – in its presentation of human behaviour.[6] This meant presenting things, and particularly things with which we are so familiar that we assume them to be naturally thus (when in fact they are the product of specific socio-historical circumstances), in such a way that they appear strange, in need of investigation rather than self-explanatory: 'A representation that alienates is one which allows us to recognize its subject, but at the same time makes it seem unfamiliar' (*BT*, p. 192). As a model of the 'cool, investigative eye' at work outside the theatre, Brecht cited the case of the scientist Galileo Galilei, who suddenly saw a swinging pendulum, something that other people had simply taken for granted, as a puzzling phenomenon in need of scientific study.

Perhaps the best-known term introduced by Brecht to describe his new conception of theatre was 'epic theatre', which again he defined in opposition to the 'dramatic' theatre of the past. Essentially, 'epic' theatre was to be a narrative form of theatre, one where a narrative voice is constantly to be heard, as it were, mediating between the events of the play and the audience, and directing the process of 'Verfremdung'.[7] The events were thus to have the status of illustrative material, by means of which the narrator would present an argument about social life to the audience. Thanks to the mediating presence of the narrator, the events on stage would lose the powerful immediacy characteristic of traditional dramatic presentation. The presentation would have the quality of 'epic calm'. Freed from the emotive pressure of the old type of drama, the spectator would be in a position to reflect on the remark-able, question-able aspects of reality to which the various forms of 'Verfremdung' direct his attention.

In theory, then, Brecht's conception of theatre was one which respected the spectator's intellectual *freedom* and did not manip- ulate his responses as the Aristotelian, 'dramatic' type of theatre had allegedly done:

> The modern spectator does not want to be the involuntary object of any form of suggestion, nor to lose his powers of reasoning by being dragged into all manner of emotional states. He does not want to be raped mentally or to have someone else do his thinking for him. He wants to be presented with simple human material, *so that he himself can put it into order.*
>
> *(GW*, 15, p. 221)[8]

Having outlined the main claims Brecht made for his projected 'theatre of the scientific age', we ought now to examine these claims critically, taking Brecht at his word when he says that the most 'productive' attitude is a critical one.

The first difficulty with Brecht's conception of a 'theatre for the scientific age' is that it is not internally consistent. The second difficulty is that the main line of the theory does not describe Brecht's dramatic and theatrical practice adequately. In particular, I shall argue, his theatre cannot escape the accusation he himself levelled at 'Aristotelian' theatre, namely that it manipulated the responses of the spectator and 'did his thinking for him'.

To take the point of theoretical self-consistency first. Amongst Brecht's earliest and best-known attempts at a systematic summary of his theory of epic theatre are the 'Notes on the opera _Rise and Fall of the City of Mahagonny_'. In their first published version (1930) these notes contained a table opposing the characteristics of 'dramatic' theatre to those of 'epic' theatre. The antitheses included the following:

Dramatic theatre	_Epic theatre_
suggestion	argument
feeling	reason

This is exactly what one would expect to find in a self-styled theatre for the scientific age. However, in later editions Brecht qualified his position very considerably by adding a footnote to the table:

> This table does not show absolute antitheses but mere shifts of accent. Within the process of communication we may choose whether to stress the element of emotional suggestion or that of plain rational argument. (_BT_, p. 37)

Everyone is entitled to change his mind, of course, but this change seems to me so fundamental as to undermine the supposed central difference between epic or scientific theatre and dramatic theatre. How is the spectator to retain his freedom to reason and criticise if epic theatre is allowed to subject him to emotive suggestion in the 'process of communication' just as dramatic theatre is alleged to have done? On a number of occasions Brecht tried to defend his position against the charge of inconsistency by claiming that reason and feeling were not necessarily mutually exclusive opposites. Excitement about a new discovery, he claimed, had a proper place in science. This may be true, but there is an important distinction to be made between being emotional _about_ science and the idea that feelings have anything to contribute to scientific practice. Feelings can provide the motivation for conducting science, and they may well be aroused by the _results_ of scientific work (such as the invention of the atomic bomb), but the characteristic of scientific truth is that it can be replicated by anyone who follows the correct, rationally explicable procedures.

A similar distinction needs to be made in another area of activity to which Brecht liked to relate epic theatre. In his essay entitled

'The Street-Scene: A Basic Model for an Epic Theatre' (*BT*, pp. 121–9), Brecht argued that theatre should have a practical purpose, such as establishing right and wrong, as in a court of law. The actors should be like witnesses to an accident who are asked to reenact exactly what they saw so that the court can reach a verdict and place the blame where it should lie. This forensic conception of theatre is consistent with Brecht's original position. But that position becomes inconsistent again when he argues that 'anger about injustice' has a proper place in his new theatre. Of course the man in the street is often angry or shocked when it is established that a person has committed an act of injustice. But no such feelings should influence our judgement if we are involved, as members of a jury, in establishing *whether* someone has committed a crime. In court the only thing which can – or should – determine guilt or innocence is rationally presented evidence, and any judge or jury would act very improperly if it allowed its feelings about the case to interfere with a purely rational assessment of the evidence. Since Brecht's theatre intends to put the audience precisely into the position of judge or jury (hence the many trial scenes within the plays themselves), feelings such as 'anger at injustice' do not have a theoretically defensible place in the epic theatre, if Brecht was serious about wanting to ensure the spectator's independence of mind.

A further, very serious objection to this analogy between epic theatre and a court of law is the lack of opposition between prosecution and defence on which the process of justice as we know it rests. In Brecht's theatre we are only shown the 'evidence' he wants to show us, and only in the form in which he chooses to show it to us. There is no evidence from any other source. Nor can we test that 'evidence' by cross-examination. Despite his claim that epic theatre 'arouses the capacity for action' (*BT*, p. 37) in the spectator, he is actually expected to be as quiet and passive as in any other theatre, and not to intervene as a judge might during an advocate's presentation of his case.

Even if one accepts, for the sake of argument, that Brecht's intention was simply to bring about a significant shift of emphasis from 'suggestion' to 'argument' in the theatre, the question remains to be answered as to how – or whether – this aim was realised in his theatrical practice.

How, for example, does the narrative voice in epic theatre actually function? The narrative, mediating presence of the epic narrator can be found in virtually every element of dramatic and theatrical presentation. To put it in Brecht's own terms, the 'general gesture of showing' – 'der allgemeine Gestus des Zeigens' – accompanies each of the particular social gestures shown in the play (*BT*, p. 203). This 'gesture of showing' is readily evident, for example, in the two main types of play preferred by Brecht, the historical play, such as *Mother Courage and her Children* or *The Life of Galileo*, and the parable play, such as *The Good Person of Szechwan*. In the parable play there is often a prologue, epilogue or 'Zwischenspruch' addressed directly to the audience, which spells out the general problem or lesson the play deals with, while the action and characters in this type of play are so stylised that they clearly present an illustrative model rather than a picture taken directly from life. In fact, the presence of this generalising, parabolic quality in all Brecht's plays has led one critic to describe him as a modern 'allegorist'.[9] In Brecht's history plays the pointer, or 'Zeigestock', with which the fairground ballad-singer ('Moritatensänger') would once point at pictures illustrating the scenes of his tale, finds its verbal equivalent in the captions introducing scenes, such as the following:

> January ten, sixteen ten
> Galileo Galilei abolishes heaven.[10]

The term 'gesture of showing' is, however, too neutral a description for this narrative function. Here, in Brecht's theatre, a type of narrator comes back to life who, in an age of uncertainty and relativism, had largely disappeared from the modern novel. This is the type of the omnipresent and omniscient narrator, who can convey things of which the characters are unaware, as for example when he points forward to the consequences of actions before the characters have even carried them out. In an 'epically' constructed play like *Mother Courage*, where there is no dynamic of plot leading from one scene to the next, the spectator has to tune into the consciousness of the epic narrator in order to grasp the unity of the events being enacted; in the case of *Mother Courage* this unity is constituted by an argument about the nature of war and the role played in it by ordinary people. This has very important consequences for the arguments surrounding the role of 'empathy' in the theatre, and particularly for Brecht's attack on traditional theatre for allegedly depriving the spectator of his independence of judgement ('Bevormundung').

Through his introduction of the epic narrator, Brecht has *not* driven identification out of the theatre. Rather, he has simply shifted the focus of identification.[11] Whereas, as Brecht claimed, the spectator was traditionally invited to see the world from the perspective of the *protagonist*, the spectator in epic theatre is invited to see things from the point of view of the *narrator*. What is more, the manner in which this narrative voice functions and expresses itself makes it very difficult to avoid such identification. Firstly, as we have seen, adoption of this point of view is necessary in order to perceive the coherence of the events of the play. Furthermore, the narrative voice is endowed with an air of authority, not only in the sense that it knows the facts (such as the date and place of actions), but also through its claim to a wisdom higher than that of any of the characters. This is expressed often in a moral commentary on their behaviour, for example:

No one's virtue is complete.
Great Galileo liked to eat.   (*CP*, 5i, p. 19)

These lines exemplify the kind of linguistic technique which is often cited to support Brecht's claim that his theatre encouraged a rational response in the spectator. It is the technique of the missing logical link.[12] The sentence speaks about two distinct things: greatness – or the lack of it – and fondness for food, linking them simply with the word 'und'. The connection between the two things is not made explicit, but must be supplied 'by the spectator himself'. The connecting thought runs roughly as follows: 'Fondness for food could certainly lead a great man, and even more probably a "big man" (since "Großer Mann" is ambiguous, referring as much to physical size as to moral stature), to do something unworthy simply in order to satisfy his appetite.' But, of course, we have not really come to this insight by our own efforts. We have simply made explicit what was implicit in the poet's words. It is not unlike joining up the dots in those puzzles we have all done as children, so that 'we' seem to draw a rabbit or a snowman which has actually been pre-formed for us. By the suppression of the logical link we are drawn into the perspective of the narrator, for in supplying a materialist explanation to connect his two statements we are thinking along lines – *his* lines – which will be reinforced again and again in the course of the play.

A more complex example of Brecht's skilful steering of the spectator's responses is to be found in the caption introducing the first scene of *Mother Courage*:

> Spring 1624. The Swedish Commander-in-Chief Count Oxenstierna is raising troops in Dalecarlia for the Polish campaign. The canteen woman Anna Fierling, known under the name of Mother Courage, mislays a son.   (*CP*, 5ii, p. 3, adapted)

Here again, an *implied* connection has to be worked out in the spectator's mind in order to supply the missing link between the recruitment of soldiers and Mother Courage's loss of her son. But the spectator's identification with the implied *thought*-process is just one element in a more far-reaching process of identification with the epic narrator. The language of the caption has many attractive aesthetic qualities, a number of which could not be retained in the translation (itself a sure sign that we are dealing with an intrinsically poetic kind of language). In German the two main sentences are structured by parallelism and antithesis: Mother Courage is paralleled with Commander Oxenstierna, since both are the main referents of each sentence and both occupy the initial position in each sentence (even though they are in different grammatical cases). Gain ('Oxenstierna raises troops') is balanced by loss (Mother Courage 'mislays' a son). A man of high rank (Commander Oxenstierna) is contrasted with a woman of low rank ('canteen-woman'). The fate of one individual (Mother Courage's son) is paralleled by the fates of many others ('troops'). The parallelism of great and small implies a challenge to conventional historiography, since this would normally record the actions of Oxenstierna but have no record of the individual experiences of Mother Courage; she is just as much the centre of her world (and sentence) as the general is of his. But this parallel is simultaneously undermined by the sequence of the sentences. Oxenstierna is mentioned first because it is the actions of men like him which largely determine the lives of little people like Mother Courage and her children. Appropriately, then, he is the subject of his sentence whereas (in the original) she is put in the dative case in her sentence – as the indirect object of the impersonal verb, 'kommt...abhanden'. At the same time, the playwright's criticism of Mother Courage's view of her own position in the war, which will be made clear in the scene that follows the caption, is already hinted at in the use of the verb 'abhandenkommen'. It is a very odd verb to apply to the loss of a human being, for it means 'to mislay' and is more likely to be used with reference to an object. And yet it is an appropriate word here for several reasons. First, it reflects the fact that, in wartime, human beings are often reduced to the status of objects (as in the term 'Menschenmaterial'). Secondly, Mother Courage herself uses her son as if he were an animal, making him pull her cart for her. Thirdly, the verb reflects Mother Courage's belief that what happens to her family in wartime is an unfortunate accident, not something for which she herself is responsible.

This detailed analysis of just a few lines of Brechtian text ought to have made it clear that Brecht's language has the rich, complex density of all good poetry. These aesthetic qualities have an important influence on our response to the narrative persona in epic theatre. Far from his being someone who merely 'shows' what is happening, the wit and rhetorical elegance of the narrator make him an attractive object of identification. Just as the emotional – and intellectual – complexity of a Hamlet or Macbeth or Lear draws us powerfully into their perspective on the world, the complexities buried in the epic narrator's words require us to enter into his mental world – and spend some time there – in order to grasp all his implications. Added to this is the attraction of the narrator's irony, which invites us to share his superior standpoint above the limited perspective of the characters who are enmeshed in the contradictions of their lives. What we are offered, then, as a reward for identification with the epic narrator is a feeling of *power*. Thus, the emotive 'suggestion', which, in theory, Brecht rejected in favour of 'argument', is in fact just as much at work in his *practice* of theatre as in the 'Aristotelian' theatre he tried so hard to discredit.

The role played by the Singer in *The Caucasian Chalk Circle* is perhaps the clearest example of the way Brecht invests the narrative voice in epic theatre with persuasive power. At times Brecht enhances the narrator's authority by giving him a style of speech which draws heavily on the pathos of classical rhetoric. Here, he is addressing a deposed Governor on his way to the scaffold:

O, blindness of the great! They walk like gods
Great over bent backs, sure
Of hired fists, trusting
In their power which has already lasted so long.
But long is not forever.
O, wheel of Fortune! Hope of the people!   (*CP*, 7, p. 155)

Having earlier shown this governor to be a selfish, cruel man, Brecht now offers the audience the opportunity to vent its anger by sharing the sarcasm of the Singer – 'Walk, Your Highness, walk even now with head up' – and to enjoy the witty and malicious antitheses in which he spells out to this man the consequences of his behaviour:

> You no longer need an architect, a carpenter will do.
> You will not move into a new palace, but into a little hole in the
>   ground.   (*CP*, 7, pp. 155–6)

Underlying all these gestures is power, power which the narrator uses here to command the governor's behaviour, making him turn round to look at his palace and then sending him off with a last piece of bitter wit to meet his fate:

> Just look about you once more, you blind man!
> (The arrested Governor looks about him)
> Does all you once possessed still please you? Between the Easter
>   Mass and Easter Meal
> You are walking to that place, from which no one returns.
>   (*CP*, 7, 156)

Brecht exercises influence on the spectator not only directly, through the language or gestures of the epic narrator in his various guises, but also indirectly, through the kind of language he gives the characters to speak. There are times, for example, when a figure expresses views which Brecht would endorse. In such cases the character may speak with the kind of pathos we have just observed in the Singer. In a satire on American capitalism entitled *Saint Joan of the Stockyards* (1931/2), for instance, the heroine speaks these lines at an important moment of insight into the capitalist system:

> And there are two languages, above and below
> And two measures for weighing
> And that which bears a human face
> Knows itself no longer.[13]

This kind of unqualified pathos would not be out of place at the climactic point in a German classic drama such as Schiller's *Maid of Orleans*, which Brecht's *Saint Joan* parodies. On the other hand, when Brecht wants us to respond differently, to withhold our sympathy from certain characters, he will subject the same style to comic, parodistic distortion, as when he has two scheming, ruthless meatpackers (in *Saint Joan*) discuss the crisis in the meat trade:

> Recall, friend Cridle, how some days ago –
> Across the slaughter-yard we walked, 'twas evening –
> We stood by our new canning-machine...[14]

At such moments Brecht again makes the spectator feel superior to the characters. Sharing the critical perspective of the epic narrator, we 'see through' the hollow pathos of the language to the hypocrisy it attempts to conceal. The parodistic language produces the verbal equivalent of the 'banana-skin' effect as two rich, powerful characters are reduced to the status of comic figures.

Brecht was not only a master of language. He also used the visual resources of the theatre to excellent effect. And here too his work has the rhetorical, persuasive and suggestive qualities we have seen in his texts. A clear example of this is his presentation of the three gods who visit Szechwan. When they first appear they are clean, well-dressed and speak the language of superior beings. In later scenes, however, when they have been made to experience the harsh realities of the lives of poor, angry people in a competitive society, they appear with torn clothes, and one of them even has a black eye. Here again, Brecht's comic effect is of the kind which harnesses the aggressions of the spectators, inviting them to take malicious pleasure in the 'punishment' that is dealt out to these wilfully ignorant defenders of the established order of things.

The masks Brecht had made for his production of *The Caucasian Chalk Circle* at the Berliner Ensemble provide another example of his visual rhetoric. These masks were of different sizes and made from a variety of materials. Brecht's own explanation for the use of masks was that they defined the degree of alienation produced in the characters by their social position and function.[15] Thus, the moral and psychological deformation of a man like the Governor, who has identified fully with an exploitative social order, was expressed by a large mask made out of hard material which covered his face almost completely. Servants who had only partly identified with the class system were given masks of softer material or masks which covered much less of the face. Grusche, the very lowly servant, who is not very clever but has a good heart, wears no mask at all because, exceptionally, she has not been deformed and hardened by the system. Brecht's account of the use of masks refers only to what they are intended to denote. Yet such masks do not only function referentially. In itself, the contrast of an artificial mask with a natural face produces contrasting feelings of withdrawal and identification, feelings which are intensified by such opposing qualities as soft and hard, mobile and immobile, round and angular, which Brecht carried over from the masks to the costumes worn by characters from different social ranks. 'Distancing' is a misleadingly bland description of the effect of these presentational devices. The contrasting responses produced by them are as simple and powerful as those often evoked by popular art, which makes no bones about where its sympathies lie. In fact, the face and costume Walt Disney drew for the Wicked Queen in *Snow White* has the same narrow eyes, the same hard edges and angular lines as those of the Wife of the Governor in *The Caucasian Chalk Circle* (which, incidentally, was intended for production on Broadway). Just how deep-seated are the instinctive feelings which such textural contrasts produce in us, and which Brecht exploits in order to push our sympathies in the direction he wants, is illustrated by a well-known experiment conducted on baby rhesus monkeys. The monkeys were presented with two artificial mother monkeys side by side. One of the 'mothers' was covered in fur and looked fairly like a monkey, but it had no milk for the babies to feed on. The other 'mother' had milk, but it was made of metal and did not look or, more importantly, feel like a mother monkey. The monkeys would drink its milk, but to do so they would climb up onto the furry mother and cling to her fur while leaning across to suck the milk from the artificial teat of the hard 'mother'. Such effects of involuntary empathy were not an inherent evil in stage presentation which Brecht simply could not eradicate from epic theatre; his use of their suggestive potential was pervasive and calculated.

Brecht frequently criticised traditional theatre for offering the audience misleading illusions rather than showing reality truthfully. What he meant by 'truth', of course, was the Marxist interpretation of history and society. But in order to persuade the audience of this truth he was perfectly happy to create a quite illusory reality on the stage. In the historical play *Life of Galileo*, for example, he wanted to focus attention both on the class-conflicts of the period and on the link between religious orthodoxy and the maintenance of the existing social order. Because Galileo's astronomical discoveries challenged the old 'Ptolemaic' model of the world, which the Church wanted people to accept, Brecht makes Galileo say 'blasphemous' things which fundamentally challenge the teachings of the church. Yet the historical Galileo was a devout Catholic, who drew no such revolutionary theological conclusions from his scientific work.[16] Many of the opinions, both social and religious, attributed to Galileo in the play are unhistorical or anachronistic, and Brecht's attitude to historical fact shows practically the same sovereign disregard of documented fact as that of Schiller, despite the fact that Brecht, unlike Schiller, insisted that truth was concrete and historical.

One last example from the same play will reinforce the point. Brecht wanted to make the social differences of the period clear by carefully distinguishing the costumes worn by characters in different social positions.[17] But the visual sources from the period offered insufficient evidence of such clear differentiation, so that he had to produce an artificial construct for the design of the costumes, drawing on sources from different times and places and then modifying them significantly to make 'history' *appear* to say what he *wanted* it to say. This sort of thing was far from uncommon in the productions of the Berliner Ensemble. The swords used by the Roman soldiers in Brecht's adaptation of Shakespeare's *Coriolanus*, for example, were in fact modelled on a *Finnish* knife owned by Helene Weigel, with which the desired emotive effect of energetic, brutal stabbing could more easily be suggested than with authentic historical evidence.[18]

To sum up: Brecht's theory of a 'theatre for the scientific age' is neither internally consistent, nor is it a comprehensive, or in some respects even a reliable guide to his actual practice in writing texts and producing plays. His theatre does not in fact dispense with audience identification by the introduction of the epic narrator and the 'Verfremdungseffekt'; rather, these devices merely shift the focus of identification away from the protagonist and onto the various expressions of the authorial point of view. Nor did Brecht create a type of theatre which dispensed with 'suggestion' in favour of 'argument'; rather, he used a whole range of suggestive and emotive devices to align the responses of the audience with the ideological positions he wished to advocate. Nor did Brecht dispense with illusion in favour of truth; rather, he produced meticulously crafted illusions (like the faded blue blouse worn by Wlassowa in *The Mother*) designed to make us believe in the truth of his interpretation of reality. His theoretical position was that 'the modern spectator does not wish to have his thinking done for him or be raped emotionally. He wants to be presented with simple human material *in order to order it himself*. If this indeed were the case, the critical modern spectator attending a play by Brecht would simply be disappointed to find that here, too, the theatre was largely doing his thinking for him, even where it left him some gaps to fill 'of his own accord'. On the other hand, the spectator who goes along to a Brecht play expecting that here, as in many other forms of theatre, he will meet situations and arguments presented with great elegance, cunning and rhetorical force, will find much to challenge and delight him.

NOTES

1.   *Gesammelte Werke in 20 Bänden* (Franfkurt a. M.; Suhrkamp, 1967), vol. 15, p. 173. All further references to this edition will be indicated in the text in the form: '(GW, volume, page)'.
2.   Brecht developed these ideas in 1927–8 in conversations and correspondence with the sociologist Fritz Sternberg. See Fritz Sternberg, *Der dichter und die ratio* (Göttingen: Sachse und Pohl, 1963) and the 'Kölner Rundfunkgespräch' between Brecht, Sternberg, Herbert Jhering and Ernst Hardt (GW 15, pp. 146–53).
3.   John Willett (ed. and trans.), *Brecht on Theatre* (London: Methuen, 1978) p. 30. Subsequent references to this translation will be given in brackets after the quotation in the form: '(BT, page no.)'.
4.   Brecht first used this phrase in the 'Kölner Rundfunkgespräch' in 1928, where he praised Georg Kaiser for writing in a manner which 'made possible that wholly new attitude in the audience, that cool, investigative, interested attitude, namely the attitude of the audience of the age of science' (GW 15, p. 153).
5.   In their *German Ideology* Marx and Engels wrote: 'Consciousness is thus in its origins a social product and will always remain such as long as human beings exist' (Karl Marx and Friedrich Engels, *Werke* (Berlin: Marx–Engels Institute, 1957) vol. 3, p. 31).
6.   See the essay 'Alienation Effects in Chinese Acting' (BT, pp. 91–9).
7.   'So what ought our major form to be like? Epic. It must report. It must not believe that one can identify oneself with our world by empathy, nor must it want this' (BT, p. 25).
8.   Brecht reaffirmed this principle in the best known of his theoretical statements, the 'Short Organum for the Theatre' (1948): 'It is only that his [i.e. the actor's] feelings must not at bottom be those of the

character, so that the audience's may not at bottom be those of the character either. The audience must have complete freedom here' (*BT*, pp. 194–5).

9. Francis Fergusson, 'Three Allegorists: Brecht, Wilder and Eliot', *Seewanee Review*, LXIV (1956) pp. 544–73.

10. John Willett and Ralph Manheim (eds), *Bertolt Brecht: Collected Plays*, vol. 5i, p. 22. All subsequent references to this edition will be in the form: '(*CP*, vol., p. no.)'.

11. In the essay 'Alienation Effects in Chinese Acting', Brecht himself described the relationship between the spectator and the actor using the alienation effect as one of identification: 'The audience identifies itself with the actor as being an observer, and accordingly develops his attitude of observing or looking on' (*BT*, p. 92).

12. One of the earliest, but still one of the best analyses of the various forms of 'Verfremdung' is Reinhold Grimm, *Bertolt Brecht: Die Struktur seines Werkes* (Nürnberg: H. Carl Verlag, 1959); see, particularly, the discussion of 'apparently wrong logic' in ch. 4.

13. *Saint Joan of the Stockyards*, trans. F. Jones (London: Methuen, 1976) p. 106 (adapted).

14. Ibid., p. 4 (adapted).

15. See the essay by Joachim Tenschert, 'Über die Verwendung von Masken', in *Brechts Theaterarbeit: Seine Inszenierung des 'Kaukasischen Kreidekreises' 1954*, ed. W. Hecht (Frankfurt a. M.: Suhrkamp, 1985) pp. 151–62.

16. G. Szczesny, *Das Leben des Galilei und der Fall Bertolt Brecht* (Frankfurt a. M.: Suhrkamp, 1966).

17. See W. Hecht (ed.), *Brechts 'Leben des Galilei'* (Frankfurt a. M.: Suhrkamp, 1981) p. 82.

18. 'Dialogue: Berliner Ensemble', *Drama Review*, vol. 12, no. 1 (1967) pp. 114–15.

4

Witkiewicz and the Theatre of Death

ROGER HOWARD

'It seems that we are watching and hearing the ravings of a syphilitic in the last stages of creeping paralysis. ...Witkiewicz's play is a total absurdity from which nothing can ever arise. It is an unnatural clinical abortion. It should be put in alcohol and studied by psychopathologists.'[1]

Such a critical reception for a first play frequently guarantees the playwright instant box-office success and automatic elevation into the canon. But the production of *Tumor Brainiowicz* at the Slowacki Theatre in Krakow in June 1921 was no breakthrough for Stanislaw Ignacy Witkiewicz (Witkacy, 1885–1939), playwright, painter, critic, aesthetician, novelist, philosopher and writer on drugs, whom his American translator and biographer, Daniel Gerould, has described as 'one of the most amazing artistic geniuses and personalities of the modern period'.[2]

During Witkiewicz's lifetime, only twelve of his nearly forty plays were produced on Polish stages and they closed after two or three, or at the most seven, performances. His major theory of theatre was published in 1920–1 but drew little attention. Most of his plays were written between 1918 and 1925 but some had to wait fifty years for their premières. After 1928, in the period of the 'democratic' thirties, the Nazi occupation of the forties and the post-war Stalinist regime, his plays disappeared from the professional repertory in Poland until 1956 when Tadeusz Kantor launched his Cricot 2 theatre in Krakow with a production of *The Cuttlefish*. There followed, according to the critic Konstanty Puzyna, 'a Witkacy vogue, riding the crest of a wave of violent reaction to socialist realism'.[3] Puzyna brought out a two-volume edition of 22 plays in 1962, inaugurating a period of rapid rediscovery, by student and professional theatres, of all his major work.

Abroad, his reception has been late, sporadic and piecemeal. A production of *The Mother* in Paris in 1970 by the Compagnie Renaud-Barrault, with Madeleine Renaud in the title role, established Witkacy's reputation in European theatre, and his work was staged in many countries of Europe in the next two decades. In the English-speaking world Gerould's translations of six plays, under the title *The Madman and the Nun* (1968), introduced him to drama specialists. In his preface to the collection *Tropical Madness: Four Plays*, published in the United States in 1972, Martin Esslin proclaimed Witkiewicz's place 'important' and 'secure' in the modern tradition from late Strindberg, through the Surrealists and Artaud, to 'the masterpieces of the dramatists of the absurd – Beckett, Ionesco, Genet and Arrabal – of the late 1940s and 1950s'.[4]

However, although the first production of Witkiewicz in English (of *The Madman and the Nun*) took place as long ago as 1967 at San Francisco State College Theatre, under the direction of the Polish critic Jan Kott, his plays have reached no closer to London's main stages than the Half Moon Theatre in Stepney (*The Shoemakers*, 1973), Essex University Theatre (*The Pragmatists, The Cuttlefish, The New Deliverance* and *Gyubal Wahazar*, in 1982–4), and the Polish Centre in Hammersmith (*They*, 1984). *They* was received with familiar scepticism. It was less 'interesting' than 'significant' (Giles Gordon, *Spectator*). It was a 'curiosity' and 'hardly a vital case for resurrection unless, heaven help them, someone is pinning political significance to this nutcase' (Ros Franey, *City Limits*). It 'has the limitations of much anti-realist theatre; it deals in generalities rather than specifics' (Micheal Billington, *Guardian*). 'Stanislaw Witkiewicz is not a name that leaps to mind', wrote Martin Hoyle in *Financial Times*. Hoyle had problems pronouncing the author's names.[5]

Yet the difficulties Witkiewciz's plays have experienced in becoming established cannot entirely be explained, abroad, by the fact that he wrote in one of the 'small' European languages or, at home, by the hostility of critics of the 1920s to what they thought was avant-garde, or by the activities of the censors of either Nazi occupiers or the home-grown Stalinists in the 1940s and 1950s. A thread of puzzlement at his dramatic aims, and confusion over his theatrical means, runs through the reviews of productions of his work, as much in Poland as in England. Even so devoted a contemporary Witkacy scholar as Janusz Degler admitted to certain reservations over whether 'a true Witkacian theatre style' has yet been discovered for his plays, even in Poland. 'The numerous methods and styles used by directors are only half-measures or they backfire, causing fresh disappointments and provoking yet another controversy.'[6] Puzyna agreed: 'Today (1985) Witkacy's plays remain as much a challenge to directors and actors as in the past.' Puzyna cautioned against 'flashy, hollow and boring' productions, and a heavy use of the 'grotesque', lacking 'a light touch'. He favoured those productions which maintained a balance between conveying Witkiewicz's aesthetic and philosophy, and using original, non-naturalistic forms of staging.[7]

The problems of reception are deep-seated. England's philistinism and fear of Marxism has kept the plays of, for instance, Heiner Müller and Volker Braun – whose names are comparatively easy to say – out of the major English theatres. Yet the plays of Havel, Mrozek and Rózewicz, whose 'dissident' political positions English liberals found easy to accept in the years of the Cold War, have been adopted by major British theatres despite their 'un-English' theatrical techniques. Witkacy's plays are, after all, politically perplexing in Poland, and will remain so in the emerging society of the 1990s, since Poland's renewed search for alternatives to Stalinism will be as confused and contradictory as that artistic reaction to socialist realism which arose in 1956, at the very beginning of Witkacy's rediscovery, and his plays are unlikely to do much to help clarify matters on this occasion any more than they did in the 1960s.

Witkiewicz's theatre is a Theatre of Death. His catastrophism and his aesthetic of Pure Form meet together in his theatre to produce a nullity. His plays succeed not only in destabilising naturalistic illusion but, through a deformation of objects, they 'extirpate the sense of "life" from the action on stage'.[8]

It is not merely that Witkacy's attitudes to capitalism, which he regarded as a cancer, and to democracy, which he thought was a sham, alienate him from present-day Thatcherite Polish free-marketeers and putative social democrats alike, just as his virulent hatred of collectives of workers – the masses of people he called 'pulp' – made him hostile to communism, or his fascination for strong men, attended by an equal revulsion at their ineffectiveness, made him deride fascism. The underlying feeling of unease which so many actors, directors, critics and audiences have had for his work is surely to be attributed to his uncompromising metaphysics, a catastrophic metaphysics which has little appeal to exponents of either a renascent Catholicism or a resurgent capitalism. What is more, his plays confuse the scholars, since, as Gerould has written, they go 'far beyond the categories of expressionism and surrealism'.[9] Neither do they conform to Esslin's notion of the 'absurd'. Witkiewicz synthesised different genres and styles, combining features which in much modern drama have been kept separate. He brought the mysterious, fantastic and dreamlike together with a historical, social and political vision, employing, according to Gerould, 'a mocking, irreverent humour and grotesque style built on parody and irony'.[10] But his plays are perhaps most disturbingly problematic because the accounts they give of totalitarian power and the collapse of mechanised democracies do not appear in the form of prophecies or warnings. Instead, they are imbued with a feeling that it is too late. The catastrophe is not impending; it has already occurred.

This seemingly somewhat aristocratic view of early twentieth-century European history is not easily identifiable as such. Rather, it appears in the form of a generalised aesthetic purism; one which, allied as it is with an obsessive aestheticisation of death, Tadeusz Kantor was quick to pick up and use in his abstracted versions of the plays, from *The Cuttlefish* of 1956 to *The Dead Class* of 1976. Puzyna regarded Kantor's 'tacking on to Witkacy's plot and dialogue an altogether different script of stage business and action all his own' as 'taking liberties' with Witkiewicz's originals.[11] Kantor, however, claimed he was stripping the plays of their residual naturalistic coverings and exposing the metaphysical essence of his master's 'Pure Form'.

For Kantor, acting is 'fully autonomous and should be derived from and shaped by the actor's creativity'. The author's text being a 'semantic entity', the '"surrealistic" mystery which is contained in the literary structure of Witkiewicz's plays cannot be textually transferred into another structure, theatrical or otherwise'. The objects in *The Water Hen*, produced by Kantor in 1967, had to be 'won over and possessed rather than depicted or shown'. Likewise, events and situations had to be 'derailed from the track of realness, given autonomy, which, in life, is called aimlessness, and deprived of any motivation and effects'. Process was all. 'The germ of my concept was to reject the idea of a COMPLETE and FINISHED WORK OF ART, and to focus on ATTEMPTS and nothing but ATTEMPTS!' True creativity was 'to deprive those ATTEMPTS of their CONSEQUENCES'. 'Fully autonomous artistic endeavour (in theatre, I mean) does not exist according to principles or norms of everyday life.'[12]

Kantor's constitutes a most zealous application of Witkiewicz's theories, taking them further than his master did into the spatial and physical arts of the actor. By comparison with Kantor's theatre, Witkiewicz's plays (although their author was a painter) are determinedly literary, word-bound and story-centred. Kantor's theatrical context is stage directing and the fine arts, whilst Witkacy's was philosophy and literature; Kantor's is the body and the eye, Witkacy's was the mind and the tongue. Yet they both sought to take possession of theatre in order to propound their metaphysics. 'Theatre is a place where people are supposed to experience art', wrote Witkiewicz, 'and not to be presented with the imitation of life.'[13]

As such, Witkiewicz's theory is implacably coercive. His plays make sense – that is, they achieve the intended result of removing all possibility of the word 'sense' from having any meaning – only if the audience accepts the author's absolutist manner of thought. 'In the theatre', he wrote in 'On a New Type of Play' (1920),

> we want to be in an entirely new world...(and) create a performance in time not limited by any logic except the logic of the form of that performance. ...On leaving the theatre, the spectator ought to have the feeling that he has just awakened from some strange dream, in which even the most ordinary things had a strange, unfathomable charm, characteristic of dream reveries.[14]

Pure Form was to reveal the Strangeness of Existence and to elicit the Metaphysical Shudder. His plays were not designed to provide spaces in which an audience may realise its freedom to choose to differ from what is in front of it, spaces which Brecht offered even in his most didactic plays (*The Measures Taken*, for example, purposely provokes its audience not to accept what is being presented to it). In its appeal to absolutes, metaphysical theatre is implicitly authoritarian. The oppressiveness of spirit and intellect thus induced is a feature of much of the theatrical tradition within which Esslin situated Witkiewicz's plays, that of Strindberg's dream plays. They are plays of stasis. Journeys may occur, but they go nowhere, as in dreams. They are plays overtaken by nullification (to use Kantor's 1963 term) or by Death (to use his 1975 term).

Maeterlinck, whose plays Witkiewicz's admired, came to think that in absolute inaction was to be found 'deeper reality'. His 'static theatre' eschewed story and plot. In *The Intruder* (1889), a room is invaded by a stranger who brings to a family circle an eternal secret from another world. 'Fitfully the talk drifts, ebbs lightly, and falls silently back, while all the time we feel death's presence drawing closer.'[15] In *The Blind* (1891), a group of blind men are lost in a forest, desperate because their guide, a priest, has died in their midst. In *The Interior* (1895), as Manfred Pfister has pointed out, dialogue no longer represents 'the tension that exists in the interrelations between various figures'. Lacking 'semantic changes of direction', dialogue collapses into a verbal consensus which resembles 'a monologue divided into a number of parts'.[16] The realist drama's use of personal and social differences by which to distinguish characters is replaced in Maeterlinck's theatre by what Gerould called 'structures of the soul', 'psychic differentiations determined by one's receptivity to the unknown and awareness that we are "playthings of the vast and heedless forces that surround us"'. Maeterlinck's characters are not individuals but 'victims of malevolent powers, to which they passively surrender',[17] or, as Artaud put it, 'puppets manipulated by destiny'.[18] The exterior world, as in Strindberg, is reconstituted as a reflection of one's interior state.

Artaud was eager to liberate theatre from the compulsions of psychological characterisation obtaining in realist theatre, which, he said, 'works relentlessly to reduce the unknown to the known'. In *The Theatre and its Double* (1938), he recommended, instead, a theatre which 'makes metaphysics' out of sounds and movements designed to 'induce trance', where words are given 'approximately the importance they have in dreams'.[19] Beckett's theatre reduced the scope of dramatic action to non-events taking place at the edge of death – waiting in *Waiting for Godot* (1953) and ending in *Endgame* (1957), where what Hamm and Clov experience is the impossibility of time and timelessness ever meeting in the consciousness. Genet's *Deathwatch* (1949), his stage direction tells us, 'must unfold as if in a dream'. Rejecting both naturalistic staging and 'real-life' characterisation, Genet wrote, in a letter to Roger Blin in 1966, 'If we maintain that life and the stage are opposites, it is because we strongly suspect that the stage is a site closely akin to death, a place where all liberties are possible.'[20] In Genet, these are the liberties of the profane, and, in Witkacy, those of the demonic, liberties of a psychic theatre which, wrote Artaud, 'like the plague, is collectively made to drain abscesses'.[21]

The art of theatre here replaces religion in taking on a ritual and mystic function. It does not admit of an objective world except as one originates from the subconscious motivations of human beings.[22] The theatrical act here resembles poetic language, which, according to Heidegger, is not an expression of human reality; it constitutes it. It is a phenomenon, that which shows itself in itself.[23] It is to be manipulated 'like a solid object',[24] as is speech in Artaud's theatre. It is a theatre closer to the one promoted by the Russian Symbolist, Viacheslav Ivanov, writing in the first decade of this century, for whom theatre, like poetry, was a religious apprehension of life rather than as aesthetic activity, whose gift was to create a mystery through which audiences would achieve a mystic communion.[25]

'Art works are negative per se', wrote Adorno in *Aesthetic Theory*, 'because they kill what they objectify, tearing it away from its context of immediacy and real life. ...This is particularly true of modern art, where we notice a general mimetic abandonment to reification, which is the principle of death.'[26] Indeed, the death principle is to be found in the very genesis of the modern metaphysic of theatre. It appeared in Nietzsche's 'temple' of theatre, and in the symbolist Sologub's '*The Theatre of the Single Will*' (1908) which, deriving its philosophy from Schopenhauer and denying that 'different people' existed, espoused a drama of 'a single being, a single I that wills, acts, suffers, burns with unquenchable fire and seeks refuge from the rage of life, with its horror and ugliness, in the comforting embraces of the eternal consoler – Death'.[27]

'Why, it may be asked, should we submit ourselves to so grim an imagination?' wrote Clive Hart of Beckett. Because, Hart replies, Beckett explores 'the shape of experience...the patterns that make things hang together'. The beauty of this shape affords us 'the experience of aesthetic joy'.[28] A delight in Pure Form is a prime object of Witkacy's theatre. The 'new type of play' he envisaged in 1920 was one that was 'extraordinarily closely knit and highly wrought in the way the action is tied together'. The emphasis was on formal integration, while the material arose from psychic disintegration: 'The actor, in his own right, should not exist; he should be the same kind of part within a whole as the colour red in a particular painting or the note C-sharp in a particular musical composition.' All the elements of performance – sound, decor, movement and dialogue – should combine together to create a formal whole so as to 'put the spectator in the position to experience metaphysical feeling. ...This method can create works of previously unsuspected beauty.' Such a play would exist, in performance, 'independently in its own right and not as a heightened picture of life'.[29]

Here is discarded that illusionism to which Ibsen referred in a letter to Edmund Gosse, of 15 January 1874. Objecting to Gosse's claim that *Emperor and Galilean* ought to have been written in verse, Ibsen replied that verse would have made his ordinary characters 'indistinguishable from one another', and therefore unnatural, thus defeating his purpose. He wished to create the impression that what happened in the play was something that 'had actually happened'. 'The illusion I wished to produce was that of reality.'[30] What Ibsen's plays had in common with Brecht's – despite the latter's qualified rejection of illusion – and with much of the dramatic, as distinct from the theatrical, tradition, was their indirect impact on an audience. Whether by combining the elements of staging in order to create illusion, or by separating the elements in order to distance the action, drama utilises the power of producing effects on an audience indirectly in the course of the process of intellectual cognition. Witkiewicz, by contrast, aimed to displace cognition by exercising theatre's power of producing effects on an audience directly. The subject and content of the work – its residual relations to 'real life' – were subsumed into the form, and the form worked directly on the audience's senses in order to create the impression in their minds that they had been dreaming.

As a result, the principles of drama were no longer valid. The flow of fictional time in a dialectical relation to the flow of time in the auditorium, the construction of a plausible story, the psychologically authentic development of characters' personalities and their consistency of behaviour, were all to be disposed of. Once the principle of imitation of life was abandoned, the theatre freed itself, wrote Witkiewicz, from the sin of lying.

The point is to make it possible that the audience – while perceiving the confused stream of becoming, constructed by the author and consisting of the characters' actions and utterances, of images and musical impressions – find themselves in the world of Formal Beauty, the beauty which is endowed with its own meaning, with a logic of its own, and with the TRUTH of its own. And this truth is not the truth characteristic of a piece of realistic painting in relation to some real landscape, or of a "love nest" presented on stage in relation to an event in real life. The truth involved here is the absolute truth.[31]

It is questionable how fully Witkacy applied this theory to his plays. Many features of realist drama remain in them. His settings seem to suppose a proscenium-arch stage. Furniture and props are usually 'real', although often strange. He divides his plays into acts. Characters speak lines of dialogue, and stage directions indicate their look or their emotion. The dialogue is coherent, gramatically conventional and apparently sequential. There is a story, however implausible, that certainly progresses, often ending in a surprising dénouement.[32] An impression of history is created both by story and by setting. Much of the action is everyday to the point of ordinariness, plagued as many of the actors are by inertia and boredom. Even the long philosophical discussions in which his artists and thinkers earnestly engage have the air of accurately-rendered transcriptions of the conversations to be heard in the writers' cafés of Krakow of Warsaw of the time. At the time when he was trying to stage his plays in Zakopane, in 1925, he wrote in a local journal, 'I'm not condemning either realistic painting or realistic theatre – I'm simply saying *it is not art*.'[33]

As Degler has suggested, Witkacy's negation of naturalistic conventions was only his point of departure. He concentrated on restructuring the dramatic text. He did not entirely discard it, as Kantor was to do; he attempted to 'de-form' it.[34] Indeed, he seemed more interested in synthesising realism and fantasy, transforming both by subverting either's pretensions to truthfulness. 'The realistic elements should exist for the sake of the purely formal goals', he wrote. They should be 'so transformed [that], when viewed realistically, the performance seems utter non-sense'. A greater truth than that of reality – 'a metaphysical feeling' – is to be experienced by an audience if a play succeeds in 'deforming either life or the world of fantasy with complete freedom so as to create a whole whose meaning would be defined only by its purely scenic internal construction'.[35] This is a pursuit not of nonsense but of the transcendence of sense to a 'meaning' beyond, or outside, meaning.

Part of the fascination of Witkacy's 'deformed' dramas is precisely that they resonate with memories of the dramatic, even if the power of drama has already left them, just as the power of creation has left so many of the drained, burnt-out artists who inhabit his plays like the ghosts of dead art. It is as if we are having demonstrated before us, in the enactment of his stories, the abandonment of drama in favour of theatre, the elevation of metamorphosis and dream over metaphor and reason, and the relinquishing of consciousness and cognition in favour of the experiential and the phenomenal. Plot, as cause-and-effect, is destroyed. Characters lose their motives and their wills and are driven by, or drift on, purely unconscious forces. Events are divested of meaning by being cut off from rational explanation or even from any causal context. Emotions exist in a vacuum devoid of feeling. Thoughts have no direction except to complete a sentence. Actions are related to each other only in so far as they make an impression on the form. Characters are removed from the laws of psychology, physics and biology (the dead frequently reappear as living). The impossible happens, making nonsense of the material world, yet creating 'formal sense'.

In his defence of the husk of dramatic text which he wanted to continue to utilise, Witkiewicz was as firm in his rejection of the 'avant-garde' as he was adamant in his subversion of realism. It is not at all certain that he would have approved of Kantor's scenographies, his complete erasure of the literary–dramatic text. He expressed himself opposed to those who, primarily concerned with the·reform of stage production, relegated or denied the dramatic text and gave supremacy to the musical, pictorial and design elements, to create a spectacular mêlée of sounds and images devoid of form and 'reducing an audience to stupefaction'. The 'single internal idea of form', which 'cemented' the elements, was lacking, and it was the writer's, not the director's or actors', creativity which provided this in the form of the dramatic text. 'It is the spoken word which is most important in a theatrical performance and the other elements must be subordinated to it.' It was his task, as the writer, to 'split' the realistic theatre 'from the inside', that is, from within the literary–dramatic text. Consequently, directors of his plays should not 'construct something stranger than the text itself suggests'.[36]

As for the actors, they should be Stanislavskian in applying to his plays the principle of ensemble playing. But they should be un-

Stanislavskian in that he wanted them never to 'experience' the inner life of the role through their own, or to attempt to identify themselves with it. The actor should 'forget completely about life' and, having first understood the formal conception of the work as a whole, 'build his role in such a way that – quite independent of his own frame of mind, his own inner experiences and state of nerves – he can execute with mathematical precision whatever is required by the purely formal conception of the work in question'. However fantastic the action or emotional the lines, the actor's delivery 'must be very restrained'. Actors must 'give up their ingrained habit of displaying emotions'. They should 'forego the desire to impersonate, to pretend to be somebody real'.[37] Freed from this desire, the actor may become a true artist who constructs his role according to 'his own creative intuition'. Relieved of the need to be plausible, he may express his 'artistic thoughts devoid of any connection with the somatic aspect of feeling', or he may simply 'use the technique of dissonance, of speaking gloomily about what is funny or laughing when delivering something tragic'. The positioning of actors on the stage should not be accidental, as in real life, but should be 'related to the scenery' and 'arranged according to the rules of composition in painting'. The set designer, however, should not allow scenery to dominate the action or to 'kill the actor and the words he utters' by its excess.[38]

In this he is far away from expressionism. Although Witkacy, the fantastic painter, used paint expressionistically on his canvasses, his use of colour in his sets and costumes, as suggested by his stage directions, bears more resemblance to Kandinsky's abstract and musical colours in his play *The Yellow Sound* (1909) in its quest for formal and emotional wholeness, and it differs from Kokoschka's colours in his expressionist settings for *Murderer, Hope of Womankind* (1909), with their aggressive, eruptive power. But Witkiewicz would not have approved of the reduction of the word to the basics of tone and rhythm in either of these works, or their abandonment of the supremacy of the dramatic text.[39]

In his theoretical statements of 1920–1, Witkiewicz was guided by a conviction that the 'mechanised' society which history had created led, in Degler's words, 'to the total extinction of metaphysical needs, the extinction of our ability to experience those higher feelings which make direct contact with the Mystery of Being possible'.[40] To propose a Pure Theatre – 'this temple of metaphysical feelings' – said Witkiewicz, was, in such a situation, to engage in 'an act of despair' directed against the 'grey life of triteness and commonplaceness' engulfing mankind. In this theatre, through 'the flow of events, funny, sublime or monstrous, the gentle, unchanging light would shine, the light of the Eternal Mystery of Being radiating from Infinity'. As he reflected on the formal relations of each moment to the flowing movement, each member of an audience would come to an awareness of the 'principle of Unity in Multiplicity governing his being', just as the author had in composing his dramatic text.[41] Witkacy was not, of course, alone or original, in expressing such sentiments. In 1904, in an essay on Chekhov's *The Cherry Orchard*, Andrei Bely speculated on how realism is 'imperceptibly transformed into symbolism' by one's concentrating 'all the powers of his soul' onto the theatrical moment. 'The power of the moment is a natural protest against the mechanisation of life.'[42]

Witkiewicz's aim of 'making strange' in order to change the materiality of expression (as the critic Christine Kiebuzinska put it), thus violating the projection of reality and forcing the audience to take note of signs and their operation, has certain affinities with Wordsworth's aim, according to Coleridge, of giving 'the charm of novelty to things of every day',[44] with the Russian formalists' theory of 'defamiliarisation', with André Breton's investment of reality with a surrealist 'marvellousness' and with Brecht's 'estrangement' or 'alienation' of subjective and objective by a separation of theatrical elements. Perhaps there was a common rebellious desire in these writers to confront habit, to register a disgust with the complacency of jaded perceptions and to use images, as the formalists saw them, to 'bring about a special perception of a thing, bring about the "seeing" and not just the "recognising" of it'.[45] Witkacy's deforming techniques, by which he 'violated the rules of the code' and created ambiguity,[46] produced their own, somewhat psychotic, 'splitting' of reality.

The undoing from within of naturalistic staging and realistic characterisation led Witkiewicz to create a synthetic theatre, fashioned from a unity of disconnected connections, or what Kott has called a 'theatre of signs without significance'.[47] In *The Mother* (1924),[48] we can see this subversion of late-nineteenth-century dramatic convention clearly operating in the structure of the play. Act One has a coherent story, Act Two has not, and the Epilogue reduces both acts to a nonsense which, paradoxically, 'makes sense' of the way in which the represented world has been deformed. Taking from

Ibsen's *Ghosts*, Strindberg's *The Father* and Przybyszewski's *The Mother*, Witkacy parodies the conventions of the naturalistic family drama and makes them absurd. While the two acts represent the illusion of a real and particular world, whose situations derive respectively from melodrama and from romantic drama and farce, the Epilogue collapses the naturalistic pretence.

The eponymous Mother's existence is knitting, while her idle, neurotic 30-year-old son, Leon, engages in utopian fantasies of saving mankind from the threat of standardisation, cretinisation and the machine. Bound to each other psychically, mother and son suck each other dry. While her eyesight fades and she seeks refuge in drink, Leon becomes rich. He spies for a foreign country, prostitutes his wife and receives money for services rendered from an ageing cocotte. The family moves from a shabby room to a glittering salon. Act Two ends with an orgiastic cocaine-sniffing party joined by Leon's accomplices and his wife's customers. The Mother goes blind and after taking a dose of cocaine dies from heart failure. The Epilogue is set in a black room which has neither doors nor windows. The Mother's body is lying in state. All the characters of the play are assembled, seated on red chairs, together with a young woman who is Leon's mother, pregnant with Leon. The body on the catafalque is a dummy filled with sawdust. Six mechanised workmen enter the room by means of a pipe in the ceiling and vaporise Leon.

Janusz Degler has analysed the ways in which six productions of *The Mother* in Poland, in the ten years following its première in Krakow in 1964, handled this theatrical sleight of hand.[49] While, in three productions, the acts were played for laughter and a style of grotesque buffoonery was employed, no satisfactory convention was found for the killing of Leon, the Epilogue appearing to provide something of an embarrassment in its tragic and political implications. A reaction against an exaggerated style of acting and design had set in by 1970 and attempts were made to apply the principle of restraint called for by Witkiewicz. Historically specific, realistic stage settings and an ironised naturalism in acting style were achieved by Erwin Axer's production at the Teatr Współczesny in Warsaw, where the celebrated actress Halina Mikolajska turned the role of the Mother into one of her greatest artistic achievements. Axer gave the Epilogue a realistic motivation in the shape of a revenge murder of Leon by one of his enemies, Calfskin, ironically the manager of a realist theatre, The Illusion. Further productions took a middle way between the extremes of the bizarre and the real. The internal subversions within Witkacy' s dramatic text became clearer as staging became more controlled. The manic became more intense through an economy in the use of stage signs. The Epilogue could then move closer to the metaphysical coercion Witkacy required.

The audience has to give itself up to Witkacy's derangements if it is to feel itself transported into a new dimension. The reappearance, on the stage, of characters who have died earlier in the play is only a problem if one takes Witkiewicz's plays to be about the living. If one understands that they are about the dead, it is of no significance, though it remains a sign. In the dramatic tradition one had his corpses at the end of the tragedy. In Witkacy's 'comedies with corpses', as he called them, one has them from the beginning, perhaps providing a running joke on the implications of the title of Tolstoy's play *The Living Corpse* (1911). In *The Water Hen* (1921), the heroine is shot in the first act and comes back in the second. In the third act she is shot again, but this time with more certainty.[50] In *The Beelzebub Sonata* (1925), the red-haired demonic opera singer, Hilda Purebrid, is shot by Baron Hieronymous Jackal in a violent gale in Act One. In Act Two she is awakened from her coffin in order to seduce Istvan St Michael, a composer. In Act Three she is shot again, this time by Istvan at the mouth of Hell.[51]

Yet, curiously, his characters still refer to the 'real' world that they have left. The psyches that Witkacy deforms and 'splits' are of those who possess power, sexually, emotionally and politically, and who use their possession of it to attempt to possess more, endlessly. They are insatiable. Consuming others, they consume themselves. Witkacy's catastrophism has the energy of extraordinary events which appear to refer to actual historical forces as well as to the 'real' psychic states of individuals. At the end of the 'Spherical Tragedy in 3 Acts', *The Water Hen*, three old Jews, Typowicz, Evader and Spectre, are playing cards. Albert Valpor, a wizened old sea captain, has suggested a game, since 'At our age it's the only way of whiling away the time during a social upheaval. Whist or bridge? "That is the question".' – 'Why not whist?' says Typowicz. And the stage direction reads, 'Burst of machine-gun fire'. The following are the last lines of the play:

TYPOWICZ: One club.
EVADER: Two clubs.

VALPOR: Two diamonds. (*A red glare floods the stage, and the monstrous boom of a grenade exploding nearby can be heard.*) Banging away in fine style. Your bid, Mr Spectre.

SPECTRE   (*in a quivering voice*):   Two hearts. The world is collapsing. (*Fainter red flashes, and two shells exploding a little further off.*)

TYPOWICZ: Pass.

In *They*, Witkiewicz establishes the rich connoisseur of the visual arts, Callisto Balandash, apparently at home in his country house with his huge Picasso, his nudes and an aroma of quince, absorbed in a critical discussion of Pure Form with his 'very beautiful' actress-mistress Spika, Countess Tremendosa.[52] Looking forward to overcoming his feeling of inner desolation by experiencing 'the wild perfection of the entire universe' in a night of love with her, while looking at his Picassos and eating mushrooms in cabbage kvass and a pâté made out of the legs of black-haired new-born goats, he is disturbed to find that, in the house next door, 'They' have arrived – the sinister other, the destroyers of his sort of art and the grotesque and fanatical believers in an egalitarian society. 'They' prove to be everywhere, even where you don't expect them. Even the theatre where Spika is to appear in a 'pure nonsense' play, *The Independence of Triangles* by Witkiewicz, is run by a gentleman called Pandarsome Vigour, who may be working for the secret committee to bring about the collapse of all art, and the play Spika is to appear in is reputedly written by someone who goes by the name of a Turkish general, Banga Tefuan, who turns out to be Richard Tremendosa, Spika's husband; his extreme avant-garde dramas are a cover for him in his job as head of the committee for destroying art.

They follows the process of Balandash's gradual destruction, the piece-by-piece stripping away of his pretensions. Tefuan, the revolutionary mind behind the new society 'They' represent, wishes to annihilate the Balandashes of the world. Since they are useless, they should no longer have the right to indulge their frustrations and sense of emptiness. He vows that in five years' time 'we will convert all the theatres into orphanges for handicapped children'. Tefuan, too, is diabolical. He, too, lives in the void; automatism will relieve him of his metaphysical anxiety. He collects women just as Balandash collects paintings. He destroys the theatre because he loves it. He appears to be motivated by an even more frenzied self-destructive psychic energy than Balandash himself. He seems to be consumed in jealousy and vengeance because of his love for Spika.

During a performance of a play one night, Spika is killed by the leading actor, Bamblioni, who plunges a knife into her heart. (Needless to say, the play is by Witkiewicz, *The Metaphysics of a Two-headed Calf*.) At this, Tefuan gives up his battle and retreats into a philosophical nihilism, leaving the Commander of the President's Guard, Colonel Fondoloff, in power, a good-hearted fellow who is quite happy to establish a heaven on earth, however meaningless it may be. 'Nothing exists', says Fondoloff at the end of the play, when 'They' have won the battle, 'But we remain. Our little revolution is hanging by just a hair. We'll come to the surface yet! We'll turn life into commedia dell'arte in Pure Form, pure as crystal.'

This death-dance of a class of people historically superfluous demonstrates a forceful dynamic operating within the dialectic of the self. The opposites in society, with which Witkacy confronts his characters, are transpositions of opposites which are tearing the self apart. As Gyubal Wahazar, the mad dictator, says, 'My system transposes my own torments into universal values.'[53] Witkacy's characters never emerge from self-containment, but the way he makes them operate inside themselves causes their inner workings to pour out into the real world and meet it, as do the traindriver's guts at the end of *The Crazy Locomotive*.

Witkiewicz's last surviving play, his longest and most complex work for the stage, is *The Shoemakers*,[54] 'a Theoretical Play with Songs in 3 Acts', written between 1927 and 1934. Gerould characterises the play as 'monstrous, frightening – a grotesque vision of Europe at the time of Hitler', yet it is so inventive, dynamic and full of 'digressions, polemics, philosophical discussions, invective, gags, literary criticism, references to his friends, obscenities and ironic parodies', that it promotes a theatrical energy which belies the absolute nihilism and despair of its underlying philosophy.[55] The structure of the play is a Hegelian triad of thesis, antithesis and synthesis, passing through three revolutions.[56] Act One presents the dead world in which 'Mankind is suffocating, squashed under the body of the rotting malignant tumour of capitalism', as Witkacy depicts it, 'on which fascist governments swell and burst like putrefying blisters, discharging foul-smelling gases from the faceless mass of humanity gone rotten from stewing in its own juice.' This world is divided by class – the bourgeoisie, who are in power, the aristocracy and the workers. At the end of Act One a fascist coup takes place, organised by an upper-middle-class attorney-general, Robert Scurvy, described as having 'a broad face as if made out of red cheese, in which are encrusted eyes pale blue as the buttons on underpants'. Act Two is set in a hall of compulsory unemployment, where the shoemakers are tortured by institutionalised boredom. The old socialist, Sajetan, leads the shoe-makers in a revolution of sexual and creative desire. Act Three shows the consequences of this second revolution. The old oppressors and the utopian revolutionaries go mad or are killed as obsolete and two technocrats, Comrade Abramowski and Comrade X, step over the corpses on their way to automating the new social relations.

The three main characters represent the three forces locked in mutual destruction in a type of rapacious ménage à trois: Sajetan, a dreamy idealist; Scurvy, or Bitchson, the bourgeois, a crass opportunist; and the Duchess, the aristocratic nymphomaniac. The character Mulch, symbolising the marriage of aristocracy and peasantry, and taken from Wyspianski's *The Wedding* (1905), is exposed as a fraud for suggesting that the nobility could rejuvenate itself by such a contract. The Duchess uses her capacious sexuality to enslave men and subvert all values and philosophies. The men who seek power, seek her, while at the same time hating her. The terror of the play is in its equation of power with lust and killing. The unity of the classes in a nation is made by rape, not by marriage.[57]

The end of the last act provides a series of violent images. The Duchess, dressed in a short green transparent slip and red pants, green bat's wings and a plumed three-cornered hat, dances a tango to music coming from London's Savoy Hotel, as Scurvy, in a dog's skin and a pink woollen cap and bell, howls and jerks on the chain that holds him to a dead stump. A bird-cage is lowered over the Duchess as the dying Sajetan crawls on his belly towards her. A Hyperworkoid throws a red cloth over the cage. The Hyperworkoids have earlier terrified them by one of them entering, brandishing a bomb and throwing it amongst them. While they all throw themselves to the ground, the Hyperworkoid picks the object up, unscrews its lid, and pours himself a cup of coffee.

The excitement of Witkiewicz's plays, Gerould has suggested, comes from a proposition that history works by dynamite.[58] 'The new social order', says Sajetan ('calmly but firmly') in Act Three, 'will come about all by itself, by spontaneous combustion, explosion, eruption, forged out of the dialectical struggle of everyone's guts in the human boiler; we're sitting on the lid.' In *The Shoemakers*, Witkiewicz moved away from a Theatre of Pure Form, with its distanced relation to life. The theatrical corpses in this play have much closer correspondences to the real corpses which litter the landscape of twentieth-century Europe. Indeed, their fates reflect quite accurately the conditions under which Witkacy himself became a corpse. On 1 September 1939, the Nazis invaded Poland from the west. With a woman friend, Witkacy fled to the east. On 17 September, the Russians entered Poland from the east. On 18 September, in wooded countryside near a small village in what was then Poland but is now in Russia, Witkiewicz slit his wrist with a razor. Even then there was some hesitation over the relation of the real and the unreal. His companion, who survived, recorded that the blood somehow did not flow.[59] Then he cut a vein in his leg, also to no real effect. 'I felt drowsy', she wrote. ' "Don't leave me alone," Stas cried out. "If you fall asleep, I'll cut my throat".' She fell asleep, and when she awoke, he was dead. This corpse did not get up. Material reality had finally had its way.

NOTES:

1. Quoted in 'Theatre Checklist No. 6', compiled by Daniel Gerould, *Theatrefacts*, vol. 2, no. 2, 1975, p. 5.
2. Introduction to Stanislaw Witkiewicz, *The Madman and the Nun and Other Plays*, trans. and ed. by Daniel Gerould and C. S. Durer (Seattle: University of Washington Press, 1968) p. xxiii. Three plays from this collection, with the Introduction, and Foreword by Jan Kott, have been reprinted as *The Madman and the Nun and The Crazy Locomotive (including The Water Hen)* (New York: Applause Theater Book Publishers, 1989).
3. Konstanty Puzyna, 'Witkacy in the Polish Theatre' (paper delivered at the ITI Witkiewicz Centenary Symposium, Warsaw, 1985).
4. Martin Esslin, 'The Search for a Metaphysical Dimension in Drama', introduction to *Tropical Madness* (New York: Winter House, 1972) p. 4.
5. *Spectator*, 3 March 1984; *City Limits*, 24 February – 1 March 1984; *Guardian*, 23 February 1984; *Financial Times*, 21 February 1984.
6. Janusz Degler, 'Witkiewicz on the Polish Stage, 1921–1984', *The Theatre in Poland*, no. 10–12 (1984) p. 32.
7. Puzyna, op. cit.
8. Degler, op. cit., p. 28.
9. Gerould and Durer, op. cit., p. xxiv.
10. Ibid., p. xxiii.
11. Puzyna, op. cit.

12. 'The Writings of Tadeusz Kantor, 1956–1985', trans. Michael Kobialka, *Drama Review*, vol. 30, no. 3 (Fall 1986) pp. 125, 136, 155, 169.

13. Stanislaw Witkiewicz, 'A Refutation of Anatol Stern's Objections' (1924), quoted in Janusz Degler, 'Witkacy's Theory of Theatre', *Dialectics and Humanism* (Polish Scientific Publishers) vol. XII, no. 2 (Spring 1985) p. 85.

14. From the last section of Stanislaw Witkiewicz, 'An Introduction to the Theory of Pure Form in the Theatre', *Skamander*, nos 1, 2 and 3 (1920) trans. in Gerould and Durer, op. cit., pp. 293, 295–6.

15. Allardyce Nicoll, *World Drama* (London: Harrap, 1949) p. 621.

16. Manfred Pfister, *The Theory and Analysis of Drama* (Cambridge: Cambridge University Press, 1988) p. 129.

17. Daniel Gerould, introduction to *Doubles, Demons and Dreamers* (New York: Performing Arts Journal Publications, 1985) pp. 13, 15.

18. Antonin Artaud in 1923, in a preface to Maeterlinck's 'Twelve Songs', quoted in Eric Sellin, *The Dramatic Concepts of Antonin Artaud* (Chicago: University of Chicago Press, 1968) p. 77.

19. Antonin Artaud, *The Theatre and its Double* (New York: Grove Press, 1958) pp. 46, 77, 94, 95.

20. Jean Genet, *Reflections on the Theatre* (London: Faber, 1972) p. 12.

21. Artaud, *The Theatre and its Double*, p. 31.

22. Esslin, op. cit., p. 4.

23. L. A. C. Dobrez, *The Existential and its Exits: Literary and Philosophical Perspectives on the Works of Beckett, Ionesco, Genet and Pinter* (London: Athlone Press, 1986) pp. 265–6.

24. Artaud, *The Theatre and its Double*, p. 72.

25. See Michael Green (ed.), *The Russian Symbolist Theatre* (Ann Arbor: Ardis, 1986) p. 110.

26. Theodor Adorno, *Aesthetic Theory* (London: Routledge, 1984) p. 193.

27. In Green, op. cit., p. 152.

28. Clive Hart, *Language and Structure in Beckett's Plays* (Gerrards Cross: Colin Smythe, 1986) pp. 17–18.

29. Gerould and Durer, op. cit., pp. 292–3, 295.

30. Henrik Ibsen, *Letters and Speeches*, ed. Evert Sprinchorn (London: MacGibbon & Kee, 1965) p. 144.

31. From Stanislaw Witkiewicz, 'Pure Form in the Theatre', tr. in Degler, 'Witkacy's Theory of Theatre', *Dialectics and Humanism*, p. 90.

32. Story, however, is residual. Following the Russian formalists' distinction between plot and story, Christine Kiebuzinska suggests that in Witkiewicz's plays, story, as the objective reality reflected in the work, is clearly absent, and instead plot – the means of reflecting and organising that reality through language, gestures, costumes, scenery and so on – takes its place and becomes the content. I would agree that, in his version of the relation of the fantastical and the real, Witkiewicz's dramaturgy 'hesitates' (to use Todorov's term) between story and plot, suspended as his characters are in a limbo of Death–Life. See Christine Kiebuzinska, *Revolutionaries in the Theater:*

Mayerhold, Brecht and Witkiewicz (Ann Arbor: UMI Research Press, 1988) pp. 112, 117.

33. Gerould and Durer, op. cit., p. xiiv.
34. Degler, 'Witkacy's Theory of Theatre', *Dialectics and Humanism*, p. 87.
35. 'On a New Type of Play', in Gerould and Durer, op. cit., p. 292.
36. From Witkiewicz, 'Pure Form in the Theatre', trans. in Degler, 'Witkacy's Theory of Theatre, *Dialectics and Humanism*, p. 91.
37. Stanislaw Witkiewicz, 'A Few Words about the Role of the Actor in the Theatre of Pure Form', trans. Daniel Gerould, *Theatre Quarterly*, vol. V, no. 18 (1975) pp. 94–5.
38. Witkiewicz, quoted by Degler in 'Witkacy's Theory of Theatre', *Dialectics and Humanism*, pp. 94–5.
39. See Victor H. Miesel (ed.), *Voices of German Expressionism* (London: Prentice-Hall, 1970); Dorothy Pam, 'Kokoschka's "Murderer, the Woman's Hope" ', *Drama Review*, vol. 19, no. 3 (September 1975) pp. 5–12; J. M. Ritchie and H. F. Garten, *Seven Expressionist Plays* (London: Calder, 1968).
40. Degler, 'Witkacy's Theory of Theatre', *Dialectics and Humanism*, p. 98. See also, Konstanty Puzyna, 'The Genius of Witkacy', *Gambit*, vol. 9, nos 33–4 (1979) pp. 60–1.
41. Witkiewicz, quoted by Degler, ibid., pp. 86, 99.
42. Green, op. cit., p. 131.
43. Kiebuzinska, op. cit., p. 117.
44. Samuel Taylor Coleridge, *Biographia Literaria* (London: J. M. Dent, 1906) ch. XIV, p. 147.
45. Boris Eichenbaum, 'The Theory of the Formal Method', quoting Victor Shklovsky, *Russian Formalist Criticism*, trans. Lee T. Lemon and Marion J. Reis (Lincoln: University of Nebraska Press, 1965) p. 114.
46. Umberto Eco, *A Theory of Semiotics* (Bloomington: Indiana University Press, 1976) p. 268.
47. Jan Kott, 'Witkiewicz and Artaud: Where the Analogy Ends', *Theatre Quarterly*, vol. V, no. 18 (1975) p. 70.
48. In Witkiewicz, *The Madman and the Nun*.
49. Janusz Degler, 'Witkacy in Poland: Finding a Style for "The Mother" ', *Theatre Quarterly*, vol. V, no. 18 (1975) pp. 74–9.
50. In Witkiewicz, *The Madman and the Nun*.
51. In Stanislaw Witkiewicz, *The Beelzebub Sonata: Plays, Essays and Documents*, ed. and trans. Daniel Gerould and Jadwiga Kosicka (New York: Performing Arts Journal Publications, 1980).
52. In Witkiewicz, *The Madman and the Nun*.
53. In Stanislaw Witkiewicz, *Tropical Madness*. For an analysis of Witkiewicz's techniques in dramatising Wahazar's violent monomania, see James W. Parker, 'Witkiewics's "Gyubal Wahazar" and Riebout-Dessaigne's "L'Empereur de Chine"', *Polish Review*, vol. XVIII, nos 1–2 (1973) pp. 35–6.
54. In Witkiewicz, *The Madman and the Nun*. He wrote *The End of the World* in 1928, whose manuscript was lost during the destruction of

Warsaw by the Nazis. He was working on *So-Called Humanity Gone Mad* in the year of his death.

55. Gerould and Durer, op. cit., p. 215.
56. Daniel Gerould, *Witkacy: Stanislaw Ignacy Witkiewicz as an Imaginative Writer* (Seattle: University of Washington Press, 1981) p. 325.
57. See Kiebuzinska, op. cit., p. 136.
58. Gerould and Durer, op. cit., p. xxxiv.
59. Czeslawa Korzeniowska, quoted in 'Theatre Checklist No. 6', *Theatrefacts*, vol. 2, no. 2 (1975) p. 8.

5

Beckett's Stage of Deconstruction

LANCE ST JOHN BUTLER

Beckett is the poet of the poststructuralist age. In his plays, as in all his work, we are offered something like a version of the world according to Derrida. Where Beckett has already given up the search for determinable meaning, in the 1940s and 1950s, as a vain pursuit, poststructuralism would proclaim, in the 1960s and 1970s, the ultimately undecidable nature of meaning, and would celebrate meaninglessness as an objective correlative for a new vision of the world.

Beckett started as a Modernist, offering in the poem *Whoroscope*, of 1929, and in the stories *More Pricks Than Kicks*, of 1934, formalistic constructs in the manner of Joyce which, though socially anarchic, operate according to the Joycean equation of world-order to word-order. He did not seem able to find his voice as a playwright before the Second World War, although he had dabbled, as a student and later, in dramatic experiments. His parody of Corneille's *Le Cid*, entitled *Le Kid*, written in collaboration with the French *lecteur* at Trinity College Dublin, Georges Pelorson, was performed in 1931, while, according to Ruby Cohn, a single scene of a play about Dr Johnson, *Human Wishes*, was completed in 1937 (and is published in *Disjecta* of 1983).

By 1945 Beckett had also written the two novels, *Murphy* (1938) and *Watt* (1945). These strain the Modernist project to breaking point, *Watt*, in particular, developing a style of presentation of language that becomes opaque, even insane. Reading *Watt*, the literary experiments of William Burroughs come to mind, and we should also remember that Beckett was soon to form part of the group (if he ever formed part of *any* group) around the publisher Jerome Lindon, whose *Éditions de Minuit* published the *'nouveau roman'* of Robbé-Grillet, Pinget, Duras and others in the 1950s as well as Beckett's own novels.

Then, from about 1947, Beckett began to find his own voice, to see his own vision most clearly and to write it most forcefully. Interestingly, he claimed that the idea that enabled him to make this breakthrough was connected with the word 'monologue'. During the six years after 1947 he produced his trilogy of novels, *Molloy*, *Malone Dies* and *The Unnamable*, and his most famous and influential play, *Waiting for Godot* (written probably in 1948–9). This great period of activity can be seen as continuing through *Endgame* (written in 1956) and on to the novel *How It Is* (written in 1960) and the play *Happy Days* of 1961. Which means that the 'classic' Beckett texts belong to the first half of his writing career, 1934–61, while the remainder of his texts (I choose the word 'remainder' with some care) take up the second half of his active life as a writer, 1961–89. This splitting of his career, although somewhat arbitrary, applies to his plays as much as to his novels and it suggests that we consider *Godot* (first performed in 1953), *Endgame* (1956), the radio play *All That Fall* (1957), *Krapp's Last Tape* (1958), *Happy Days* (1961) and perhaps *Play* (1963) as 'classic' Beckett, while seeing as 'residual' the plethora of shorter dramatic pieces, including a few that came as chips off the block (what the French call *déchets d'atelier*) during the great creative period.

These shorter plays, sometimes called 'dramaticules' by Beckett, include, contemporaneously with the major pieces, the two *Acts Without Words*, *Embers*, *Words and Music* and *Cascando*; then, subsequently, *Come and Go*, *Eh Joe*, *Breath*, *Not I*, *That Time*, *Footfalls*; and the latest pieces, including the television plays, *Ghost Trio* and *…but the clouds…*, and a partial reversion to an earlier manner, *Catastrophe*. This is not an exhaustive list (which is best found in, for example, the Faber *Collected Shorter Plays of Samuel Beckett* or, indeed, Faber's *Complete Plays of Samuel Beckett*) but if offers a map of Beckett's career as a dramatist that is reasonably accurate.

I have foregrounded the two terms 'remainder' and 'residual' in listing the later plays. In doing so I am partly following Beckett's own usage; among the titles he used for his collections of later texts (he produced a considerable number of non-dramatic texts as well as plays) we find *Fizzles* and *Disjecta* and a collection subtitled *Other Residua*. He answered a query of Brian Finney's about the word 'residua' with the gloss that texts following *How It Is* were to be considered residual, '(1) Severally, even when that does not appear of which each is all that remains and, (2) In relation to whole body of previous work.'[1] Clearly he sees these pieces as supplementary to a main body or corpus of work already accomplished, and, at first blush, one might well ask how on earth we would approach this later work, much of it 'difficult', if we did not know that it came from the pen of Samuel Beckett. Would such utterly static pieces of theatre as *Ohio Impromptu* or *A Piece of Monologue* ever have seen the light of international production, for instance, if they had come from an unknown? They are extraordinarily effective pieces of theatre but their minimalism sends the reader or audience back to the relatively more solid ground of the 'classic' work. They are the last few building blocks of the house that Beckett deconstructed for so long but could never finally abandon.

Yet, if the later work is rendered comprehensible by the earlier, it can equally well be claimed that the earlier work is illuminated and, as it were, confirmed by the later. We do not perhaps know how to read *Godot* until we have read, or rather seen, *Quad*, nor *Endgame* until we have seen *That Time*. That is the first proposal I have to make for reading Beckett's plays, that we should allow them to bounce off one another in both directions, imagining perhaps a circular, even centripetal, motion in Beckett's mind, round and round the same obsessive topics, refining on but never escaping from his 'pensum', churning again and again his 'whey of words'.

Besides this dialectic between 'the essential works of the canon', as John Fletcher calls them, and the 'residua', another dialectic can be established between the plays and the novels. Here again there is a circularity rather than a hierarchy, but a useful first move might be to see the plays as simpler or more schematic versions of the material of the fiction. Beckett himself said something to this effect with reference to a production of *Endgame*: 'Theater ist für mich zunächst eine Erholung von der Arbeit am Roman. Man hat es mit einen bestimmten Raum zu tun und mit Menschen in diesem Raum', that is, that theatre is for him a 'relief from working on novels'; in the theatre you have to work 'with a definite space and with people in this space.'[2] The illimitable freedom of the blank page where the 'wordy-gurdy' of the novelist churns away ('Where now? Who now? When now?', as Beckett asks of the first page of *The Unnamable*), is replaced by the discipline of the set, the stage, 'the Board' as Pozzo calls it, and by the limits of the human figures on it: one man, one woman, two men...four at most at any one time. Compared with the novel, theatre *is* a minimalist art.

The plays can thus be seen as parables, shorter and perhaps pithier versions of what has been elaborated in the fiction. But, once again, although this has an explanatory power, it is as well to canvass the opposite possibility too, for if the plays are a concise version of longer texts it may be that they contain the quintessential features of the novels. An example here might be the stunning monologue, *Not I*, of 1973, which reproduces in miniature something of the essence of many earlier monologues, especially perhaps the cascade of words that constitutes the second half of *The Unnamable*. Although this seems to put *Not I* into the junior position, one might want to use that play to help one understand the nature of the Unnamable's voice and the orientation of his concerns. Equally, the shortest of all Beckett's plays, *Breath*, of 1969, contains in its thirty seconds' duration a concrete parable that illustrates the many places in Beckett where the dual nature of time is explored, from *More Pricks Than Kicks* to *Godot* (here a residual play illuminates a classic play) and the trilogy.

*   *   *

Having had a 'little canter' around these ways of seeing Beckett's plays in relation to each other and to his novels, we come face to face with their enigmatic presence. What are we to make of them?

They are, first and foremost, no freer than any other cultural objects from the historical moment in which they were produced. They are situated at a particular point in the 'general text' of twentieth-century culture and speak the language of their environment. Thus the 'problem' of meaninglessness has been prioritised in intellectual discourse at least since the First World War (Beckett was born in 1906), and since the 1920s writers have had, as a possible model solution, the aestheticist escape: the function of art for Proust and Joyce in the 1920s (and for Joyce until his death in 1941) was not to give meaning to reality but to *be* a reality in itself. *A la recherche du temps perdu* and *Finnegans Wake* offer substitute realities, not explanations of what Beckett would call 'this one'. Beckett himself, writing of Joyce's magnum opus in 1929, when it was still called *Work in Progress*, pointed out that *Finnegans Wake* 'is not *about* something; *it is that something itself'*.[3] The incipient word-mountains that are Beckett's early texts, as well as his essay on Joyce from which this quotation comes, testify to his temptation to take this path, but by the time of the trilogy at least, he was also aware of the alternative pull towards silence, something unthinkable to his mentors. (The word 'mentor' is justified by Beckett's essay on Joyce, by their friendship in Paris in the 1920s and 1930s and by Beckett's most spectacular piece of criticism, the essay on Proust of 1931.)

Beckett shows signs of having been aware of many of the various strands of the reaction to meaninglessness both from the twentieth century and earlier: Buddhism, Cartesian doubt, Surrealism, Existentialism.[4] His statements about the classic topics of nihilism are surprisingly open, ranging from the first line of *Godot* ('Nothing to be done') to the poem that is printed among the notes at the end of *Watt*, which includes the query, 'Who may...Nothingness in words enclose?'

This directness has encouraged Beckett criticism to start from the assumption that it is with 'nothingness' that it has to do, and that its task is to account for the meaning that emerges from this insistence on meaninglessness. This essay is no exception, for it now seems to me that Beckett, as much in his plays as in his fiction, is best seen as offering an artistic version of the most recent philosophical expression of the void, poststructuralist relativism.

We can take, as itself a 'classic' text of this style of thinking, Derrida's essay 'Structure, Sign and Play in the Discourse of the Human Sciences' of 1966.[5] It is in the opening pages of this text that Derrida launches his attack on the 'centre' and on metaphysics in general, in an effort to give full value to the Structuralist enterprise on which he is commenting in the essay (notably on the anthropology of Lévi-Strauss). He wants to draw the necessary inferences from the new realisation of 'the structurality of structure' and these include, notably, the abandoning of the notion of the centre as the ground of explanation. Until the Structuralist revolution, according to Derrida, Western thought substituted one centre for another; committed to the notion of some invariable *presence*, it has filled this notion with names: essence, existence, substance, subject, truth, the transcendent, consciousness, God, man ... the list of 'fundamentals' could be extended. Since Structuralism, however, we have not been able to find another satisfying 'metonymy' of this sort and have been left in a wilderness without centre.

This 'decentring' of our possibilities of thought, with its roots in Nietzsche, Freud and Heidegger, reaches its limit, as is well known, in Derrida's own work. He points out that no discourse can operate in a vacuum, hence the fact that his deconstruction of metaphysics will employ the vocabulary of metaphysics, but, in the end, his discourse tends to be a radical undermining of any possibility of stable meaning within discourse.

Here, rather than in the impossible silence, is surely the Sisyphean quarry where Samuel Beckett has been working too. The quarry is the world of signifiers (words upon words), floating unanchored to the signifieds that would produce a centre to guarantee their meaning; the problem is illustrated by the enigmatic picture in Erskine's room, in *Watt* ('a circle and a centre not its centre in search of a centre and its circle respectively').[6] Yet, as for Derrida, there is no alternative to words, and to speak, even of escape, is to speak in the words that are given to us. As Clov tells Hamm, in *Endgame*, 'I use the words you taught me. If they don't mean anything any more, teach me others. Or let me be silent.' The impossible silence shimmers behind Beckett's texts like a mystical mirage of an impossible completion – meanwhile we are in words, up to our necks in words like Winnie in the sand in *Happy Days*.

The silence would be the transcendental signified, the meaning that needs no mediation by signifiers to express itself; God, presence, the plenitude of being, eternity, the truth. Precisely, in fact, those metaphysical entities whose radical impossibility it has been Derrida's self-appointed task to demonstrate. We live in the alphabetic world that never begins or ends, while God would be, as has been claimed for him, Alpha and Omega. Origins and ends are what there is not for poststructuralism – as Derrida puts it, the concept of structure has done away with concepts of *arché* and *telos* – beginning and end.

Here, surely, is the philosophical analogue for Beckett's plays. What made *Godot* so stunning and so difficult for its first audiences was just the unfamiliarity of this style of thinking. Why can't Didi and Gogo remember their origins? Why is it impossible to predict for them an end that would be an end? Why, in the play, does 'nothing happen twice'? There is a possible negative theology available in this – the encounter with Godot is, since he manifests his presence by non-presence, an encounter with nothingness. But we need not become too dewy-eyed at this apparent reintroduction of the divine under a thick veil – the nothing *is nothing*; Godot does not come indeed. Yet we are here for all that, we are, as Heidegger would say, 'always already' in situation, always already with a past.

And *Endgame* is the play that starts with the word 'finished' and ends with the word 'remain', presenting us with a joke on *arché* and *telos*. It is the play that tries again and again to reach an end, that insists on its own last gasp but that approaches that gasp in an infinitely deferred asymptotic curve.

*   *   *

A good place to start when studying Beckett's drama is with the two mimes, *Act Without Words* I and II. The first of these shows us Heideggerian man 'thrown into being' and his attempts to understand the semiotic world in which he finds himself:

> Desert. Dazzling light.
> The man is flung backwards on stage from right wing. He falls, gets up immediately, dusts himself, turns aside, reflects.

Reflection is not what prompts his next move – the world is already set up for it – a whistle summons him:

> Whistle from right wing.
> He reflects, goes out right.
> Immediately flung back on stage he falls, gets up immediately, dusts himself, turns aside, reflects.

The laws are already in place, the system of rewards and punishments – what Lacan would call the tyranny of the signifier – is immediately operational, the individual does not create his own world. On the contrary, he responds to signs, signals, signifiers within it, looking for meanings that are constantly offered and just as constantly withdrawn from him:

> A tiny carafe, to which is attached a huge label inscribed WATER, descends from flies...
> He looks up, sees carafe, reflects, gets up, goes and stands under it, tries in vain to reach it, renounces...

The renunciation of meaning is quite explicitly suggested in this parable of human frustration; the carafe offers the water of grace, of baptism, of salvation, but, in the intellectual context within which Beckett wrote this image, must itself give way to notions of *explanation* – the divine would *explain* what Beckett has called 'the mess'.

Derrida has called the structuralist revolution the 'moment when language invaded the universal problematic'[7] and this is the invasion that Beckett, too, will undergo. In the novels the 'wordy-gurdy' ploughs on, unable ever to 'get it all said', unable ever to 'say the word that will be me'. In the plays with words the same process is apparent: Lucky's speech, in *Godot*, is a parody of a lecture that offers an explanation of the decline of the human species; it has to be silenced. Hamm's stories, in *Endgame*, are transparent inventions designed to pass the time. The trouble is in the words; Clov hints that 'they don't mean anything any more'. People, too, are merely signifiers, representatives rather than originals, as Vladimir puts it when the tramps are considering whether to help up the fallen Pozzo: 'It is not every day that we are needed. Not indeed that we personally are needed. Others would meet the case equally well, if not better.' When, a few lines later, he boasts that they have kept their appointment (with Godot) and asks, 'How many people can boast as much?' Estragon answers, 'Billions.'

Unoriginal, then, and decentred, mankind becomes analogous to the signifiers of Structuralism themselves, that is, detached from the sort of properly-grounded meaning that Western thinking has always sought. In one of this questions to Clov, Hamm puts the point farcically: 'We're not beginning to...to...mean something?' And Clov answers: 'Mean something! You and I, mean something! (*Brief laugh.*) Ah that's a good one!'

Our meaninglessness is in part caused by the routine with which we deaden our everyday lives. As Clov asks, 'Why this farce, day after day?'. It was a theme that concerned Beckett as early as the essay on Proust which mentions, among much else, the Proustian attempt to get beyond the habitual. This Existentialist thesis is apparent in the second *Act Without Words*, which works by the simple method of having a 'goad' prod into life two men sleeping in sacks on the stage. Each in turn gets out of his sack at the behest of the goad, dresses and generally prepares himself for the day, moves the sacks, undresses and crawls into his sack to sleep. Routine could be no more forcefully or claustrophobically conveyed.

What is to be done under these gloomy circumstances? Of course, and famously, 'nothing' is to be done, but, as the tramps in *Godot* might say, what are we to do while we are doing nothing? What, in other words, did Beckett find to pass the time with or, to put it another way, to fill the page or the stage with? The answer supplied by a reading of Derrida would be *'bricolage'*. Taking his cue from the Structuralist, Gerard Genette, he develops Lévi-Strauss's concept of the 'makeshift' and extends it to all writing in the following manner. The *bricoleur*, in Lévi-Strauss, is someone who uses the means which happen to be at his disposal to complete a project, who employs what is readily available rather than the tools specifically intended for the job. By trial and error, combination and adaptation, he finds the way to use his material; as Genette says, this analysis of *'bricolage'* could be applied to criticism, including literary criticism, for there is, according to Derrida, a 'necessity of borrowing one's concepts from the text of a heritage which is more or less coherent or ruined' so that now 'every discourse is *bricoleur'*.[8]

What Derrida has in mind here is the relationship of discourses to their predecessors. Just as, in deconstructing metaphysics, one must employ the vocabulary of metaphysics, so, in putting together any text, one must employ the given vocabulary (construed in its broadest sense) of other available texts. Otherwise one becomes an 'engineer' – the one who 'constructs the totality of his language, syntax, and lexicon' thus becoming 'a subject who supposedly would be the absolute origin of his own discourse and supposedly would construct it "out of nothing"'.[9]

In all this there is a way of understanding Beckett. He is playing among the ruins of the culture to which he had so impassioned an attachment as a young man. At first there were signs that he would follow Joyce in the attempt to engineer a new discourse and construct a totality of language within which he could be god, but instead he opted for the *via negativa* that leads towards the silence. This did not prove an easy passage – *Godot* tries to become the play in which the pause (the silence) works as powerfully as the words, and *Endgame* tries to create the impression that there is almost nothing left to do or say; it makes, in fact, an immense effort to *end*. These efforts, however, are only able to be made in, and with, the ruinous material of Western culture. The plays are, in the end, plays, artistic constructs that have their own shape. Didi and Gogo come as close as it is possible to do to being nothing. But there is no silence, there is no play that is not a play, there is no final possibility of 'being nothing'. The only material ready to hand for the expression, even of the void, is the material of our culture. Thus, Lucky does not *babble*, he gives a lecture; Hamm's stories, though transparently mendacious, rely on a shared culture of giving and receiving; Didi and Gogo are, if not clearly French, Irish, English or Russian, at least definitely not Chinese, or men from Mars.

Thus Beckett performs his *bricolage* among the ruins. The ruins are the remains of his reading in Dante, in Descartes, in Shakespeare and in the Existentialists. He may appear to try to jettison them but, in the end, he plays with them instead of, as Hamm would say, 'discarding'. As his work went on, I have suggested, he also played among the ruins of his own texts, thereby adding a new dimension to intertextual *bricolage*.

In the major plays, Beckett's exercising of his material in this sense is quite easy to spot and is responsible for the odd tone of *Godot* and *Endgame*, which are, as the subtitle to the former indicates, 'tragi-comedies'. The tragic side of the equation is structural – the tramps *are* lonely and abandoned, the play takes them nowhere, and almost the same words could be applied to Hamm and Clov, not to mention Nagg and Nell – but the comic side is permitted, in the face of this, by Beckett's *bricoleur* nature as a writer. For what is funny, in *Godot* and *Endgame*, are the moments of explicit reference to the models that the plays mock. It is as if Beckett says to us, 'Look! Here's the Christian religion, here's Charlie Chaplin, here's a soliloquy, here's an aside, here's Shakespeare ("My kingdom for a nightman!"), here's Bishop Berkeley, here are people also serving although they are only standing and waiting…' But none of this can, in the absymal contexts in which it is found, be taken seriously. The bits and pieces aren't the right tools for the job, they are out-of-joint, ineffective, rendered laughable. Beckett has, in other words, disclaimed all qualifications as an engineer, and the provisional or makeshift nature of the positions he adopts is intensely clear, especially in the plays where, after all, some words must be spoken, even by Lucky. Thus, the Biblical references that figure so largely in the opening pages of Godot are, simultaneously, comic in their obvious and hopeless derivativeness from a discourse that doesn't work, and tragic for precisely the same reason.

VLADIMIR: One of the thieves was saved. (*Pause.*) It's a reasonable percentage…

            Ah yes, the two thieves. Do your remember the story?
ESTRAGON: No.

VLADIMIR: Shall I tell it to you?
ESTRAGON: No.

Why does Estragon refuse to hear the story (which Vladimir, after a fashion, tells none the less)? Is the reason not connected with their agreement that 'hope deferred maketh the something sick'? Estragon cannot abide the promise of promise, the tantalising nature of what might be. It is Vladimir, in Act Two, who, optimistic as ever, greets the second arrival of Pozzo and Lucky with the cry 'It's Godot! We're saved!', thereby echoing the discussion of the Saviour in the early pages.

The Dead Sea, which seems to be most of what Estragon remembers of his reading of the Gospels, is a joke because we feel that there is perhaps more that could be remembered in those texts, and because, in his ignorance, he found the look of it make him thirsty, when it is known to be violently saline. But we are not allowed to stop at the joke. The truth is that there is something pathetic, even tragic, in Estragon's nostalgia for what he has never known ('We'll swim. We'll be happy.'). The Gospels *do* offer drink to the thirsty, salvation for the lost and so on, and the tramps *do* need it, there is no cosy alternative to their present plight which we could flatter ourselves that they might be able to retreat to once tired of waiting for Godot.

Similarly, every instant of *Endgame* is made up of the makeshift. Hamm is an actor, his stories are false, his attitudes absurd; yet they are the available ones, these are the parts assigned to us, vague memories of dramatic moments elsewhere and at another time. So much so that it is never fully possible to know when Hamm is 'putting it on' or when he is 'serious'. What value can we attach to his cries of despair (or to Pozzo's great outburst, 'Have you not done tormenting me with your accursed time?', in the second act of *Godot*) when we know that the language and the structures used are inappropriate, being the words of our culture and not of 'ourselves'? The last of the 'classic' Beckett plays, in my account, is entitled *Play*. In all his work there is this playing with the serious that undermines it intellectually without ridding it of its emotional seriousness.

*　　*　　*

I have concentrated, in what I have said so far, on the two best-known of Beckett's plays, *Godot* and *Endgame*. I think it is now possible to see his dramatic work as being all of a piece in some respects, with Beckett territory mapped out in these plays, together with *Krapp*, *All That Fall* and perhaps *Play*, and to see the later work acting as a series of refinements within this arid zone. But I also see some of the later work as achieving the quality and intensity of the great plays and, perhaps, even as advancing their arguments a little.

The word 'arguments' is perhaps wrong here, because the plays I have in mind do not necessarily appeal to the intellect. The Derridean echoes in the earlier work give place to a level that can best be described as emotional, in such works as *Not I*, *Footfalls* and *Rockaby*. It is perhaps no coincidence that these plays focus on a female protagonist (in all three cases created to Beckett's taste by Billie Whitelaw) and permitted the older Beckett to put onto the stage the slightly richer vision that the female could evoke in him at times. (We can think of Celia, in *Murphy*, or the three women who people the short piece, of 1966, *Come and Go*.) These three plays have been called 'Beckett's other trilogy' by Robert Simone,[10] and, although that is almost certainly an exaggeration of their status, they are remarkably powerful pieces with a certain continuity evident between them. I would like to close with a consideration of their significance for our overall estimation of Beckett the playwright, while signalling that I believe that, among the later plays, they should be read or seen alongside *Quad*, *That Time* and the television plays, *Ghost Trio* and...*but the clouds...*, as the essential corpus of Beckett's dramatic work of the 1970s and 1980s.

The richer vision of *Not I* (1973), in spite of the female protagonist, is hardly softer than the bleak pictures of the earlier theatre. Indeed, the humour that pervades *Godot*, *Krapp* and the other 'classic' pieces is conspicuously absent from this terrifying and hysterical monologue. I have not seen any stronger audience reactions than those experienced during and after a good performance of this play which, after all, only lasts ten minutes. But that seems to be the point – reaction is at a terrified level of powerful feeling and not a matter of ratiocination. It is as if Beckett has reached a *tone* or a *picture*[11] where the mental can be abandoned in favour of the visceral. Certainly, when Mouth emits her appalling screams at the stated intervals during her babble, the effect is of listening to pure human suffering, in the knowledge that nothing in the words spoken will account for or justify it. While working on the play, he wrote in a letter to Jessica Tandy that he was 'not unduly concerned with intelligibility' and that he hoped that his piece would work 'on the nerves`of the audience, not on its intellect'.[12]

Footfalls (1976) picks up the theme of female memory in a slightly softer mode. There is a confusion between 'V', the voice of the mother, that listens, and then talks, and 'M', the voice of May, the protagonist, whose footfalls we hear and who also talks. Each has her monologue, each seems to revolve in her mind events that took place in the past, memory is stirred by the pacing feet in the grey light. Once again it is not at all clear that we should attach much significance to what is said. Instead, the archetypal figure walks, her mother's voice sounds, perhaps in her head, and the impact is on the nerves rather than the thought processes.

Rockaby (1982) is another, softer version of *Not I*. We hear the voice speaking while the actress rocks silently except for four commands to the voice ('More'). We hear, slowly and repetitiously, what is passing in her head, but the thoughts are more impressions than thoughts and they circle around a few images so that we are able to identify a *tone* to go with the stage picture, an elegiac tone suitable to the entirely obvious fact that the old woman in the rocker, in black, is dying. There is an immense simplicity about the piece: the old woman sits, rocks, remembers, fades, dies. A few memories flit compulsively across the screen of memory, mark the life they are the epitaph to with their melancholy mood, fade, die. That is all.

It is easy to speak of the *theatre* of these late plays, and *Footfalls* has been seen by Martin Esslin as almost a new art form, while all three represent a new kind of drama,[13] but they seem far less amenable to any coherent interpretation, as texts, unless it be by a criticism that is insistently deconstructionist. Then, however, one feels that it would be the critic not so much deconstructing Beckett as merely pointing out the extent to which Beckett deconstructs the norms of Western theatre and, interestingly, himself. For the slightly softened memories of *Footfalls* and *Rockaby* are the work of an old man, himself remembering, and they provide alter egos in which Beckett can survey the past with a certain calm. In this respect the 'trilogy' would work as follows: *Not I* is the last hysterical gasp, after which we meet the woman again, calmer each time, finally surveying from the trivial Olympus of a rocking chair the unmeaning shards of a life remembered. It is the world without *telos*, but without a meaningful origin either.

*   *   *

In the end there seems no net in which to catch Beckett's theatre, although currently, along with his non-dramatic work, it seems to provoke the making of nets innumerable. The closest one comes to a catch is when one is wearing quite definitely poststructuralist spectacles. Made from the discourses of the past (our past, Beckett's own version of that past), his last plays became simpler and less inclined to try to assert their own discourses, the words have become emptier, sparer, more enigmatic, and the tendency has been towards the creation of a form of picture that can at least pretend to have escaped from the tyranny of the signifier.

NOTES

1. Brian Finney, *Since How It Is: A Study of Samuel Beckett's Later Fiction* (London: Covent Garden Press, 1972) p. 10.
2. See Michael Haerdter, *Materialen zu Becketts Endspiel* (Frankfurt: Suhrkamp, 1967) p. 88.
3. This essay is now collected in Ruby Cohn (ed.), *Disjecta: Miscellaneous Writings and a Dramatic Fragment by Samuel Beckett* (London: John Calder, 1983) pp. 19–34.
4. See, for instance, David Hesla, *The Shape of Chaos: An Interpretation of the Art of Samuel Beckett* (Minneapolis: University of Minnesota Press, 1971), and Lance St John Butler, *Samuel Beckett and the Meaning of Being: A Study in Ontological Parable* (London: Macmillan, 1984).
5. Jacques Derrida, 'Structure, Sign and Play in the Discourse of the Human Sciences', was delivered as a lecture at Johns Hopkins University, Baltimore, USA, in French in October 1966. It is available in English in Jacques Derrida, *Writing and Difference*, trans. Alan Bass (London: Routledge & Kegan Paul, 1978) pp. 278–93.
6. Samuel Beckett, *Watt* (London: John Calder, 1963) p. 127.
7. Derrida, 'Structure, Sign and Play', p. 124.
8. Ibid., p. 129.
9. Ibid.

10. R. Thomas Simone, 'Beckett's Other Trilogy: *Not I, Footfalls* and *Rockaby*', in Robin J. Davis and Lance St John Butler (eds), *'Make Sense Who May': Essays on Samuel Beckett's Later Works* (Gerrards Cross: Colin Smythe, 1988) pp. 56–65.
11. Ibid., p. 57.
12. See Enoch Brater, 'Dada, Surrealism and the Genesis of *Not I*', *Modern Drama*, vol. 18, no. 1 (1975) p. 53.
13. Simone, op. cit., p. 57.

6

Antonin Artaud and the Theatre of Cruelty

BETTINA L. KNAPP

'A true theatrical work disturbs the senses in repose, liberates the repressed unconscious, foments a virtual revolt ... and imposes both a heroic and difficult attitude on the assembled collectivity.'[1] So wrote Antonin Artaud in 1933. The father of the revolutionary theatre of cruelty, Artaud wanted to do away with the traditional theatre, whose nuclear elements were words, well-made plots, psychologically oriented and rationally understandable characters.

Artaud viewed the theatre as had the people of antiquity: as a ritual whose purpose was to stimulate numinous or religious experiences within the spectator. To achieve this end he sought to expand the spectator's reality by arousing the explosive and creative forces within man's unconscious, which, he believed, was more powerful than rational consciousness in determining man's actions. By means of a theatre based on *myths, symbols,* and *gestures,* the play, for Artaud, became a weapon to be used to whip up man's irrational forces, so that a collective theatrical event could be turned into a personal and living experience.

*   *   *

Why was Artaud so preoccupied with the unconscious, with the irrational? Because he was a sick man. An inability to think in a rational manner, and an oversensitive and high-strung nature, had led him to opt for a theatre which worked on the nerves and the senses, and reject one which sought to speak to the intellect alone. Artaud's theatre, therefore, was militantly anti-rational as well as hugely emotional; it was an attempt to spew forth venom – to scathe all those with whom it would come into contact. Artaud was not a social reformer. Artaud's theatre was apolitical. Such a stand can best be attested to in terms of his rapport with the Surrealists. When Artaud joined the Surrealist group, in 1924, he felt he had something in common with its founder, André Breton. According to Breton's *Surrealist Manifesto*, humankind was to be freed from the grasping tentacles of an overly constricting moralistic bourgeois society as well as from literary and artistic conventions. Surrealism brought forth another world to be scrutinised, one not limited by man's rational vision, but existing in the unlimited realm of the unconscious.

Two years later, however, in 1926, Artaud severed relations with the Surrealist group because its leaders had become communists. Breton, Aragon, Éluard, Peret, Unik had joined the Communist Party. The Big Five, as they were known then, wrote a pamphlet, 'In the Light of Day' in which they proclaimed the expulsion of Artaud from their group and also made their political affiliations quite clear. They did not stop there, but proceeded to attack Artaud's Achilles' heel – the weak rational aspect of his mind. Artaud could not leave the affront unanswered. He counter-attacked with 'In Broad Night or the Surrealist Bluff' and accused his former friends of treachery, declaring that Surrealism had died the day Breton and his cohorts rallied to the Communist banner. To try to reconcile freedom with constriction was impossible for Artaud. Breton and his group were merely permitting 'social armature' to pass from one form of power to another, whether the bourgeoisie or the proletariat held power made little difference to the artist in quest of the free, eternal aspects in man.

Artaud's ideas concerning the theatre were relatively simple: divest the theatre of *all* logic and verisimilitude; touch and bruise the spectator, thereby forcing involvement. The theatre must not be considered as mere entertainment, nor as a game-like activity, but rather as a 'kind of event', a totally unexpected event. The audience becomes an intrinsic part of the theatrical venture. The spectator must be shocked, react violently to the 'unprecedented eruption of a world' on stage: he must feel that he is seeing the essence of his own being before him, that his life is unfolding within the bodies of others. If a theatrical production is to be considered effective, the spectator must experience anguish, be immensely and intensely involved; so deeply affected that his whole organism is shaken into participation.

Artaud founded the Théâtre Alfred Jarry in 1926, thirty years after the creation of Jarry's *King Ubu* at the Théâtre de l'Oeuvre. Jarry's most successful failure, *King Ubu*, had rocked the Parisian theatrical world. Was it a coincidence that both of these men of vision, whose approach to people and things was uninhibited, whose humour was biting and whose imagination was keen, rebelled against what they considered to be stupidity, cowardliness, greed and hypocrisy? Was it a coincidence that Jarry and Artaud were labelled by many of their contemporaries as 'eccentric', 'mad', and were the butt of satire and ridicule?

Jarry's theatrical notions were revolutionary. He rejected the well-made play, the psychological, romantic, and naturalistic dramas so popular in his day and whose purpose was to please, entertain or elevate the public. Though the theatrical climate in Paris at the end of the nineteenth century was varied and vigorous, for some, namely Jarry, it was uninteresting and repetitious. André Antoine had created his Théâtre Libre (1887–94), and produced naturalistic plays featuring a 'slice of life', as well as foreign works. Paul Fort, who had created his Théâtre d'Art (1890–3), offered a symbolistic atmosphere with scenic adaptations of works by Mallarmé, Rimbaud, Laforgue and others. Lugné-Poë, the founder of the Théâtre de l'Oeuvre, won his first successes with Maeterlinck's *Pelléas and Mélisande*. Dramatists flooded the boards: Jules Renard, Octave Mirbeau, Porto-Riche, Henry Bataille, Henry Bernstein, François de Curel, Paul Hervieu, and Eugène Brieux, Tristan Bernard, Maurice Donnay, Georges Feydeau, Courteline, and the list is long.

Unlike most of his contemporaries, Jarry refused to write *down* or to write *up* to his audiences. The theatre for this 'Enfant Terrible of Symbolism', as he was sometimes called by his friends, was neither a civic festival nor a morality lesson, nor was it designed for relaxation. Jarry's audiences were not merely to sit back and *take in*. His theatre was one of *action*, of shock, designed for an élite and not for the 'tout Paris' who responded to flashy decor, gaudy ballets, obvious and accessible emotions. Those who did not understand or appreciate what he had in mind could leave the theatre, as far as he was concerned, or, better still, be forcibly ejected.

Artaud was as iconoclastic as his mentor. When founding the Théâtre Alfred Jarry, he wrote:

The spectator who comes to us knows that he has agreed to undergo a true operation, where not only his mind, but his senses and his flesh are going to come into play. Henceforth, he will go to the theatre as he goes to the dentist. In the same spirit with the thought that he will not die from the ordeal, but that it is something serious and from which he will not emerge intact. If we were not convinced of being able to strike him in the most serious manner possible, we would consider ourselves incapable of carrying out our most absolute task. He must really be convinced that we are capable of making him scream out.[2]

Artaud's ideas concerning the dramatic arts were inspired by Jarry; but they were also born from his sickness. Indeed, he looked upon the theatre as a curative agent; a means whereby the individual could come to the theatre to be dissected, split and cut open first, and then healed. The healing ritual would proceed as follows: the stage happenings would elicit psychological projections from the spectator. As tension was developed on stage, as events moved toward a climax, there would ensue a corresponding tension in the audience that would eventually become so great as to force the spectator to recognise the nature of his projections and anxieties. Once having permitted his anxieties to come to the light of consciousness, the spectator would now see his various problems from a different point of view and would gain, thereby, greater participation and self-understanding. This new vision would allow the fragments of the spectator's personality, which had been projected onto the stage, to return to their source, the spectator's being – nourished and renewed by the added understanding.

Artaud's first theatrical venture – the Théâtre Alfred Jarry – aborted. He had sought, unsuccessfully, to produce plays by Paul Claudel, Roger Vitrac, and himself; to break the conventions of contemporary theatre and to obey the dictates of an 'inner necessity'. He had tried to dislocate the reality to which audiences were accustomed, in the hope that they might achieve a deeper and more forthright way of considering life. Stage life, for Artaud, was a continuation of real life – his own – and a search for meaning.

Another powerful influence was to make itself felt on Artaud: the production of Balinese Theatre which he witnessed in 1931 at the Colonial Exhibition in Paris. What had impressed him most of all in Balinese theatre was the importance of gestures and facial expressions, and the relatively unimportant role of the spoken word. It was the antithesis of Western views on the subject.

The theatre, as Artaud now saw it, and as he expressed it in *The Theatre and its Double*, a volume of essays, letters, and manifestoes written between 1931 and 1935, was to be a ritual capable of evoking a religious experience within the spectator's mind and heart. What was to be dramatised? – a *Myth*, Artaud had said.

What did he mean by myth? A myth is a dramatic relating of those experiences, or a description of those qualities, which are deepest within beings. Myths are the outcome of original experiences; not always personal but, rather, impersonal or transcendental.

Just as myths have been dramatised by Aeschylus, Sophocles, Euripides, and others, so must modern authors, he suggested, dramatise modern myths. To make the spectator's theatrical experience meaningful, the myth must be enacted on stage in modern terms to suit a human being's present-day needs. New myths, therefore, must come into being, and quickly, because Western man today, as a whole, feels cut off from nature and from himself. His rational and scientific development has given him a clearer understanding of his relationship to nature, but, as a result, he no longer participates in the same mysteries as did the ancients. A cliff is a cliff – plain and simple – it is no longer a source of mystery, magic, fright and excitement, as it had been for the ancients. Primitive people became familiar with their own inner drama, through analogy, in the processes of nature. A modern person has to find his way alone, unaided by alliance with either God, Nature or even himself. But just as modern society cannot return to a more primitive level of existence, so twentieth-century authors must not worship the great writers of the antiquity. Modern masses should not be blamed for their inability to appreciate a play such as *Oedipus Rex*, Artaud indicates in his essay 'No More Masterpieces'. If Sophocles' play no longer appeals to large audiences, it is not because people are devoid of torments (murders, wars, rapes etc.) or that they no longer have a feeling for the 'sublime'. Modern man does not respond to the myths as expressed by Sophocles, Aeschylus, Euripides and Shakespeare, because they are no longer part of his living religion. They are not original experiences. They are history, fine literature, the products of genius; but they do not reach into the heart of today's people and so are no longer valid. The Judaeo-Christian myths, for example, are no longer a real source of inspiration for the artist, as they had once been in the Middle Ages and the Renaissance.

In Artaud's vital article, 'Metaphysics and the *mise-en-scène*', he discusses just this point: the decline in meaningfulness of certain myths with reference to paintings. Modern painters, when trying to depict a Biblical scene, usually turn out a dry, lifeless, and uninteresting work simply because they no longer believe in the myths of their ancestors. They are incapable, therefore, of finding a living response within their own being, and, so, within others. It is the task of the writer to discover modern man's real sentiments about life, to dredge up, from within, all of his buried forces, the fire which lives within him. With this material the writer must create or express new myths. Today, a person must search out his or her own contemporary myth, declared Artaud, force down the mask and reveal his inner sun, although it may be coated and smudged. People must find their own living religion.

Artaud called the theatre he wished to see come into being the Theatre of Cruelty. But *cruelty*, the term as used by Artaud, does not mean *blood* or *carnage*, although these might occur during a performance. Philosophically speaking, the word 'cruelty' means to create, to breathe, to cry – any *act* is cruelty.

> I employ the word 'cruelty' in the sense of an appetite for life, a cosmic rigor and implacable necessity, in the gnostic sense of a living whirlwind that devours the darkness, in the sense of that pain from whose ineluctable necessity life could not continue.[3]

> I should like to delve a bit more deeply into this concept of cruelty as being synonymous with action. For example, everything that is not dormant in life is cruel. When Brahma, for example, left his state of rest, he suffered. When a child is born, it knows pain. Death, transformation, thirst, love, appetite are all *cruelties*: 'It is cruelty that cements matter together, cruelty that molds the features of the created world.'[4]

The moment unity no longer exists, pain or cruelty or action must follow. Any change, then, in a state requires motion, and so conflict and cruelty begin: a change from dark to light, matter to spirit, inertia to movement. When God created the world he did away with the original state of unity. When he cast Adam and Eve from Paradise he further increased the division between human beings and himself; his creation and the cosmos. Before the *Creation*, and before Adam and Eve were cast into the world of antagonisms, life did not exist as we now perceive it – paradise is, in actuality, a state of union with the cosmos.

The 'Great Fable of Creation', that is, the change from un-conscious unity to conscious individuality and multiplicity, is forever being enacted on different levels and is, Artaud felt, a human being's most traumatic experience. The drama *per se*, looked upon symbolically, is one of *Creation*. It is the enactment and reenactment of the pain experienced by human beings as they are torn away from their stage of original unity, from 'Mother Earth' or from 'undifferentiated reality'. A person is then forced into a state of multiplicity where he must act and react, therefore, live cruelly.

As spectators see and hear the story of Creation enacted before them, they are filled with nostalgia for the primordial condition they once knew – and which they had nearly forgotten. To reach this deepest of levels, to discover unity with the cosmos, a march inward must be made. Such motion is shocking and painful; it is a voyage fraught with cruelty every step of the way. 'Everything that acts is a cruelty. It is upon this idea of extreme action, pushed beyond all limits, that theatre must be rebuilt.'[5] The theatre, then, is to take each and every spectator on a *journey inward*. The theatre is an active force, therefore a cruel one, which must work on the spectator always.

In the same way that our dreams have an effect upon us and reality has an effect upon our dreams, so we believe that the images of thought can be identified with a dream which will be efficacious to the degree that it can be projected with the neces-sary violence. And the public will believe in the theatre's dreams on condition that it takes them for true dreams and not for a servile copy of reality; on condition that they allow the public to liberate within itself the magical liberties of dreams which it can only recognize when they are imprinted with terror and cruelty.[6]

The Theatre of Cruelty, for Artaud, is a total experience. It is at once material and spiritual, real and imaginary. To establish such a theatre, theatrical techniques must be precise and as organised as the circulation of blood in the arteries.

*   *   *

What were the techniques involved in a Theatre of Cruelty production?

A Theatre of Cruelty *production* must contain 'physical' and 'objective' elements, capable of acting and reacting upon everybody's sensibilities: screams, apparitions, surprises, magic, beauty, rituals, harmony, movement, colours etc.

A *director* creating a *mise-en-scène* for a Theatre of Cruelty play must bring about a fusion of all these disparate elements, thereby creating unity from disunity. The director, for Artaud, was a type of 'unique Creator', who would be responsible both for the spectacle and for the action. The director was like a magician, a master, to use Artaud's words, of 'sacred ceremonies', a 'Demiurge', a high priest, a god.

If a director's function, in part, was to infuse life into the spectacle, the *actor* must do likewise when creating his role. An actor must materialise the sensations and feelings he sought to bring out in his portrayal and could effect such results through proper breathing. This technique stemmed from a complex metaphysical concept. Passion, Artaud wrote, of every type, had 'organic bases'. It was something physical and the rays emitted by a sensation from the body were likewise material. Every mental motion, every feeling, had its corresponding breath, Artaud stated. It was the actor, through training, who must discover the right breath for the proper sentiment.

Artaud considered breathing techniques to be of the utmost importance. It was a way, he felt, of linking the actor to the character he was portraying: it was also a means of associating him with the forces of the cosmos. In 'Emotional Athleticism' Artaud wrote:

> The gifted actor finds by instinct how to tap and radiate certain powers; but he would be astonished indeed if it were revealed to him that these powers, which have their material trajectory by and *in the organs*, actually exist, for he has never realized they could actually exist.[7]

Artaud's metaphysical attitude in connection with breathing led him to consider breathing as a source of creation. Indeed, such a notion dates far back into prehistory. According to the Bible, creation took place when God breathed 'a living breath' into Adam. The Orientals believe in the all-pervading Breath, the Buddha-Essence of the Buddha-Mind, the One, and that all life emerges from it and dissolves back into it.

The actor, through breathing, could also create *a being* (his double), that is, the character he wanted to personify, or an image or a mood. He could learn to commune with the forces of nature, as well as with his own disparate parts, by localising the points where his muscles were affected by the emotion he sought to portray: anger, sobs, guilt etc.

Furthermore, the actor must know how to 'touch' certain parts of the spectator's body in order to send him into a magic trance. He could succeed in this because emotion had organic origins. When breathing properly the actor cast forth certain rays which struck the spectator in the proper place, provoking him to laugh or to cry, as the case might be.

Unlike the Western actor, who looked *out*, who was 'uplifted toward God' and who 'succumbed to exaltation' when he experienced religious fervour, Artaud's actor, like the Oriental, looked *within* to find God or Self – his Breath, his Double.

Gesture was also of extreme importance in creating a momentous theatrical spectacle. It revealed the inner man. Gestures were symbolic evocations of nature's aspects. They were signs of both inner and outer activities, which could be made on stage and which acted upon the spectator's imagination.

Although gestures and attitudes on the part of the actor were of supreme importance in Artaud's theatre, words should not be 'suppressed' in creating a *stage language*. They should be given the importance they have in dreams, Artaud stated. The word was but one of many theatrical vehicles, to be combined with lighting, gestures, music, sound, facial expressions etc. Western theatre, as Artaud had already indicated, relied too heavily upon the spoken and written word as a vehicle for expression. The word, as a result, had become ossified and a frozen means of conveying feeling, magic and mystery in the theatre.

Artaud relegated the *word* to its proper place, as one of the ways of expressing and acting upon a person's inner world. If words were to be effective, they must be manipulated like solid objects, Artaud explicated. They must act and react upon each other and upon the spectator.

The word was a concrete reality for Artaud and it must be uttered with the vehemence of the emotion that gave birth to it. Words were not merely a means of communication. He sought to restore to them their primitive functions and qualities, their incantatory nature, supernatural aura, mesmerising and magical faculties (as in hymns, prayers etc.) – all lost to the modern person. (Genet has captured this quality superbly in *The Blacks*.) To recreate the role of the word necessitated first its destruction. Established words, meanings and sounds would have to be shattered before new contents could emerge. (Ionesco slashed the usual meanings of words in his early plays, such as *The Bald Soprano*, *The Lesson*, etc.) Words then become as hieroglyphics, a visual translation for certain mysterious elements within a human being and the universe.

Sound effects played a strong role in Artaud's conceptions. He made notations for background noises to be used in his dramatic productions. In fact, they were marked in such detail that they resembled a musical score. But even these notations, indicating the concrete sounds he sought to reproduce in the course of a play, could not possibly convey the sought-for impression, since no verbal description of a sound or vocal intonation or nuance is really possible. Musical instruments, if needed during a performance, should also be used as objects, symbolically, as did Orientals, as part of the decor. If modern instruments could not produce the sounds necessary, then ancient instruments should be used or new ones invented 'based on special blendings of a new metal alloys which can add new pitches to an octave, produce unbearable shooting sounds and noises'. (Such sounds are reminiscent of rock musicals, such as *Salvation*.)

Lights should be protagonists in the drama – actors. The interplay of lights on the stage could be a dramatic instrument designed to create an atmosphere capable of moving the spectator to anxiety, terror, eroticism, or love. Lighting was a force which could play on the mind of the spectator because of its vibratory possibilities. It could, Artaud declared, be cast down onto the stage in waves, in sheets, or in fiery arrows.

Costumes could be exquisite works of art, as they were in Oriental theatre; they could also capture the magic and mystery of the unknown. Modern dress, Artaud felt, should be avoided since it did not stir the imagination.

There should be no separation between *the stage and the theatre*. The theatre should be enclosed within four walls and be modified according to the architecture of certain sacred places: churches or temples, such as those in Tibet. There would be no ornamentation and the walls would be painted with lime to absorb the light. Audiences would sit in the middle of the stage on mobile chairs that would permit them to follow the play, unfolding around them. There would be galleries in the theatre, allowing the action to take place on all levels and dimensions; in height and in depth. This diffused action in space would grip and assault the spectator – as though a world were forcing itself in upon him: symbolically speaking, the outside world acting upon and stimulating the audience's inner world. (There were, therefore, few visual centres in Artaud's theatre, as in that of the Oriental: in Kabuki theatre, for example. One actor might be performing on one side of the stage while someone else might be gesturing on the other. Günter Grass did this in *The Tin Drum*; Peter Weiss in *Marats/Sade*, etc.) A performance, then, consisted of a series of 'parts of a play isolated in space'. These parts of images were usually not bound together according to a so-called rational pattern, as they were in the West. There were no situations created to develop progression, suspense or depth of character, as Westerners thought of it. The rational mind, Artaud felt, must not synthesise or order the images it saw into consecutive patterns. Life itself was in a state of flux. It was the impact of these isolated fragments upon the spectator that was important.

Objects, masks, accessories were to be used to help create a concrete theatrical language. These accessories and masks might appear on stage in the same size and shape as they did in the sleeper's dream world. They could, therefore, be huge or tiny, grotesque or beautiful, etc.

There should be no *decor*, Artaud wrote. It must be noted that in old Chinese and Noh theatre there was no attempt at realistic scenery. The stage was decorated; that is, it indicated where the action was situated (a palace, lake, etc.), but it did not represent it. Properties were used symbolically: a wooden table and two chairs might imply a banquet hall. Artaud felt that his actors, whom he called 'animated hieroglyphics' could, by the rhythmic use of their voices and gestures, express everything that was necessary.

*   *   *

It was not until August 1936 that Artaud's theatrical ideas were actually made concrete – and for him alone. It happened during his perilous journey into an 'anterior' world – in the land of the Tarahumaras Indians, 48 hours north of Mexico City.

The Tarahumaras Indians lived in the same state of development that humanity had before the flood. As Artaud journeyed up the mountain to their home, a world alive with magic, with haunting rhythms, images and artifacts, seemed to be closing in on him. He was dazzled by the extremes of colour; by the region's topography, the shapes and forms he saw about him. In some areas, these forms took the shape of men's tortured bodies; elsewhere, of gods' heads peering from behind rock clusters; of drowned men half eaten by stones; a statue of Death holding a child in its hand; a man lying on a stone, his arms open and his hands nailed as they pointed to the four cardinal points.

The Tarahumaras Indians believed themselves to be the descend-ants of a race of fire-bearing men who had served three Masters or three Kings. It was said that these Masters were on their way toward the Polar star, and had stopped amid the Tarahumaras tribe way back in time. A similar legend was related by Saint Matthew, when he declared that the three Magi, guided by celestial indica-tions, had come from Persia and were going to Jerusalem.

The Tarahumaras were not only worshippers of the heavenly fire – the visible fire god, the sun – but they imbibed peyotl, which they said opened the way to Ciguri or the Man–God. Peyotl, then, became that precious element needed to cross from the finite world to the infinite – enabling each one of them to experience God within. The great peyotl festival took place once a year and Artaud was to witness it.

What Artaud saw was so incredible as to be beyond belief: something he had known intuitively all these years, insights which had risen forth from his most primitive depths, revelations he had presented in his brilliant essays in *The Theatre and its Double* – what Paris's theatrical world had rejected en masse via blocks of unpleas-ant epithets. On a mountain top, removed from civilisation, Artaud was going to watch and partake of a religious ritual: a true Theatre of Cruelty spectacle.

The sky was ablaze, as though mirroring the intensity of what was about to occur. Artaud watched the priest–sorcerers come down the mountainside with all the accessories necessary for a religious (dramatic) ritual: baskets, crosses, 'mirrors gleaming like patches of sky'. A vision possessed his eyes: worlds far distant seemed to cling together as the past shot forth, invading the present.

The ceremony began. The faces of the initiates, who had already taken communion by eating their peyotl God, took on an almost inhuman expression: a strange glow and illumination. The stage was set; the 'ring' had been drawn. Around it glowed the forbidden area where evil breathed its destructive force. Here, no mortal was allowed to tread, so horrendous would be the consequences. Within the 'ring' a 'history of the world is danced' from dawn to daybreak, around a fire, the reflection of the eternal sun. The priest–sorcerers thumped the ground with a stick, traced magic numbers (usually an 8) in a series of intricate geometrical designs (triangles, circles, etc.) in order to 'restore lost rapports'. After this, they spat not saliva from their mouths but the 'breath' of life, the symbol of creation. They walked upon the stage, together with the dancers, armed with six hundred small bells of horn and silver, glaring, sparkling, lending dramatic excitement to this decor of magic and myth. The lighting effects dazzled; the sounds emanating from this array of beings and things devastated. Dancers whirled. They seemed to lacerate space with their 'coyote' calls, shooting through the land like bristling arrows. Their gestures became more violent, as though they wanted to taunt destiny, tempt danger; and they drew closer and closer to that forbidden area in which evil was held captive. The dancers, Male and Female symbolising the Great Principle, gestured now in a menacing and warring manner; then fled from one another, only to bump against each other once again.

Artaud watched the Ciguri Rite dance, which is essentially one of creation, as a spectator–participant, parishioner–officiant. Transfixed, as sensations from all quarters of the universe seemed to pour in on him, forcefully at first, then with bated impact; he was invaded by a sense of the sacred, of danger, of the inhuman. Slowly, virtually unconsciously, he slipped into the elements of the alchemical drama he had described so vividly in his essay, 'Alchemical Theatre' (1932). Reaching right into the heart of the Myth – the Mystery – he became part of the essential transforming process in nature.

The performance continued as actors veered about, pursuing their mimodrama; tinkling their bells; casting voluntary shadow on the stage/ground floor as they persevered in their endless gyrations, silhouetted against a blistering sun. Another series of symbols now etched themselves on stage, as though they had emerged bodily from *The Book of the Dead*: crosses, mirrors, beams, all manifestations of the Male and Female Principles which lie buried in matter. The Priest–Sorcerers, feeling compelled to obtain some tangible proof of the efficacy of their ritual, filed past the flames: bowing, curtsying, marching, crossing themselves; and the

dancers, heaving, swirling, screaming, shrieking out their an-
guished joy. The Priest–Sorcerers took out their grater, the most
sacred of all religious accoutrements used to exorcise the elements,
rattled it first on the initiate's head, then struck him with it. The
real world now became visible to the baptised, the one no ordinary
man can see, but rather, the one which Ciguri reveals to him.

The Theatre of Cruelty spectacle which Artaud had witnessed
had permitted him to merge with *actuality*, to become assimilated
with the breath of creation. It was no longer merely an abstract
notion on his part, but the Theatre of Cruelty had become a vital
and living force – experienced in the existential domain.

*   *   *

Although the Theatre of Cruelty remained only a vision (for others)
during Artaud's lifetime, it has taken root in the theatrical arts
today. The Theatre of the Absurd, the Theatre of Happenings, the
Living Theatre, the Theatre of the Ridiculous, the Guerilla Theatre,
the Street Theatre are all designed to arouse, disturb, and evoke
bizarre and powerful sensations within the spectators; visceral
reactions capable of transforming and/or distorting their
conceptions of the world and themselves. The aim is to shatter
previously held notions, to expand consciousness, to reveal the
thrilling – and perhaps horrendous – world that lies just beyond
our usual 'rational'.

NOTES

1. Antonin Artaud, *Oeuvres complètes*, vol. IV (Paris: Gallimard, 1964)
   p. 32.
2. Ibid., vol. II, p. 14.
3. Ibid., vol. IV, p. 122.
4. Antonin Artaud, *The Theatre and its Double*, trans. Caroline Richards
   (New York: Grove Press, 1958) p. 104.
5. Ibid., p. 85.
6. Ibid.
7. Antonin Artaud, 'Emotional Athleticism', in *Collected Works*, vol. 4
   (London: Calder and Boyars, 1974) p. 101.

7

Ionesco's Plays:
A Conspiracy of the Mind

MICHAEL J. HAYES

I

Ionesco's surrealism, or, more precisely, Theatre of the Absurd, is a homeopathic remedy for twentieth-century madness. It works by giving us controlled doses of the insanities that we have engendered to stimulate our own defence systems and so bring us to heal ourselves. The experiencing of Ionesco engages us in madness to bring us to sanity.

I have purposely used the word 'engages' because his plays are not about being a mirror held up to nature, or demonstrating a thesis on the human condition; they are about performers exposing audiences to, and provoking them with, madness: a confrontation that can lead to a mutual affirmation of humanity through the experiences of the plays. I do not believe that the accomplishment of that affirmation can be fully or even adequately explained, but its genesis can be described in terms of the ingredients of the plays and their evolving action, which is what I propose to describe.

The most basic terms in this description are 'audience' and 'theatre'. It is customary, in discussions of theatre, to credit audiences with a vital role in the whole event, but rarely does that role get any real explication. It is assumed that somehow, although actual theatrical experiences differ greatly, the most general descriptions will do for the audience contribution.

For example, Victorian working-class audiences loved the directness and sentimentality of melodramas, which turned into the problem plays and comedies of manners in the latter part of the century, as the theatre underwent bourgeoisification.

If, however, I am to substantiate a claim for Ionesco's importance on the basis of a capacity to heal in a way analogous to homeopathic remedies, then a much more precise definition of the audience will be necessary. If the plays are remedies – fine – but for what illness?

The first part of the overall description, then, is the pathology of the audience, who is the patient. By audience I do not simply mean those people who sit watching what the performers are doing, I mean everybody who is present at the theatrical event: watchers, performers and assistants to the performers. This redefinition of the audience is not simply an attempt to be modish or different, but a key point if we are to accept the event of an Ionesco play as a conspiracy of the mind to bring about its own healing. I am suggesting that the performers, like the audience, cannot really understand what is going on, they can only participate. How can we understand unreason? We can experience it, be affected by it, but we cannot understand it.

The audience is essentially a 'first world' audience whose consciences and consciousness are numbed by the awful scale of present inhumanity and are progressively limited by the encroachments of mass communication. The conventional recital of specifically twentieth-century horrors runs from the Holocaust to Hiroshima to the fire-bombings of Dresden and Tokyo, both of which almost certainly killed more people than the atom bomb, to Vietnam, that longest-running breakfast serial on TV, to the Gulf war, certainly the biggest and best computer game to date (summer 1991). The real horror, though, is not simply the massacres (there have always been massacres) but the progressive reduction of human moral responses, to a point where all that is left to them is to agree or disagree, win or lose, for or against.

Accompanying this naive level of moral judgement is the all too frequent indifferent recognition that 'he's using that same bloody old list again'. It is as if the price of knowledge has to be paid in an increasingly debased coinage. 'We exist within the context of a language that is our own invention but which controls us in so far we have lost sight of its origins in our day to day practice.'[1] McLuhan's electronic 'global family' ends up as a family able only to communicate in terms of + or –.

Tyrants have always had power of life and death over their subjects. In modern, first-world countries that claim universal adult suffrage (always with a few cautious exceptions written in) but depend on vast financial and industrial complexes with, if possible, nuclear weapons thrown in (for purely defensive purposes), that

'sufferage' resides in the simplification and restriction of the col-
luding individual. The protesting rage at the maltreatment of
fellow human beings is harvested in the form of protest votes, or
worse, of cheap risible headlines: 'The Sun (no less) says Saddam
Hussein must go.'

'If you go mad, by normal social definition, in psychoanalysis,
your likely fate is the usual psychiatric incarceration with all the
violent trimmings – at least until your language – words and acts –
becomes normally "grammatical" – and normally banal once
again.'[2] This description can, I believe, be taken, as David Cooper
intends, as a model for a whole range of communal behaviours in
the developed world. If we look at our theatre audience not, this
time, with what they bring with them from their lives outside the
theatre, but simply within the theatre context itself, what do we
find?

The watchers, the watched and the facilitators all have rigidly
conventionalised ideas as to what the communication event is
about and what behaviours are appropriate. We get some idea of
the underlying determinism when we recall the arguments that
greeted proposals, in the fifties, for changes in the shape and
placing of the performing areas; and more recent proposals to
diminish the director and hand back interpretation to the actors.
The seating, the not talking, the not crackling sweet papers, the
circumspect relations between watchers and watched and the
dismay if narrative conventions are offended, all signal the highly
specific code that dominates theatre communication. The very
specificity of these conventions, in our own time, mimics the re-
pressiveness of our society. The anarchic element of the Victorian
melodrama found shelter in the music hall until that too succumbed to respectability.

I have not intended to labour over long with my account of the
audience but, if Ionesco's medicine is to be described, the patient as
well as the care needs description. I believe that the drama is the
least well written about form because plays are too frequently
treated simply as texts rather than as the site for a communication
between people.

Having discussed the audience and the theatre in general, what
of the drama that Ionesco inherited? The specific origins of Theatre
of the Absurd are said to lie in Jarry's late-nineteenth-century Ubu
plays. But, in my opening sentence, I went along with the opinion
that sees the Absurd as a particular instance of surrealism. As a

major artistic force, the surreal emerged after, and partly in reaction to, the First World War. The appalling slaughter that resulted from the terrifying logic of that war (i.e., if at the end I've got one soldier living and you've got none, then I've won) turned artists inward to the non-logical.

One obvious recourse was the Freudian premise that, although our id desires, repressions and inner conflicts pertain to us alone as individuals, their expression is subject to a universal mechanism. Just as individuals go through broadly similar processes of physical growth and development to attain their individual physical characteristics, so they go through similar psychic processes in the development of individual personalities. The way to identification of this inner self is through dreams, associations and phantasies. Surrealism was an attempt, through dreamlike associations in art, to establish communication at a level beyond the rational. Though powerfully affective in its refusal to reduce art, whether verbal or pictorial, to the purely narrative structures, its impact was restricted. Worse still, it helped perpetuate notions of high and low culture. Its adherent were vocal and influential but still very much a privileged minority.

Ionesco was born of a French mother and a Romanian father. Educated in France, he went to Bucharest, returning to Paris just prior to the Second World War. To some extent there would seem to be some ambivalence about his cultural roots. Being poised, as he was, between Romania and France, no doubt played its part in prompting the kind of scrutiny of the conscious and unconscious channels of communication that characterise his work.

When his plays began to appear in small Parisian theatres at the beginning of the fifties, they were in French. The work was quickly translated for fringe and university theatre groups all over Europe. By the sixties, major national companies were performing his work and it received the ambiguous accolade of appearing on network television for wide national audiences. This is not the place to argue the differences between theatre and television presentations, the point is being made in order to demonstrate the growing level of interest in his work; the extent to which the sane voice of unreason was being heard. What is important now is to give an account of the texts as sites for communication events shared by groups of people gathered together to experience theatre.

In putting Ionesco in the surrealist tradition I am suggesting that we recognise his narrative structures as determined largely by the mechanisms of the unconscious. In augmenting that description, by invoking 'the absurd', I am suggesting first that he attacks the form of language itself, prefiguring deconstruction, and second that he attacks the presupposed commonsense relationship between language and substance. Finally and paradoxically, in spite of this sustained attack on language, our chief channel of communication, the result is not despair but a heightened and exhilarated affirmation of humanity.

II

The form of language may be taken as having two aspects, giving rise to the two main branches of Structuralism. First, it is a system containing elements, and second, these elements can only operate in certain grammatical or narrative orders. The idea that language consists of elements, and words are one good example of elements, which define each other by their presence in the same system derives from Saussure. But the elaboration of that core idea owes most to the work of the Russian, Trubetzkoy, whose work was particularly focussed on the element of sound, or the phoneme. What he pointed out was that a sound is recognised not for any inherent value in itself but because of its differences from other sounds. So the 'p' in 'pad' and the 'b' in 'bad' are made by the same movements of the mouth with one exception, 'p' is voiceless, the vocal cords not vibrating, while 'b' is voiced, the cords vibrate. This kind of difference is the most obvious, it is one of opposition, things either happen or they do not. If we now take the element, the word, difference by opposition would give us 'good' *v.* 'bad' or 'happy' *v.* 'sad'.

Naturally the polar elements, such as 'good' and 'bad', are related to families of cognate elements: 'good' with 'virtuous', 'happy' and 'peaceful' for example. It has always been one of the functions of romanticism, as opposed to classicism, to explore these boundaries to see just how far meaning can be pushed. Shelley gives us 'awful beauty', and Yeats, 'terrible beauty', for example, but it is Ionesco who goes all the way to see what happens when the elements are destroyed completely.

In *The Bald Prima Donna*, for example, Ionesco gives a virtuoso performance on the theme of how to destroy the system of meaning. Early in the play, Mr and Mrs Smith are talking about the death of Bobby Watson. Conventionally the name of someone in the system of a family distinguishes them from every other member of the family, but in this family everybody is Bobby Watson, reminding us of Pierce's saying: 'If all the world were red, red wouldn't exist.' Now Bobby Watson, wife of Bobby Watson and mother of the two Bobby Watson children,

> has regular features, but you
> can't call her beautiful. She's
> too tall and too well-built. Her
> features are rather irregular,
> but everyone calls her beautiful.
> A trifle too short and too slight,
> perhaps. (*The Bald Prima Donna*, p. 5)

The only element that is not contradicted is that she remains 'she' throughout.

What do the audience do with a piece of non-sense like this? In the first place, in spite of the piece being called 'A Pseudo-Play', both watchers and watched conspire to treat it as a play; if they do not, the watchers leave the theatre (as some have done over the years) and the watched look for work elsewhere. Secondly, having agreed that the piece is indeed a play, they try mutually to rescue what meaning they can: as human beings we are endlessly ingenious and determined to create meaning; nonsense is a pathological state normally cured by sense. From the cohort of Bobby Watsons, this particular one is a wife and a mother. Since the information about her is so contradictory, we scrutinise the language as a whole to try and retrieve some semblance of meaning. Does the phrase 'everyone calls her beautiful' mitigate the contradiction 'you can't call her beautiful', if we insert our own 'but' before it? Does the word 'perhaps' relieve the inconsistency of her being both too tall and too short, too well-built and too slight?

We make sure that the answer is yes to both of these questions by pointing out that this is a conversation going on which, of its very nature, is supposed to make sense. Moreover, the ordering of the words, that is their grammaticality, is perfectly regular. To complete our defence and return nonsense to the health of sense, we lay some blame on the speaker. Mrs Smith is really a rather silly woman, nice enough but tends to talk without thinking.

The most obvious point of entry for a critical look at the language of the play is to look at the disruption of meaning that results from ascribing, to the same thing, words that are opposite in meaning. However, this is not the only way that Ionesco sabotages the normal use of language. If we take the experimental fables of the Fire-Chief, for example, we find 'another ox asked another dog a question'.(*The Bald Prima Donna*, p. 24). Since neither a dog nor an ox has so far been mentioned, the 'another' is, to say the least, redundant. Again, it is rescuable by eliding it as a mistake, or by supposing that, in the family of fables, there are indeed other oxen and other dogs that we must be supposed to know about. Take again Mrs Martin's, 'You may sit down on the chair, when the chair hasn't any.' At first hearing, nonsense, but rescuable if we assume a psychological slip by the speaker – the omission, for example, of 'occupant' at the end of the statement. Mr Martin's use of 'whereas', in 'The pine is a tree whereas the pine is also a tree' (*The Bald Prima Donna*, p. 33), is not so easy to rationalise away, it is a gross deviation.

These are examples of the violation of rules of the code itself, words that normally have an established place in the interrelated system of meanings are thrown into the disorder of nonsense. What I am suggesting is that the participants in the act of theatre, although at first dismayed by these deviations, summon up strategies to compensate for them and complete the meaning. In the face of chaos, we stir ourselves to recover what we can of meaning. This feeling of the basic recuperability of language is supported both by the fact that, for all their nonsense, the elements are grammatically ordered and, above all, by our expectation that meaning should be there. The occasion is, after all, theatre and, though theatre does go 'over the top' at the end of the day, it is still meaningful, such extravagance is to be expected – and we applaud.

But the next level of Ionesco's critique of language is not so easy to recuperate. Its mistakes cannot be put down to those lapses of memory, errors and slips of the tongue that Chomsky says characterise language performance. In this case it is the rupture of the relationship between language and what we think of as its normal frame of reference, namely reality.

There are plenty of instances of the breakdown of the normal relations between language and reality in *The Bald Prima Donna*, for example, the young girl asphyxiated by gas because 'she thought it was a comb' (*The Bald Prima Donna*, p. 23).

We know that even the most apparently outlandish statements can be psychiatrically explained. We only have to think of Jung's patient, Babette S., who said variously 'I am the Lorelei', 'I am Socrates' deputy' and 'I am Germania and Helvetia of exclusively sweet butter', all of which statements he found explicable. But neither the context of the play nor the conduct of the language nor the general level of knowledge among the watchers would allow us to undertake such an explanatory excercise.

In *Maid To Marry*, another short play from the early fifties, a Lady and a Gentleman are talking, among other topics, about the Lady's daughter. When she arrives 'She is a man, about thirty years old, robust and virile, with a bushy black moustache, wearing a grey suit' (*Maid To Marry*, p. 188). Both the introductions and the conversation continue just as if 'he' was the Lady's daughter. The fact that s/he is said to be ninety-three, and curtsies to the Gentleman, in no way alleviates our bewilderment. The substance of the drama, a man and woman talking and the entry of the very offspring who has been part of the subject of conversation, is perfectly feasible. Even the conversation is normal, up to the point where the daughter enters and what we see and what is said are totally incompatible: the situation goes on in defiance of the language. This demonstration is given (like the best Hollywood movies) one more twist – the man curtsies as if he were indeed a maid, showing the arbitrariness of, even, codes of behaviour.

In dramatic form Ionesco is provoking us to experience what happens when reality and the codes of meaning we use to signify it, particularly language, are divided. Put in these terms, we are confronting not just a dramatist's whimsy but the breakdown between reality and its expression through 'an intellectual juggling with words'. To complete the quotation, a few lines later Jung calls our failure to encompass reality adequately 'the psychic dichotomy of our time'.[3]

Ionesco, having confronted us, like Lewis Carroll's Cheshire cat, with the tenuousness of the link between language and reality, does not simply leave us looking at the broken pieces in our heads. The various kinds of humour that he retrieves from the situations actually imply that there is something substantial in the codes. Humour of all kinds is the very human response to the adverse conditions of life, from horror to tragedy, even to irritation and discomfort. All types of humour run through Ionesco's plays, the united laughter of the watchers affirming their capacity to enter into communication with each other through the dramatist's work.

While I have no intention of analysing the different types of humour Ionesco employs in different situations, it is significant that the critique of the word-world connection gives rise to the ridiculous. For all the failure of language to embody experience adequately, the laughter that greets the entry of the Lady's daughter, complete with moustache and grey suit, asserts that there is a world and that, however much we play with it and even try to negate it, there is a core of significance in its relationship to language that the overwhelming majority of us accept and perceive in common.

Consideration of the relations between elements in the system of meaning, and the problem of the relation between the system and the real world, are age-old problems which have reappeared with particular vehemence in the twentieth century. But the broader problem is the relation of the system, in this case language, to its context of use. Our ability to use language is one not merely of knowing the words and how to order them, but of knowing the right language behaviour to fit the context. A major part of our learning of language consists of acquiring the knowledge to know which part of the language is acceptable in which context.

We speak of knowing a language as if it was one coherent entity, when what we actually know are dozens of languages under the umbrella of 'a language'. We do not know English, we know lots of Englishes. When we go to the doctor's or the pub or talk to small children, or even go to seminars on dramatists like Ionesco, we employ very different variants of English. The capacity to choose the right variant is called communicative competence. Part of Ionesco's critique of language through dramatisation consists of tackling the problem of communicative competence. It is through his sensitivity to different varieties that we are able to rescue the absurdity of his plays and espouse it to the cause of sense.

It is at the level of choice of the right variety of language that a discussion of the sources of *The Bald Prima Donna* comes into its own. The play draws on the bizarre language of what used to pass, and unfortunately sometimes still does, for language learning materials. That language is 'akin to the mad alphabet of an optician's chart', and seeing the play as a parody of that very particular kind of language certainly helps make sense of the run through from stories to poems to tongue-twisters until it finally enters the world of phonetic nightmare.

MRS MARTIN: You cacklegobblers! You gobblecacklers!
MR MARTIN: Cat's lick and pots luck.
MRS SMITH: Krishnawallop krishnawallop krishnawallop.

(*The Bald Prima Donna*, p. 35).

But what is particularly interesting is the way in which the very language we are learning, to give access to another culture, actually separates us from reality. The setting of a recognisable family group is often the source of language learning materials, but the nature of the language drills, with their simplifications and repetitions, throws real-world assumptions in doubt. Not only do we not know how long Bobby Watson has been dead – anywhere between eighteen months and four years – we do not even know what the present time of the play is, as the clock strikes randomly from two to fifteen times. Even more disconcertingly, when the visiting Martins come they only have language of a very limited kind with which to identify each other. Their conversation together consists of the attempt, by careful comparison of the similarities of their movements and of the family relationships they have, to conclude that 'there can be no mistake' they are indeed man and wife.

The destructive parody of such an artificial language is, in part, good fun. The watchers are made aware of the weaknesses of that particular variety, but they are also made aware of a more important aspect, namely how quickly and easily a simplified language runs into chaos. A real-life variant of language is parodied in *Maid to Marry*, namely the use of language between men and women.

Since Robin Lakoff published *Language and Women's Place*, in 1973, some twenty years after the first performance of Ionesco's play, a good many studies of women's language have followed. Although all her claims have not been substantiated by subsequent research, the general thesis, that women's subordinate role to men can be seen to be reflected in their language, generally holds true. In *Maid to Marry* the Gentleman completes sentences for the Lady and contradicts her, so she hastens to agree to the opposite of what she has just said. The Lady endlessly mouths agreement, even echoing his phraseology or actually repeating it, and she crowns it all with 'Oh Monsieur – After all, I'm only a woman!' (*Maid to Marry*, p. 187). The speciousness of these relative registers is not only underlined by the heavy irony of the piece but finally exploded by the appearance of the male daughter using the female register.

Most of Ionesco's shorter pieces for the theatre tackle problems of language variation or register. Where *Maid to Marry* is sharply ironic about male condescension, *The Lesson* is brutally direct in its attack on the repressive nature of education. *The Motor Show* is a wonderful extravaganza on the language of salesmanship, that cunningly puts the natural world of the farmyard against the industrial world of production. Even the conventions of theatre itself are not exempt: as Marguerite says, in *Exit the King* – 'You're going to die in an hour and a half, you're going to die at the end of the show.'

Probably the most complete exploration just of language and its place in life is that undertaken in *The Chairs*. An old man, who is a caretaker, and an old woman live in a house surrounded by water. In their isolation they are stripped down to an essential humanity and so become, as well as themselves, a universal metaphor, a Mr and Mrs Everyman. From their vantage point the follies and vanities of the world are seen as merely an intricate dance of words. The old woman, speaking of her husband's potential, says, 'You might have become a President General, a General Director, or even a General Physician or a Postmaster-General if you'd wanted to, if you'd had just a little ambition in life' (*The Chairs*, p. 9). The glittering careers are reduced to their essential madness, a verbal game played by two old people, in this case centring on the word 'general'. The old man continues the parody of the game of careers as he replies, 'Since I'm a caretaker, I am a Quartermaster-General' (p. 9).

Similarly, all their topics of discussion and recollections distil experience to an essential core of language that reverberates in the mind with the quality of myth. In recalling a visit to Paris it becomes 'the city of light and four hundred thousand years ago it faded right away.'; of this recreation of another Eden 'there's nothing left [of it] now, except a song' (*The Chairs*, p. 11).

The action of the play revolves around the relationship of the couple and the old man's mission to give the world his message. The very words they use to each other prompt notions of the archetypal and mythic, so they both refer to the old woman as the wife/mother and the old man as her husband/child. It is he who has the message for the world but it is she who must encourage and inspire him to the effort of delivering it.

In the play, beauty and truth can be arrived at neither through manipulation of the language nor through its use to represent the surface of the world. Only when language reflects the vision created by the workings of the inner self of a particular individual does it give birth to true poetic meaning. Speaking becomes, then, not just the rehearsal of meanings but a manifestation of the whole experience of a real human being, a manifestation which language itself creates. 'It's as we speak that we find our ideas, our words, ourselves too, in our words, and the city, the garden, perhaps everything comes back and we're not orphans any more' (*The Chairs*, p. 17).

An invisible audience, including a photographer, a colonel and the lovely Mrs Lovely, even the Emperor, all gather. The old couple provide visible chairs and real words of welcome for the invisible audience. The stage fills with unseen presences. In their chatter the old couple reveal contradictory lives and hidden selves. The old woman is erotic and whorish with the photographer, the old man romantic and flirtatious with Mrs Lovely. They have both had and not had a child, the old man was both a good son and a bad son. Still the invisible audience packs onto the stage.

Feeling unequal to the task, the old man has hired an orator to actually deliver his message; when he arrives he is dressed like a Bohemian artist of yesteryear. But his appearance affirms for the old couple the reality of the situation: 'He exists. And he's here all right. It's not a dream' (*The Chairs*, p. 33). As the orator signs autographs for the invisible audience the old man introduces him and explains his role in delivering the message. When the scene is set the old couple, in a double suicide, leap from the window into the waters that surround the house – they have returned to the source waters of life.

The final irony is that the orator is a deaf mute. He mouths sounds but only incoherent gibberish emerges. He writes on the blackboard, ANGELBREAD, and a series of meaningless letters, dissatisfied he rubs them out and replaces them with others. Finally acknowledging failure he departs, ceremoniously. The invisible audience shuffle and whisper audibly, as the noise fades the real audience depart.

Language at the end fails; the message, if there ever was one, is not delivered. Paradoxically the fuller life, of which language is only a part, is resoundingly affirmed. If the invited guests for the message are non-existent, the watchers of the lives enacted on the stage very much exist. In their appreciation of the stage world, in its pathos and lyricism, hopes and failures, drama has succeeded in validating the mysterious vitality of the most ordinary lives. The message of a lifetime is the life itself.

III

Generally speaking, *The Chairs* can be seen as standing between the shorter plays, where Ionesco explores the madness of language, and the longer plays, with their exploration of what it is to be human in the modern world. What saves the shorter plays from futility and nihilism is their ability to provoke laughter and their challenge to us to rescue meaning from meaninglessness. Their demands make us affirm that we are the children of meaning.

In the longer plays we have a recurrence of themes and motifs from the shorter works, but the challenge is to recognise and overcome the perils that threaten our humanity. If our lives are a struggle to create meaning, what is that meaning for? Where does the individual stand in relation to meaning? How is it that our gift for creating meaning is so often subverted?

Theatre critics and commentators alike have agreed in seeing Ionesco's plays of the late fifties and sixties as being concerned with socio-political issues: with the dangers of dictatorship and the mob. Certainly the canvas of characters is broadened from the family and intimate groups to that of the community, but the plays can also be interpreted in the light of the themes established in the shorter works. From this perspective Ionesco's major plays expose the ironies and perils inherent in our being creatures who struggle to make meaning.

In *The Killer*, first produced in 1959, Berenger, the central character, is described as 'an average, middle-aged character' (p. 63). At the opening of the play he is being shown by the Architect around a radiant city, a paradise on earth such as the old couple in *The Chairs* vaguely recall. It is a wonder of technology and progress, always sunny, the flowers always in bloom and everything perfect. Above all, in the radiant city Berenger becomes his real self, 'a smiling being in a smiling world' (p. 76). That sense of being himself is renewed because the radiant city is an outward projection of his inward self. There is harmony between his inner self and the world he inhabits, 'when there's not total agreement between myself inside and myself outside, then it's a total cata-strophe, a universal contradiction, a schism' (p. 76). Then he learns that the radiant city is being abandoned, a killer lurks. The killer, like the man showing dirty postcards, lures his victims by showing a photograph of the colonel; so that they can see better, they stand by the ornamental pool, at which point he drowns them.

Berenger, finally believing he has access to the necessary evidence, goes in pursuit of the killer. At the end of the play, in what must surely be one of the most heroic and tragic speeches about what it is to be human, Berenger confronts the killer, only to finish on his knees before him. As the author's directions read, 'In fact Berenger finds within himself, in spite of himself and against his own will, arguments in favour of the Killer' (p. 65). The final irony is that we sympathise with Berenger but, in striving like Berenger to rationalise events, we become the killer.

Early in the play Berenger remembers moments suffused with pure joy, what Maslow termed peak experiences: 'My own peace and light spread in their turn throughout the world. I was filling the universe with a kind of ethereal energy' (p. 81). The recall of these moments lightens the burden of the gloomiest days. In confronting the killer, Berenger hopes to win back for mankind this capacity for exultation. In his appeal he goes through argument after argument, he tries to understand the killer's point of view, 'After all, you are a human being. You've got reasons, perhaps'. (p. 167). The 'perhaps' underlines his own lack of confidence, his susceptibility, which marks his humanity.

Berenger appeals for tolerance of others, protesting that they should not be killed just because they do not behave as you would like. Maybe, he suggests, the killer wishes to kill from pity. He appeals to the killer's common humanity, 'you're a human being, we're the same species, we've got to understand each other' (p. 172). Still the killer refuses to speak, 'There must be one thing in common, a common language' (p. 173). An appeal to reason, the promise of economic support, even the suggestion of a shared uncertainty all fail – 'And what good are bullets even, against the resistance of an infinitely stubborn will' (p. 178). And Ionesco appears to have interpreted his own play for us. Joy is destroyed by repression and authoritarianism.

But what happens to the play if we accept that interpretation? At one level we are satisfied that the play has a theme; like Berenger, we finally know what it has all been about. At the same time, the richness of the communication event itself has been destroyed: the killer has got us – all we need is for photographs of the colonel to be on sale as we leave the theatre. But the enigmas return to puzzle us.

Does the killer actually kill Berenger? Why has he changed his method from a photograph to a knife with Berenger, particularly since everybody knew the photograph method anyway, and it still did not stop them being killed? Why drowning?

Certainly, in an historical context, the play can be seen as a critique of post-colonial wars – particularly the war in Algeria. But I believe the full richness of the play is more nearly approached if we see, as its theme, the nature of human consciousness. And human consciousness of which 'stubborn will' is born arises from our capacity for creating signifying codes, symbolic systems of which the chief is language. The more Berenger argues, the more he falls prey to his alter ego, the killer.

We go to the ornamental pool to see ourselves more clearly. It is Narcissus' pool, Perseus' shield wherein he reflected Medusa's image back to herself, Lacan's mirror phase – but we do not see ourselves; rather, a photograph of the colonel. Our image has been replaced by an endless stream of technologically produced images of the colonel, signifying repression. The image reflected back to us is necessarily distorted by the very fact that we consciously sought it out. Heisenberg's indeterminacy principle, which says, broadly speaking, things change as you look at them, refers just as much to ourselves as to the physical world. The microscope of language necessarily distorts – as Berenger rehearses all his arguments to the killer, their speciousness becomes apparent to himself. The 'stubborn will' is the ambivalence of language which, under the pressure of human experience, either deconstructs or becomes a prison-house. As Berenger says of his moments of joy, 'I don't even know if the experience I had can be communicated' (p. 79). By the end of the play he realises that not only can it not be communicated, but the attempt kills it. The only escape from the killer is to stay with the group and to avoid his importunities to go off alone with him – to settle for the untidy, cacophonous, boring voices that flood the beginning of Act Two.

In the theatre, watching Ionesco's play, we have individual interpretations like the one offered here. These disintegrate under the pressure of alternative close analyses; what does not evaporate is the experience we had as a watcher among watchers. Audience and actors alike, confronted by Ionesco's enigmas and lyricism, join together in a communion that defies the depradations of my stifling pen as it insistently draws a moustache on the colonel's photograph.

The central character of *Rhinoceros*, first produced in 1969, is again named Berenger. His concern for humanity is as strong as in the former play: 'I feel responsible for everything that happens. I feel involved, I can't just be indifferent' (p. 78). But this time it is expressed in his refusal to tolerate the views of others concerning the rhinoceroses. Character after character, in different ways, express a willingness to understand the point of view of the rhinoceroses. Berenger sees them as ugly and an affront to humanity – he refuses to acquiesce. At the end of his curtain speech he defiantly says: 'I am the last man left, and I'm staying that way until the end. I'm not capitulating' (p. 107). And of course the end has come, the play is over and Berenger, in his obstinacy, has survived: he has not succumbed to the grunts and roars of the rhinoceroses.

But the dangers Ionesco is explaining are as real as the dangers of self-consciousness. In order to communicate with each other we need a common language – we need to recognise in each other a common core of reference on which to base our communion. In arriving at that common core we have to guard our autonomy, otherwise our individual humanity is destroyed, 'A firm sense of one's own autonomous identity is required in order that one may be related as one human being to another.'[5] The rhinoceroses remind us all too readily of those dreams that threaten engulfment, recorded by both Jung and Laing: a small shape, say a ball or triangle, grows and grows until it threatens to engulf us. The characters in the play, starting with those peripheral to Berenger and steadily encroaching on those close to him, are transformed into rhinoceroses that in their power and bulk threaten to overwhelm him. We, the watchers of the scene, experience their claustrophobic might and bulk as well. At the end of the play our autonomy and humanity are preserved in so far as we remain watchers, distant from the actions on the stage. In refusing to identify with the action of the characters, in maintaining our right to argue about the piece as a whole, we preserve our obstinate individuality.

Of course the one attack that none of us is immune from is death. In *Exit the King*, produced in 1963, Berenger has metamorphosed into that most renaissance of theatrical figures, a king. A king whose kingdom, as he approaches death, has shrunk to almost nothing; his subjects have dwindled to a doctor, a domestic help and a guard.

In spite of this outward decay, which counterpoints his inward decline, King Berenger resists death with all his failing strength. Even in realising his own mortality his plea is, 'Let them cry my name throughout eternity' (p. 48).

It is Marie, his second wife, who encourages him not to be afraid. '"Exist" and "die" are just words, figments of your imagination. Once you realize that, nothing can touch you' (p. 50). It is knowledge, the ambivalent gift of language, which makes us question life and death, which actually creates the endless questions. 'Escape from definitions and you will breathe again' (p. 50). But, if language creates a questioning self-consciousness that undermines our capacity to experience life, that prevents us from '[Diving] into an endless maze of wonder and surprise' (p. 50), it is also language that holds us in communion in the theatre. It is language that allows us to recapture 'that morning in June we spent together by the sea, when happiness raced through you and inflamed you' (p. 52).

Ionesco's theatre gives us palatable doses of the madness of language. It disrupts our expectations of meaning, it mocks the conventions by which we try to say the right thing in the right context. But in tweaking our ears and twisting our tongue it reminds us of the subtlety, humour and lyricism that are the children of language. Paradoxically, by subjecting us to the sickness of language, Ionesco turns sickness into health.

NOTES

All quotations from Ionesco's plays are from the following editions: *The Bald Prima Donna*, trans. D. Watson (London: Samuel French, 1958); *Ionesco, Three Plays*, trans. D. Watson (London: Jupiter Books, 1963); *Eugene Ionesco Plays*, vol. iv, trans. D. Watson, vol. v, trans. D. Prouse (London: Calder and Boyars, 1970).

1. D. Cooper, *The Language of Madness* (Harmondsworth: Penguin, 1980) p. 19.
2. Ibid., p. 23.
3. C. G. Jung, *Memories, Dreams, Reflections* (London: Flamingo, 1990) p. 166.
4. V. Nabokov, *Speak, Memory*; quoted in R. Norrman, 'Reflections on the Non-text and *The Bald Soprano*' (off-print) p. 366.
5. R. D. Laing, *The Divided Self* (Harmondsworth: Penguin, 1976) p. 44.

8

The Heroic World of Jean Anouilh

ALBA AMOIA

Women are the dominant figures in the theatre of Jean Anouilh, around women rotates the axis of his world of heroism, and to women does the author ascribe the epithet, 'flowers in the midst of garbage'.

The cast of Anouilh's preeminent female characters ranges from the uncouth and sublime 'lark' (Joan of Arc) to the pure and untamed 'sauvage'; from the uncompromising Antigone to the adamant, hunchbacked 'daisy' (*Ardèle, ou la Marguerite*). Anouilh's intransigent heroines are willing to die in defence of a cherished principle; they refuse all happiness, love or romance that is not 'pure'; and they take an ethereal view of existence in their struggle against all forms of compromise and deceit. Often guided by compassion for the victimised and downtrodden, they fit into Joan of Arc's 'ordered world' of the poor, the ill, the aged, and the wounded. (Becket is perhaps the one male heroic exception in Anouilh's theatre, for he inspires the love of the downtrodden masses of Canterbury by championing them against the power of the Crown, the rich, and the Normans.)

Opposite in kind to the unyielding heroines, are the men in Anouilh's plays – distorted, depersonalised, degraded roués, who make a mockery of lofty goals, seek money and power, and are motivated by selfishness and baseness. Even historical giants such as Napoleon and Louis XVIII are doing nothing more, in *La Foire d'empoigne* (1962), than playing a petty game of grab, catching as catch can, unmindful of their unheroic demeanour. Male heroism for Anouilh? It is encapsulated in the ironic title of his 1970 play, *Les poissons rouges ou mon père, ce héros*. The 'hero's' highest form of self-expression as a child was urinating in the goldfish bowl. It is no wonder that, grown man and established author that he now is, he

109

comes under attack from all sides, albeit by equally contemptible and ridiculous characters: his wife, mother-in-law, children, mistress, physician, and friend. The only figure in the play worthy of esteem is the pale little servant, Adele – a stock character in Anouilh's theatre, whose place is in the ranks of the downtrodden but who remains always generous and pure. The naive Adele is relentlessly ordered about by her mistress and made the victim of street urchins' pranks, but she is the only person in the household who refuses to be caught up in the accusations and insults cascading against the sorry hero, defending him even at the cost of rough banishment to the kitchen. Humble Adele, no less than Antigone, Eurydice, Medea, or Joan of Arc, attempts to modify the role she is destined to play during her life on earth. Unlike Gaston, for example, in *Le Voyageur sans bagage*, who can only weep when he discovers the role he is expected to play in the Renaud household, and seeks to escape moral responsibility for his horrendous past actions, Adele does not fear to defy society, face up to reality, and shoulder her own identity. Resistants rather than Collaborators, Anouilh's heroines champion realities and truths which reveal the hollowness and falseness of the male characters' compromises. Banishment or sentencing to death seems devastating to these heroines, but they walk steadily and undramatically off stage, while the anti-hero is left to decay morally in a corner from which he cannot escape nor even desire to escape. Anouilh's plays without heroes have acquired unforgettable heroines, who are ultimately vindicated and emerge triumphant in their implacable 'purity'.

Anouilh's 'pièces noires' and 'nouvelles pièces noires' are pessimistic, bitter, and permeated with gloom. They display most clearly his lack of faith in humanity and its institutions. His pessimism stems from the realisation that neither the so-called joys and comforts of life reserved for the happy few, nor the invitations to unsavoury adventures, promiscuity, and immorality extended to all, lead to real happiness. Concomitantly, resignation to abject poverty, rigid acceptance of one's role in life, strict morality, and punctilious observance of a code of honour, can lead only to tragedy or death. Purity and love cannot prevail on this earth, because of the intrinsic impurity of happiness. Anouilh's heroines, seeking a happiness known only to themselves, a 'purity' of self and an 'absolute' love, are faithful in their search even though they know that none is attainable in life. Heroines cannot be 'happy'. Because they reject 'le sale petit bonheur' reserved for the mediocre, they are condemned to a solitude that admits of neither love nor friendship. Their task of finding or creating the ambience in which their truth can thrive is limited to the realms of illusion and of death, where real love and purity do exist.

For Anouilh's heroines, offerings or worldly gain are meaningless. In their search for the realisation of an ideal far beyond the horizons of the masses, the temptations of the so-called good things in life do not sway them from their perpetual task of refusing mediocrity. Antigone's retort to her family's assurances that happiness awaits her because she is young, beautiful, and engaged to be married, is: 'You all disgust me with your happiness. With your life that has to be lived at any cost. And that daily ration of good fortune, which suffices as long as you're not too demanding.'[1] In words that echo Joan of Arc's 'I don't want to have a happy ending...an ending that never ends',[2] she rejects Creon's image of a marriage that will permit her to live happily ever after. The heroine's rejection of a love that is less than perfect is incomprehensible to the mediocre masses, for whom 'love and marriage' are an integral part of life. Joan of Arc's disappearance from her father's farm to keep her divine appointment provokes her mother's prodding for explanations of the long absence, and her father's 'Ah! you're losing track of time now! I hope to God you haven't lost something else that you don't dare mention!' (*PC*, p. 26). It would be inconceivable for Joan to answer 'Saint Michael' to parents such as these. In *Antigone*, the uncomprehending Nurse immediately assumes that her charge's absence from the palace in the middle of the night can only be explained by a tryst with a common boy. Again, it would be absurd for Antigone to answer that she had gone to cover the body of her dead brother. Joan might avoid her father's violent thrashings and be 'happier' if only she would try to appear attractive to a village boy who will marry her, thereby easing her father's mind and his blows. She recognises her parent's right to destroy her physically, but maintains her spiritual rights: 'Beat me hard; you have the right to. But it's my right to continue to believe and to say no to you' (*PC*, p. 87). After an especially hard paternal drubbing, she refuses her mother's consolatory offer of an embroidered scarf: 'I don't want to look pretty, mommy...I don't want to get married' (p. 32). Later in the play, her words express even more clearly her renunciation of 'happiness' and her desire for nonconformity: 'I don't want things to turn out all right. ...I don't want to live your time' (*PC*, p. 131).

Medea has already experienced marriage – that short, happy union which is soon followed by the inevitable period of non-communication that eventually culminates in silence and hatred. Medea's Nurse tells her mistress that 'the earth is still full of good things: the sun on the bench at the resting-place, hot soup at noon, the coins you have earned in your hand, the drop of booze that warms your heart before you doze off'.[3] Medea, nauseated by the mediocrity of the Nurse's criteria, banishes her to unheroic realms: 'You have said too much, with your carcass, your drop of booze, and your sun shining on your rotten flesh. Get back to your dishes, your broom, your peelings, you and the rest of your [mediocre] race' (*NPN*, p. 367). Turning toward Corinth, where people are celebrating boisterously, Medea says: 'Something in me is stirring...and it says *no* to happiness' (*NPN*, p. 359). Her own children revolt her, for she already sees them as sly, deceitful adults who are, worst of all, anxious to 'live and be happy'. Jason predicts that there will never be other Medeas on this earth, that mothers will never name their daughters Medea, and that the Medea he knows will stand alone until the end of time. At the close of the play, as she and her children are being devoured by flames, she will proclaim: 'I am Medea, finally and forever.' A young woman of the lesser race who carries her head high, clenches her fists, scornfully spits on the ground, and stamps her feet in defiance, Medea is almost a stock character in Anouilh's plays. She survives through the ages in the dramatist's work as Antigone, Joan of Arc, 'la sauvage', Jeannette in *Roméo et Jeannette*, Adele (of *La Grotte*), and others – all of whom are atavisms of Medea.

Nowhere in Anouilh's plays does a heroine seek to satisfy a maternal instinct. Children are never portrayed as a delight or a comfort, but rather as tiring, vociferous mini-adults. In one play, *La Répétition* (1950), Anouilh is unsparing: his characters find deaf-mute children perhaps tolerable, but rose bushes preferable. The caricatural figure of the typical male child, Toto, who reappears in numerous plays, is a mixture of mime, prankster, and liar, who plays grotesque games of love to parody his parents. The female child is usually portrayed in her earliest teens, pregnant, preten-tious, and possessed of some ridiculous name such as Camomilla.

Jason had formerly been the ideal for whom Medea had sacri-ficed all. After their marriage his love was lost and that love now repels her. When he tries to save her from the many enemies she has made because of him, she protests: 'What are you trying to save? This worn-out skin, this carcass Medea, good for nothing except to drag around in its boredom and its hatred? A little bread and a house somewhere, and she'll grow old in silence until nobody mentions her name any more, right?' (*NPN*, p. 359). The acceptance of 'happiness' means submersion in the eternal oblivion of conformity, which is the equivalent of vegetation. Electra, in Anouilh's *Oreste* (1945), describing Aegisthus's and Clytemnestra's marriage as a slow process of watching the approach of old age, the onset of coldness, lack of desire, and ultimately hatred, exclaims sardonically: 'Oh, the indissoluble sanctity of marriage!'[4] Electra pursues her vengeance by becoming a child of hate and destruction. She purposely makes herself ugly and dirty, tears her dresses, and rubs her skin against the lepers huddled at the walls of the palace of Argos. She has taken all mirrors out of her room because she knows and fears the self-created monster of destruction that will call Aegisthus and Clytemnestra out of the palace to die.

It is in his 'jarring' plays ('pièces grinçantes') that Anouilh expounds most discordantly upon the subjects of life and love, marriage and children. The plays end on a displeasing, disconcerting note, expressing total cynicism that love can exist between a man and a woman. Even the marriages of the wealthy, although based on the solid foundation of money, are not happy. The nefarious influence of money on love, which the poor heroines fear, is lived out each day by the rich: a routine of boredom, hostility, hatred, deception, hypocrisies and extravagances of all kinds. Anouilh's heroines, refusing orchids, champagne and furs, will request baser beverages and seek instead the warmth of a supportive hand in their revolt against society's hypocrisy. No truly happy couple is portrayed in any of the plays, and whatever pleasure might have existed in the premarital state is soon destroyed by marriage. Anouilh describes marriage as a chemical experiment in which ' a mixture at first bubbles and sparkles; then happiness volatilises, leaving in the retort nothing but a big grey lump of [marital] obligations.'[5] The stock figure of General Saint-Pé (in *Ardèle, La Valse des toréadors*, and *L'Hurluberlu*), as well as Antoine de Saint-Flour in *Les poissons rouges*, are symbolic of the pathetic, disillusioned, humiliated, and unheroic married man.

Anouilh's heroines are true to themselves, isolated in their contemporary world, persistent in their sincerity and fidelity, lacerated by the conflict between their ideal and the hypocrisy that underlies sordid reality. In the 'pièces noires', the antagonism between the 'pure' heroine and perverted society results in either actual or symbolic death, while, in the 'pièces roses' and 'brillantes', escape from the convulsed world takes the form of either the creation of an illusion that triumphs over reality, or a refuge in one's multiple personalities. The author is deeply concerned with this idea of the multiplicity and mutability of the human personality, and with the realisation that the human being cannot be reduced to a unity that will afford him inner peace and contentment. He is aware of the relativity of human sentiments and emotions to social, sociological and economic conditions, and of the disturbing feelings of disunity that result from the conflict between them. Perhaps the most forceful example the author has given us of a heroine for whom changing human opinions have no significance is Joan of Arc: in the face of the relative truths of her parents, the people of France, and her executioners, she remains a symbol of absolute truth.

Anouilh's distinction between the heroic and the mediocre is often explained in terms of the 'poor' and the 'rich' races. Of the two, it is the poor race that can father heroines – not the wealthy nor the nobility. The lower class produces remarkably courageous women, while the upper class spends its unheroic life taking futility seriously. By the very rottenness of family life among the wealthy, with its inaneness, its ménages à trois, or à quatre, its hypocrisy, and its debauchery, the growth of heroism in the 'rich' race is stunted. Within the poor race, Anouilh distinguishes between the happy and the unhappy, the mediocre and the heroic. He describes the former as 'an exploding, fertile race, a flabby mass of dough that eats its sausage, bears children, uses its tools, counts its *sous*, year after year, in spite of epidemics and wars, until old age catches up with it; people living life, everyday people, people it's hard to imagine as dead'. The latter he describes as 'the noble ones, the heroes. Those whom you can easily imagine stretched out dead, pale, with a bullet hole in the head – the cream of the crop'.[6] The 'flabby masses of dough' take the form of the Rouen mob awaiting the spectacle of the burning of Joan of Arc, or the spitting, stenching Thebes mob described in *Antigone*, with its thousand arms and its thousand faces, but only one indistinguishable expression of mockery and laughter.

The heroines look disdainfully on the mediocrity of those who inhabit the realms of superficiality, conformity, and weakness; this majority is analogous to the 'rich' race in that it masks truths and is afraid to face absolutes. Rather than daring to dream the impossible dream of something better, the mediocre take refuge in their petty maladies, their banalities, and their stomachs. The heroines, instead, seek answers to metaphysical questions and are eternally dissatisfied with themselves. Their conscience and concept of order, clearly conceived and stated, form the sharp dividing line between the rigorous demands of heroic honour and the mediocre satisfactions of the masses. Anouilh's heroines love honour not for honour's sake, but for the sake of an *idea of honour* which they have created for themselves. Whereas honour, for the author's anti-heroes, is something to be remembered or forgotten at will, to be bought and sold, soiled and washed, the heroine's idea of honour can be neither improvised nor defiled by compromise. The concept of an honour to be defended unto death is basic to the plays in which a heroine champions nonconformity, purity, and refusal to compromise. A truly sorry figure is King Charles of France, in *L'Alouette*, who has neither wealth, nor courage, nor anyone to defend his person, much less his title. For this pusillanimous king, the concept of honour is nonexistent, and it is Joan who will illustrate what the pursuit of honour is all about. Joan's duty is to remain loyal to her intransigent race and to her search for purity, regardless of how absurd or how grotesque her role may be. The sole commandment for Anouilh's 'insolent breed' of heroines is to do what has to be done, when it has to be done, and to do it wholeheartedly and completely, even though it is unpleasant and difficult. Cauchon, the Bishop of Beauvais, pleads with Joan to recant during her trial for heresy: 'Joan, try to understand that there is something absurd about your refusal' (*PC*, p. 112). Likewise, Antigone persistently tells Creon that she must return to her brother's grave to replace the earth that the guards have removed. Creon replies: 'You'll return to make such an absurd gesture again?...Even if you should succeed in covering the grave again, you know very well that we'll uncover the cadaver. So what are you accomplishing except dirtying your fingernails with blood and getting yourself hanged?' Antigone answers: 'Nothing but that, I know. But at least I can do that. And everyone must do whatever he can' (*NPN*, p. 76). The 'insolent ones' are confident that God or the gods favour them and will grant them sufficient time in which to accomplish, with appropriate dignity, their absurd duty. Antigone will have time to perform the funeral rites for her dead brother with her tiny, rusty spade before she is hanged. Anouilh's heroines find lies repugnant, deception indecent, compromise inelegant. They insist on being aesthetically 'pure', on playing their role down to the last detail. The heroine is willing to adopt the commandment to do what has to be done, even though it may be absurd because she has been unable to find a solid truth in society on which she can base her definition of self and of her actions. The roots of her tragedy lie in the disjointed relations between herself and others: Antigone cannot accept Creon as her true authority; Medea could be happy in a world without Jason (who symbolises compromise), but she knows that the world contains both Jason and herself and, therefore, the seeds of conflict. She will have to oppose him unarmed in a losing battle, because he is of the 'rich' race. She cries out to him: 'Race of Abel, race of the just, race of the rich, how calmly you speak. It must be good to have the gods on your side, and the police, too' (*NPN*, p. 389). The serenity of the mediocre race is denied to the frenzied heroines who obstreperously reject the maxim that physical, political, or military might makes right. Antigone's position, vis-à-vis the king, who demands compromise, is identical to that of Medea. Antigone loves both life and her fiancé Haemon, but will nevertheless persist in performing the burial rites for her brother in the full knowledge that death will be her groom.

Rejecting all concepts of compromise and conformity, Anouilh's heroines starkly delineate and label their every action or sentiment of honour; nowhere do they see a grey area offering refuge, nor any opportunity to avoid justification of their acts. While the heroic figures refuse to accept the definition of happiness proffered by the mediocre, the mediocre, in turn, can understand neither what it is that the heroines are seeking, nor why, in their mental anorexia, they choose to absent themselves physically and spiritually from the routine of life's banquet.

The lifespan of the mediocre race is nothing but an endless and ugly vegetation. So powerful is the heroine's scorn for life's 'sale espoir' that, just as Joan of Arc is about to recant and Antigone is about to accede to her uncle's reasoning, the allusions to 'happiness' by Warwick and Creon, respectively, are enough for the women once again to prefer death to an act of compromise. The 'happiness' formula automatically antagonises the heroine; the picture of the 'petit bonheur' of the masses as a life of compromise and mediocrity, contrary to her demands for a state of perpetual happiness, shocks Antigone into reasserting her defiance. She thereupon taunts her uncle, the king, until he is forced to call in the guards. Only then does Creon understand her revolt. Polynices was merely a pretext; Antigone's *raison d'être* is to be put to death – to be a heroine. It is not difficult for Antigone to renounce even Haemon, because the idea that he will grow older and make compromises is unbearable: 'I love a young and hard Haemon, a Haemon demanding and faithful, like me....But if the wear and tear of your life, your happiness, must change him in any way...then I no longer love Haemon' (*NPN*, p. 187). Antigone is reminiscent of Ibsen's uncompromising Brand, for whom 'the enemy' is personified as the spirit of compromise, the spirit of the *juste milieu*. Death, then, becomes a refuge and deliverance from this damnable existence. The vicarious experience of 'living' makes the heroines even more determined, at the crucial and decisive moment, to refuse to understand, to refuse to be 'reasonable'. 'Moi, je ne veux pas comprendre', is Antigone's rejoinder throughout the play, and it is echoed in other plays by heroines who refuse to be 'reasonable' by conforming to society's norms. Refusal to 'live', to 'grow up and understand', is a dominant theme in Anouilh's theatre, but the desire to remain childlike is not a form of desire for regression; it is, rather, a reasoned and deliberate decision not to conform when an ideal or a concept of honour is threatened.

Persons in power attempt unsuccessfully to dissuade extremists from their nonconformity by demonstrating the absurdity of their ideal. Creon tries to destroy Antigone's illusions by smearing the image in her mind of her brother Polynices and revealing that it may even be Eteocles' body that she has buried instead. Her sister Ismene tries to dissuade her from covering the body, arguing that he was not a good brother. Antigone, however, stands firm: 'What do I care for your politics, your necessities, your miserable stories. I can still say "no"...and I am sole judge' (*NPN*, p. 177). The concept of an absurd duty to be fulfilled can be judged only by a superior race of 'imbeciles'. Cauchon, in an attempt to destroy the will of the imprisoned Joan, tells her that all of her good soldiers have abandoned her and, weary of war, have fled Rouen. Even La Hire, her closest companion in battle, has hired himself out as a mercenary, she is told; but higher voices than Cauchon's also speak to Joan and those are the only ones she hears. Count Tigre, in *La Répétition*, is defamed by a debauched nobleman who attempts to disabuse the heroine, Lucile. Obstinately refusing to leave the château, for she cherishes the Count and her own illusions about him, Lucile persists in believing in the superiority of her ideal

Tigre, despite most convincing evidence of his incorrigible flightiness.

Although Anouilh's heroines will accept death, if necessary, in order to fulfil their concept of duty, they nevertheless love life and cling to it humbly and sentimentally. Unabashedly seeking ways to lessen their fear, they are not at all like Corneille's classical feminine protagonists, who would die without openly expressing their innermost feelings. The Prologue in *Antigone* tells us that, as the heroine sits silently on the stage, she thinks about the fact that she is going to die, that she is young and would have liked to live, but that there is no changing the role that she must play. Later in the play, the following exchange takes place between Antigone and her sister: '(Ismene:) I don't want to die. (Antigone:) I too would have liked not to die...(Ismene:) I'm not very courageous, you know. (Antigone:) Neither am I. But what difference does it make?' (*NPN*, pp. 140,143). An almost identical scene is to be found in *Medea*: '(Nurse:) I am old, I don't want to die. (Medea:) I too...would have liked to live' (*NPN*, pp. 366–7). Joan, when asked by Cauchon whether she is afraid to die, admits that she is but that it makes no difference. Invariably, the heroines must bear their emotions and fears alone. They stand firm in the knowledge that they have been abandoned by all and that, in the end, society will destroy them. Antigone, after Ismene's renunciation of her part in the burial of Polynices, realises that it is up to her alone to defy Creon's edict. Creon, as the author of that edict, is also alone, but he can never reach the stature of the heroine, who has made no compromise with life. Electra had learned hatred and revenge all by herself and she, too, is the sole judge of her actions. Her mother's infidelity, and the assassination of her father, have given her an inflexible concept of duty and honour which will drive her unflinchingly to vengeance. Solitary, inaccessible heroines, abandoned by gods and by men, they all, like Joan, 'continue...with that curious mixture of humility and insolence, of grandeur and common sense, even up to the stake;...it is this solitude, in this silence of an absent God, in this deprivation and this bestial misery, that...[they are] great and alone' (*PC*, p. 56). Like Joan, they are 'little skylark[s] immobile against the sun, being shot at' (*PC*, p. 83) – an image that greatly disturbs those who have power but not glory. The Inquisitor in *L'Alouette*, for example, explains that the smaller, the frailer, the more tender, the *purer* the enemy, the more formidable he/she is. When Creon is told that it was a young girl

who defied his orders, he muses over the dialogue that he anti-
cipates between himself and the pale, intransigent rebel, knowing
well that haughty contempt awaits him.

Describing George Bernard Shaw's Joan of Arc, Harold Clurman
has written:

> She has to be stopped, done away with, because like all fana-
> tically persistent moralists, she is a pest, a threat, unbearable to
> the ordinary. ...Though she wins in history, she must lose in her
> person. She herself recognizes this, but cannot and does not wish
> to curb her force and fail her fate.[7]

Only when the fragile little 'enemies' of the Church or State are
removed from the scene does stability again reign, but only
temporarily, until the next heroine is conjured up. After each new
heroine falls under the Inquisition or the gallows, silent calm
descends upon the State, until the next gunshots are heard being
fired at a skylark.

Anouilh gives the name of the shameless, dissolute and
notorious wife of Ahab, King of Israel, to the anti-heroine of his
play, *Jézabel* (1932), whose immorality and atrocious behaviour
deny her son, Marc, the happiness he seeks. Opposed to Jézabel is
Jacqueline, a paragon of purity, innocence and serenity, whom
Marc loves and would like to bring into his home – but this is
precluded by the fat, lazy, alcoholic, promiscuous, murderous
woman that is his mother and for whom he feels responsible. In
desperation, and clinging to the squalor that links him to his
mother, Marc roughly expels Jacqueline from his life, refusing to
understand her love, her gentleness, her pity, and the invitation to
happiness that she extends to him. Once his beloved has left,
however, Marc dashes out of his home, stricken with madness and
suffering. The glimpse of purity provided by Jacqueline prevents
him from remaining any longer with Jézabel. The reader must
believe that Marc will overtake Jacqueline and achieve the purifica-
tion that can be wrought through the heroine.

La Sauvage (1934) is in many ways similar to *Jézabel*. Thérèse
Tarde, whose sordid life is evoked in relentless detail, is loved by
the wealthy Florent, who offers her (as did Jacqueline to Marc)
marriage, happiness, and forgetfulness of things past. Thérèse
refuses the happiness Florent offers, convinced that suffering must
be her vocation and her only hope for redemption, echoing

Baudelaire's 'Je sais que la douleur est la noblesse unique'. The heroine is faced with the option of 'le sale petit bonheur' that money offers, and she derisively rejects it. Revolt stirs within her; she cries out that she simply does not want to understand certain things, that she will not be domesticated, and that she will not be tricked into looking only at the pleasant things in life. Thérèse envisions all the people of her sordid past as though banded together to receive her in their midst and thus prevent her from making any compromise with the rich. She can reach no comprehension of Florent and his 'race'; she can, however, understand that it is only through extreme violence or in supreme gestures that the 'poor' come a bit closer to the 'happiness' that is heroism or, vice versa, the heroism that constitutes true happiness.

Similarly, the heroine of *Roméo et Jeannette* (1945), reminiscent of the central character in Saul Bellow's *The Last Analysis*, is determined to undergo a baptism of filth and squalor in order to recover her true self. By shamelessly exposing her immorality to her Romeo, she believes she will find the path of self-renewal. Jeannette, in the end, will drown herself in her symbolic white gown, taking the lead in the final tragedy in which the man she loves follows suit, both choosing sacrificial death for the sake of the 'pure' love denied to the mediocre.

La Grotte (1961) is one of the plays in which the stock character of the young servant, Adele appears. Downstairs in the 'grotto' (the kitchen), she is trying desperately and with much physical pain to abort, after having been raped and become pregnant, by imbibing bitter brews. She is further martyrised by the Cook, who has discovered that her illegitimate son (the Seminarist) loves Adele; by the Seminarist, who insists that Adele remain 'pure'; by the despicable valet, who tries to 'sell' her to a café owner in Oran; and, finally, by the Author himself – a character in the play – who deafens her by shouting that her mentality is all wrong! Adele is miraculously 'a being who still remains pure and innocent in the filth in which she wallows'.[8] Up to a certain point in the play, Adele is a self-negating, timid creature, who submits whenever anyone raises a voice to her – a pathetic peasant girl without the mettle of Joan of Arc. But in the dramatic scene in which she finally rejects with scorn both the downstairs and the upstairs worlds that surround her, she shows herself to be of the ilk of a true Anouilh heroine. Her scathing contempt is directed against her father, who had made her a victim of his drunken desires; the coachman, who had seduced her in the filth of the stable; the Cook, who prepares concoctions to induce abortion and serves them with violent blows; the Count and the Countess 'upstairs'; the nuns who used to punish her in winter by forcing her to sit outdoors on a pail of cold water and ask for God's pardon; the Seminarist, whom she loves; and God, whom she does not love. Adele represents the innocence and purity of 'la sauvage' in the midst of corruption and abasement. The Author in the play says: 'It is for her, too – to render homage that she never would have received in her misery – that I wanted to write this play, and I wanted it to be a beautiful play' (*La Grotte*, p. 51).

If, in the 'pièces noires', society triumphs over the absolute ideal and compels the heroines to tragic escape, in the 'pièces roses', Anouilh's characters flee black reality through fantasy, illusion, and changing personality. It is as if the author felt that the world, with its fiendish problems, lacked and needed the sense of humour that he attempted to provide in 'rosy' situations, dexterously managed and manipulated by women, who give their audiences a sense of confidence and optimism. With sparkling humour, the English Lady Hurf (in *Le Bal des voleurs*, 1932), an old 'belle', bored in her sumptuous villa, plays out a comedy of errors, for her only escape from loneliness is into the realm of the illusion created on the evening of the thieves' ball. The aura of fantasy enveloping Lady Hurf and her entourage is carried over to Isabelle, in *Le Rendezvous de Senlis* (1937), in which Georges Delachaume, ashamed of the hypocrisy and avarice of his parents and harassed by the hysteria and jealousy of his wife, creates a world of dreams and fantasies into which he leads the naive young provincial girl, Isabelle, who symbolises detachment and purity, and with whose simplicity, happiness, radiance, and grandmothers, Georges falls fancifully in love.

Another of Anouilh's purely poetic fantasies is *Léocadia* (1939), in which the humble milliner, Amanda, succeeds miraculously in substituting for the dead dramatic actress Léocadia in the heart of the inconsolable Prince Albert Troubiscol. Amanda's magic is that she can render the repulsive attractive, the complicated simple, the unreal real, and the hypocritical sincere, just by being her honest and modest self.

Likewise, in the pleasantly jumbled fairy tale *L'Invitation au château* (1947), it is the poor, insignificant dancer, Isabelle, playing the role of a dazzling socialite, who is the heroine in the château and in the comedy. This young girl's indomitable pride bids her to refuse money: as useful as it is, it cannot replace her values, which are friendship and love. Similarly, Lucile, in *La Répétition*, emerges as the character possessed of the purest and most noble sentiments. Governess of the twelve orphans being raised in a wing of the château, the generous, self-giving Lucile holds herself apart from the sordid liaisons being played out in the aristocratic household. She has faith in higher values of romantic purity and true love. This 'pièce brillante' is delicately and scintillatingly fashioned around the tragic theme of the destruction of that love and Lucile's exile from the château, combined with the rosy theme of the jaded Count's love for the humble governess – a love that goes beyond time and circumstance, beyond good and evil.

Ardèle is the hunchbacked old maid, whose love for the hunchbacked tutor in the Saint-Pé household is genuine and sublime. A symbol of pure love, Ardèle is kept locked in her bedroom, whence she undertakes a protest hunger strike, remains invisible throughout the play, and is ultimately destroyed, for the night that her door is accidentally left unlocked, her lover slips into her room and the two commit suicide. Ardèle is the daisy whose petals wither and fall on too close contact with the grotesque loveless love scenes of the other couples in the play. What Anouilh has said about Joan of Arc applies also to *Ardèle ou la Marguerite*:

> 'You cannot explain Joan any more than you can explain the tiniest flower growing by the wayside. There it is – just a little living flower that has always known, ever since it was a microscopic seed, how many petals it would have and how big they would grow, exactly how blue its blue would be and how its delicate scent would be compounded.[9]

Anouilh's heroines are exceptional women united in a troubling, tragic destiny. In the story of their lives there is a dramatic constant – an enigmatic discomfort which modern psychiatry defines as 'mental anorexia'. Ardèle's refusal of food until the soul in her hump is recognised by those who will not see, Antigone's persistent defiance and refusal to obey edicts, indicate their indomitable perseverance in their search for self-annihilation. Anouilh's heroines are rebellious women with a will to self-sacrifice, in protest or on principle. Through the famous examples in his plays, Anouilh brings rich imagination to descriptions of adolescents, or mature and intelligent women, who refuse the food of life, choose to renounce 'happiness' and die, thereby giving expression to their hunger for something else – perhaps a hunger for 'nothingness'.

If the theatre of Jean Anouilh is destined to survive in future panoramas of French literature, his fame will unequivocally rest on those plays whose heroes are heroines.

NOTES

1. Jean Anouilh, *Nouvelles pièces noires* (Paris: La Table ronde, 1958) p. 188. Subsequent page references are given in text as: '(*NPN*, p.)'.
2. Jean Anouilh, *Pièces costumées* (Paris: La Table ronde, 1960) p. 131. Subsequent page references are given in text as: '(*PC*, p.)'.
3. Anouilh, *Nouvelles pièces noires*, p. 366.
4. Jean Anouilh, *Oreste* (fragments), in Robert de Luppé, *Jean Anouilh, suive de fragments de la pièce de Jean Anouilh: Oreste* (Paris: Editions universitaires, 1959) p. 115.
5. Jean Anouilh, *Pièces brillantes*, (Paris: La Table ronde, 1951) p. 493.
6. Jean Anouilh, *Pièces noires* (Paris: Calmann-Lévy, 1945) p. 360.
7. Harold Clurman, *The Naked Image: Observations on the Modern Theatre* (New York: Macmillan, 1966) p. 142.
8. Jean Anouilh, *La Grotte* (Paris: La Table ronde, 1961) p. 141. Subsequent page references are given in text.
9. In the programme of the French production of *L'Alouette*; quoted in Christopher Fry's translation, *The Lark* (New York: Oxford University Press, 1956) p. ii.

9

Arrabal's Theatre of Liberation

CLAUDE SCHUMACHER

'Un théâtre qui aspire seulement à être infiniment libre et meilleur.'[1]

The theatre is the art of the present. This cliché is repeated over and over again and every critic, at some point or other, is quite happy to state this obvious truth as if s/he had just discovered something profound. But, more often than not, the truism is forgotten as soon as uttered and the clever critic goes on to criticise the playwright, play or production under review *sub specie aeternitatis*. Too often, if not always, the implicit question underlying theatrical criticism is: 'How does this play compare with *Oedipus*, or *Hamlet*, or *Phèdre*, or...*Waiting for Godot?*' Why these eternal touchstones? Because they are 'masterpieces that will speak to all wo/men for all eternity'. In other words, what turns a play into a masterpiece is its degree of abstraction, its timelessness. Yet another cliché proclaims that theatre is, *par excellence*, the art of physical presence. Since Artaud was 'discovered' by, mainly, non-practising theatre scholars in the 1960s (some twenty years after the poet's death), statements like the following are being repeated ad nauseam: 'I maintain the stage is a tangible, physical place that needs to be filled and it ought to be allowed to speak its own concrete language',[2] or the theatre must provide 'the audience with truthful distillations of dreams where its taste for crime, its erotic obsessions, its savageness, its fantasies, even its cannibalism' can be satisfied.[3] Quoted with approval, such statements are also accompanied by a lament: 'there aren't any authors bold enough to carry out Artaud's soaring vision!' Artaud was a dreamer who articulated many of the aspirations of his contemporaries in the 1930s and, prophetically, the aspirations of the generations that came of age or were born immediately following the Second World War.

If Artaud was the dreamer whose ideas became fashionable in the 1960s, Arrabal is the playwright who put the theory into action, and it is perhaps because the latter owes no literary or theatrical debt to the former that Arrabal has not yet achieved the critical recognition that is due to him.

SOME BIOGRAPHICAL POINTERS

'I am a mirror of my time. A mirror. The mirror is not to be spat upon.'[4]

The circumstances of Arrabal's life, from his birth in Melilla (Spanish Morocco) on 11 August 1932 to his incarceration in the notorious Spanish jail of Carabanchel during July and August 1967, are inexorably linked with his writing. But the event that was to shape Arrabal's personality was the arrest of his father, an officer in the Republican army, on 17 July 1936, eve of Franco's coup d'état, for 'military rebellion'. Arrabal senior was first condemned to death, but the sentence was commuted to 'thirty years and one day' in jail. Then, on 4 November 1941, the prisoner was transferred to a mental hospital in Burgos, whence, according to the authorities, he escaped 54 days later, in his pyjamas, across a snow-covered landscape, never to be recaptured. The young Arrabal saw his father once or twice in prison, but the boy could not understand the reasons for his incarceration. The absent father and the tragic events surrounding his life became an inescapable obsession for Arrabal when, in the late 1940s, he discovered letters that his father had written from prison, some notebooks, and family photographs from which his mother had cut out her husband's face. This chance discovery coincided with Arrabal's refusal to apply for a place at the Military Academy, and that decision confirmed the rift between mother and son and contributed to his eventual exile.

Brought up by women (his mother, her sister and, initially, nuns in a convent school), the young boy worshipped his mother. The brutal revelation, in late adolescence, of what he perceived to be her betrayal of his father, led him to reject all that she stood for – Catholicism, Franquism, patriotism – and he became convinced that she was directly responsible for her husband's death.[5] His sexual awakening, described in his autobiographical novel *Baal Babylone* (1959; later to be adapted for the screen as *Viva la muerte*), must have been particularly distressing too. Arrabal dates his first erotic stirrings back to pre-adolescence, when his sexually frustrated aunt would enlist the participation of the boy in her eroticoreligious penitent ceremonies, mixing masturbation and flagellation, following prayer sessions that had assembled the whole family around the kitchen table.

All the elements of Arrabal's obsessional inspiration are the result of a traumatic childhood, and his later work was to become an exorcism, a vast psychodrama in which all the primeval forces at war in his innermost being are given theatrical expression. For that reason, some eminent critics tend to dismiss his theatre as too personal or even self-indulgent.[6] Such an assessment is unnecessarily reductive, as Arrabal's theatre reactivates the great Freudian and Jungian archetypal myths in the context of the chaotic history of the twentieth century.

To conclude this brief bio-presentation one should add the following brief outline in order to help a more immediate understanding of Arrabal's theatre:

1952   Reads avidly Dostoievski, Kafka, Carroll, Saroyan, Mihura. Writes the first version of *Picnic on the Battlefield* (first published in French in 1958; original title: *Los soldados*).

1954   Hitches to Paris to see the Berliner Ensemble's *Mother Courage*. Meets Luce Moreau, his future wife, then studying Spanish at university.

1955   Wins a bursary to study in Paris, where he is diagnosed as suffering from tuberculosis; long stays in sanatoria and surgery (1955-8).

1956   In the sanatorium at Bouffémont, near Paris, writes: *Fando and Lis, Ceremony for a Murdered Black, The Two Executioners, The Labyrinth.*

1957   Completes *The Car Cemetery.*

1958   29 January: *The Tricycle* is given a single performance in Madrid.

        1 February: Arrabal marries Luce Moreau. His wife works in close collaboration with him, translating his writing into French. Completes *Baal Babylone*. First publication of his plays in France. Writes *The Solemn Communion.*

1959 Publication of *Baal Babylone*. Writes *Guernica*.
25 April: *Picnic on the Battlefield*, directed by Jean-Marie Serreau, first professional production in France.

1962 Creates the 'Panic Theatre' movement. Meets André Breton and the Surrealists. Lectures on 'the panic man' ('el hombre pánico') at Sydney University.

1964 Plays performed all over the world directed by the best directors. Wins several prizes.

1966 Victor Garcia's production of *The Car Cemetery* at Dijon (incorporating *Orison, The Two Executioners* and *The Solemn Communion*) plays to critical and popular acclaim. Completes *The Architect and the Emperor of Assyria*.

1967 Jailed in Spain for having written a blasphemous inscription on a copy of *Arrabal celebrando la ceremonia de la confusión* bought by an *agent provocateur*. On his release writes *The Garden of Delights* and begins ... *and they put handcuffs on the flowers*.

1968 April: publishes the first volume of *Le Théâtre*, a journal of theatre research.
May: takes part in the very first occupation (sit-in) in Paris at the Collège d'Espagne.
June: writes *Aurore rouge et noire* (Red and Black Dawn).

1969 Publishes Volumes 6 and 7 of his *Théâtre*; completes...*and they put handcuffs on the flowers*, writes Guerilla Theatre.

Since 1969 Arrabal has devoted more of his time to directing his plays, in France and abroad (especially...*and they put handcuffs on the flowers* in the USA). He has written and directed films (*Viva la muerte*, 1970; *J'irai comme un cheval fou*, 1973; *Guernica*, 1975). He wrote two 'open letters' to two dictators (to Franco in 1972 and to Castro in 1983), has written several books on chess, a game which fascinates him as much as mathematics (a fascination to be borne in mind when analysing the structure of his plays). He has published over fifty plays, which, with rare exceptions, have all been performed in French and in numerous translations, and which have attracted leading directors across the world. Since the late seventies, Spanish productions have also been staged, even if sometimes edulcorated versions are offered to Iberian audiences by timid managements.

1990 September: *La Charge des centaures* premièred in Paris (Accatone 19). The cinema attached to the theatre screened five of Arrabal's films and exhibited his paintings under the title: 'Viva Arrabal!!!'

ARRABAL'S THEATRE

Arrabal's career spans four decades and, forty years on, his approach to his craft is as fresh, as daring and as experimental as and when he started. Unlike the leading playwrights of the preceding generation (e.g., Beckett and Ionesco), who became classics in their own lifetime, Arrabal remains the enfant terrible of the French stage. Despite his anarchist/libertarian attitude, however, Arrabal the playwright has a very meticulous approach to his craft, and three more or less clearly defined main periods can be identified: (a) the 50s, characterised by a concern for the lost individual in some abstract, but hostile and nightmarish world; (b) the 60s, and their infectious theatricality as exemplified in the 'panic movement'; and (c) Guerilla Theatre, dramatising political issues in which the individual is inserted in the socio-political reality of our time.[7]

(a)   The Pre-60s

Arrabal's early plays are often discussed alongside the works of the so-called 'absurd' playwrights.[8] And there are clear affinities between these plays and the writings of Beckett and Ionesco, although the Spaniard had never heard of them when he penned his first texts. *Picnic, Guernica, The Two Executioners*, dramatise the plight of the individual lost in a hostile world which he cannot comprehend, which appears to be meaningless, and which directly threatens his life. But, whereas the authors of *Waiting for Godot* or *The Bald Prima Donna* remain 'outside' their fictional worlds, Arrabal's presence is strongly felt within his dramatic creations.

Picnic on a Battlefield, set on a stage 'covered with barbed wire and sandbags', opens with a cacophony of battle noises ('rifle shots, exploding bombs, machine-guns'). When the din subsides, a frightened soldier who was taking cover picks himself up and starts knitting a pullover. Zapo, the boy soldier, then receives the visit of his mother and father (a sentimental veteran of past wars), who have decided to join him for a picnic to help him pass the time. Soon they are joined by Zépo,[9] another childish soldier from the opposing army, who has lost his way and strolled along, attracted by the record Mr and Mrs Tepan play on their portable gramophone. The lads fraternise and the foursome enjoy themselves, eating, drinking, dancing. Mr Tepan, who loves philosophising, tells the boys how they should end the war: '(*To Zapo*) You just tell your pals that the enemy soldiers don't want to fight a war, and you (*to Zépo*) say the same to your comrades. And then everyone goes home.'[10] Forgetful of what is happening around them, they go on dancing to celebrate peace, when 'a burst of machine-gun fire mows them all down'. The play ends with the return of two happy stretcher-bearers who had previously interrupted the merrymaking because, however much they tried, they could not find a 'stiff', as they say, anywhere.

Picnic is a succession of games: play on words, party games, social and domestic ceremonies, which are most incongruous on a battlefield. But the games Arrabal's characters play are not playful games which the audience is invited to enjoy. They are informed by a deep anger and corrosive irony, directed against man's stupidity and his propensity either to butcher his fellow humans or, altern-atively, to bury his head in the sand, pretending that evil does not exist.

Lira, the old woman never seen in *Guernica*, is buried alive under the rubble of her house while sitting on the lavatory. Fanchou, her husband, ineffectually messes about outside – and, all the time, an air raid is going on around them and bombs keep falling ever closer. Their flirtatious word games and amorous clichés are so many absurd attempts at escaping from the inescapable: they both end up, for ever silenced, under the debris of their home. Oblivious to the old couple's plight, a 'Writer' is researching the Spanish Civil War, and what he is witnessing inspires in him an 'extraordinary' work: 'What a novel I shall make out of all this. What a novel! Or a play, perhaps, and even a film. And what a film!' The device of introducing a writer into the fabric of the play is neither gratuitous, playful nor self-indulgent. It poses the question of the legitimacy of creating 'works of art' out of people's sufferings, and questions directly the reasons for the public's presence at the performance of the play. More effectively than any Brechtian *Verfremdungs* device, the effete aestheticism of the writer's attitude forces the spectator to look inside himself and search for personal answers to the problems raised by the play.

The Two Executioners (subtitled 'Melodrama in one act') is the most harrowing of all Arrabal's plays, as it is also his most painfully autobiographical. Having discovered the truth about his father's fate (or, at least, as much truth as was available to him), Arrabal turned violently against his mother, whom he had worshipped, and became convinced that she had denounced her husband to the fascists. In *Baal Babylone*,[11] the mother defends her collaboration with the judges and the fact that she testified against her husband, by saying that her intervention could only have been beneficial and that she told the judges 'only what he should have confessed immediately in order to escape a harsher condemnation'. In *The Two Executioners*, the theme which remained implicit in the novel, namely the wife's betrayal, becomes explicit. The play opens with the arrival of Françoise into the den of two bored and apathetic torturers: she informs them that her husband 'is guilty' and gives them his name and address. The thugs, stirred into action by the word 'guilty', exit without a word (they never speak or interact with the other characters in the play and they are completely anonymous).[12] After their exit, Françoise beckons her two sons, Benoît and Maurice, into the room. As befits a melodrama, one son is 'good', the other 'bad': Benoît idolises his mother and agrees with everything she does; Maurice is revolted by her behaviour and rebels. The family squabble is interrupted by the return of the thugs, 'carrying Jean, feet and wrists tied together and hanging from a stick in the way captured lions are carried in Africa. ...Françoise looks at her husband attentively, avidly even, as he is taken into the torture chamber.' At the sound of the whiplashes and at her husband's muffled cries, the woman becomes wild and hysterical and joins the men offstage to rub 'vinegar and salt on his wounds to disinfect them'.

When the tortured corpse is carried out, still tied to the pole, Maurice finds the courage to speak out and to accuse his mother of murder. The mother defends herself by saying that the 'father compromised the future of his children and of his wife'. Although Maurice, at first, vehemently rejects her hypocritical explanation, he is eventually unable to resist the arguments she and his brother put forward:

Maurice goes up to his mother and kisses her.
FRANÇOISE: My son!
BENOIT (*to Maurice*):   Ask Mother to forgive you.
MAURICE (*nearly crying*):   Forgive me, Mother.
Maurice and Françoise embrace. Benoît joins them and all three stay enfolded in each other arms while the
       Curtains falls.

Angel Berenguer[13] convincingly argues that the very ambiguous and even shocking ending, in which the faithful son betrays his father and joins the enemy, transcends the personal and obsessional concerns of the author: Arrabal himself refused to kiss and forget and, therefore, he had no option but to exile himself from Spain and his family. But Franco and his regime survived for forty years, thanks to the cowardly silence of the Maurices of this world.[14]

Other plays belonging to this first period (*Orison, The Solemn Communion, Fando and Lis, The Labyrinth...*) are more abstract and have no obvious links with the social or political situation of the 1950s. These works probe human relationships at a subconscious and obsessional level; they are structured by childhood and childish games, elaborate word games and arcane ceremonies invented by the characters as so many devices to pass the time or to make sense of a senseless world. The main characters in these plays, usually a young couple tied together by a sado-masochistic relationship, speak and behave childishly and philosophise endlessly about good and evil, salvation and damnation, sexuality and religion, crime and punishment, earthly delights and human misery...

Orison is a brief 'mystical play' performed in a black box containing 'a child's coffin (black), four candles and an iron Christ'. The coffin contains the body of a child, which two young adults, Fido and Lilbé, have just killed out of sheer boredom to pass the time. Nothing is said about the child, but it could just as well be the couple's own as some kid they might have befriended recently. Now, for no reason at all, they decide 'to be good and pure' and 'to keep God's laws' as set out in the Bible. They reflect that they could even try to achieve sainthood, although, as they say, that might be asking too much. The ceremonial presentation, the evocation of the Creation and of 'baby Jesus', recall unmistakably – but in a derisory fashion – Christ's destiny, the cradle/coffin bringing together, in one daring image, Christ's birth and death.

The Solemn Communion is another inverted Catholic mystery play, taking place in the same funereal space, but the coffin is now of adult size and contains the body of a naked women, which two male undertakers try to whisk out of the way of a marauding necrophiliac. The play opens with a mad dash of that bizarre trio across the stage, followed by the shy entrance of a young girl, equally naked but for a pair of pants, accompanied by an old woman: a grandmother is preparing her grandchild for Holy Communion and, as she ceremoniously dresses her for church, she proffers advice on how to become the perfect submissive housewife. At intervals, the smooth operation is interrupted by the macabre rush across the stage of the coffin, followed by the necrophile, whose sex assumes ever more monstrous proportions. On their third passage the undertakers drop the coffin and run off. In ecstasy the necrophile jumps into the coffin and defiles the corpse under the stern gaze of the girl, who watches intently. The communicant is then led off by her grandmother, only to return alone: she stabs the necrophile and bursts out laughing at the sight of the spurt of blood reddening her white dress, while red balloons float out of the coffin. The surrealist oneirism of the play lends it a nightmarish quality which defies rationalisation, and Arrabal triggers in his spectators responses based on the association of conflicting images: communion dress/wedding dress; naked corpse/laced-up virgin; coffin/wedding bed; grandmother/bawd; virgin/voyeuse; victim/murderess...

In such plays nothing is clear-cut, nothing is sure, nothing is what it seems to be. The issues of good and evil are hopelessly confused and Arrabal's characters try desperately to latch on to 'something'; and in their desperation to be good, or sincere, or faithful or whatever takes their fancy, they behave with an in-human, mechanical precision in which the exercise of free will is not permitted.

(b)   The 1960s: Panic Theatre and Confusion

A prolific writer and an active promoter of his own work, Arrabal was none the less shunned by the French cultural and theatrical establishment, at a time when his plays became more and more successful everywhere else. So it was that, in 1962, with his friends Alexandro Jodorowsky, a Mexican theatre and film director, and Topor, a French designer and painter, he created the 'panic movement': a playful stunt to attract media attention, an act of derision directed against bourgeois and academic pomposity, it was also a sincere desire to try to define their art even if, as Beckett would have said, their art was striving all the time to avoid defini-tion. Arrabal had been labelled an 'absurdist' and, since he did not accept the tag, he decided to impose a more accurate label to characterise himself and his art. 'We got together one afternoon, Topor, Jodorowsky and I', writes Arrabal, 'and we thought: "today nobody knows us, but one day we'll be well known. Let's create the Panic Movement. Since we succeed in everything we do, Panic will succeed too."'[15]

Even if the idea of a movement was born out of the whimsy of some artists, the notion helps to understand Arrabal's theatre, and his 1963 Sydney University lecture on 'the panic man' is most illuminating.[16] He told his Australian audience that he particularly enjoyed the game of free associations of ideas and that he had recently come up with the following sentence: 'L'avenir agit en coups de théâtre' ('The future acts through chance occurrences'). He then commented: 'I was enchanted by that sentence. I reckoned that the future is determined by chance and I came to the conclusion that confusion (undistinguishable from chance) ruled our future and therefore our present and our...past (ex-future).'

To the concepts of chance and confusion just outlined, Arrabal added the notion of memory, and claimed that these 'three catalysts' rule human destiny and that authentic artistic creation should also allow itself to be ruled absolutely by these three forces. He concluded that 'since all that is human is confused *par excellence*', any attempt at achieving perfection would yield artificiality (i.e., non-confusion) and that such an attempt was therefore 'inhuman'.

In theatrical terms Arrabal was greatly helped in his panic endeavours by his two associates and by a group of talented directors, known as the Parisian 'Latin-Americans' (chiefly Victor Garcia and Jorge Lavelli and, to a lesser extent, Jérôme Savary). Arguably Garcia's greatest success was achieved in 1966, when he staged *Le Cimetière des voitures*, or 'The Passion According to Arrabal', at the Festival Dramatique de Bourgogne (Dijon, 1966). Garcia's production is most memorable for its use of space, and his subversion of the traditional actor/spectator relationship, in a huge hangar inside the Palais des Congrès.[17] The space (18m × 12m × 5m) was transformed into a chaotic 'car cemetery' with broken up cars hanging from the ceiling at various angles and different heights. The action unfolded at all levels, inside, on top and beneath the cars and all around the spectators. As well as exploding the space and exploiting the three dimensions creatively, Garcia abandoned the linear story-telling approach and made use of simultaneous staging, developing parallel actions in locations scattered around the hangar. Although the name of Artaud was often invoked by critics, Garcia – like Arrabal – always maintained that the French poet had had no influence over him. It is true that both men were inspired by the same 'exotic' theatre forms (Indian folklore, Brasilian traditions, Peking Opera, Kathakali, Kabuki, Nô...), but

Garcia had the advantage of knowing some of these traditions at first hand and of having seen a rich variety of Far-Eastern performances, whereas Artaud had to be content with a single visit of a Balinese dance company to Paris.

Arrabal's most successful and most often performed play is *The Architect and the Emperor of Assyria*, completed in 1965 and first directed in Paris in 1967, by Jorge Lavelli, before being produced by major theatres throughout the world. In London, Garcia directed Anthony Hopkins in the Emperor's role at the National Theatre in 1971, and Lavelli revived it in 1975. More than any of Arrabal's plays, *The Architect* defies summarisation. 'The action takes place in a small clearing of some island where the Architect lives alone.' The play opens with the sound of a plane crash, of which the Emperor of Assyria is the sole survivor. The enforced companionship of this latter-day Robinson/Friday couple turns into a series of ritualised games and ceremonies, in which the two men play a succession of dual roles (teacher/pupil, master-slave, fiancé/fiancée, mother/son, soldier/enemy, father confessor/penitent, judge/matricide...). They discuss philosophy, religion, art, morality, theatre...They pray and they blaspheme; they play amorous and erotic games, either as 'themselves' or by assuming other, male or female, characters; they fight, they insult one another, they threaten to leave the island and leave the other alone...There isn't a fantasy they don't indulge in, or a nightmare that isn't haunting them.

Act I of *The Architect*, in its apparently unfocused proliferation, leads to the trial of Act II, during which the Emperor confesses to the murder of his mother, before pronouncing his own sentence: 'I want you...to eat me. I want you to be both you and me. You will eat me up, Architect, is that clear?' The cannibalistic ceremony is duly performed, but it does not allow the 'Architect/Emperor' to accede to a higher plane of consciousness, as the Emperor had hoped. Deliberately the play comes to no conclusion, as it ends where it began, with an air crash. The play can start all over again, the only difference being that the roles are now reversed.

To compound the confusion, Arrabal explains: 'At certain moments the Architect thinks that the Emperor is playing a role, when in fact he is not, and vice versa. And when the Emperor decides to die, having confessed his sordid past, he is no longer playing a role, but only he knows it.'[18] The play, adds Arrabal, contains moments of truth which anchor the action into recognisable reality; but Arrabal's 'reality' encompasses all contradictions and, like Jarry, he subscribes to the equations: good = bad, + = –, 0 = ∞... *The Architect and the Emperor* is meant to activate in the spectator a myriad of conflicting emotions and to stir up jarring thoughts. The psycho-drama taking place on stage should, insidiously, prompt the spectator to ask for himself all the questions raised in the play, and thus undergo, in the innermost recesses of his heart, a similar experience.

(c) 1968 and Beyond

In the summer of 1967 Arrabal returned to Spain for a holiday. In early July he signed his book *Arrabal celebrando la ceremonia de la confusión* in a Madrid library. A young 'admirer' requested a 'Panic inscription' and the author obliged: 'Me cago en Dios, en la Patra[19] y en todo lo demás' (I shit on God, on Patra and on everything else). The admirer turned out to be an *agent provocateur* belonging to the police, and in the night of 20–1 July Arrabal was arrested and charged with blasphemy and insult to the fatherland. While he was kept in solitary confinement, the fascist press ran a campaign of vilification, one newspaper calling for his castration to prevent him from fathering anti-Spanish children![20] Thanks to the intervention of well-known artists and writers (Anouilh, Beckett, Ionesco, Mauriac, Weiss...) Arrabal was released on 14 August and ac-quitted the following month. The short stay in Franco's jails proved to be very traumatic and it had an immediate impact on Arrabal's writing. He turned away from the more abstract and metaphysical concerns of his earlier theatre to include contemporary events and topics into the fabric of his plays. He left Spain determined to bring the plight of the political prisoners to the attention of the world, but, before he could write the play he had in mind, more dramatic and more immediately pressing events were to require his atten-tion.

The student uprising of May 1968 saw him in the forefront of the conflict, and he was among the 'groupuscule' which started the occupation of the Collège d'Espagne at the Cité Universitaire in Paris. But the exhilaration and enthusiasm of the early, heady days of the youthful revolt were soon followed by street violence, police brutality and repression. *Aurore rouge et noire* (Red and Black Dawn, subtitled Théâtre de Guérilla), the play Arrabal started writing during the student uprising, is appropriately divided into four parts, alternating between exhilaration and despondency. True to

its anarchist inspiration, the play indicts every aspect of the
Establishment's policy (authoritarianism reeking of neo-fascism in
the state, the church, the army, the police, as well as in financial,
educational and political circles...) in powerful and unforgettable
images set against idyllic pictures of idealistic youths, youthful love
and sexual liberation.

Aurore (especially *Tous les parfums d'Arabie*) became the first draft
of what I consider to be Arrabal's finest and most important
achievement:...*et ils passèrent des menottes aux fleurs* ('...and they put
handcuffs on the flowers'),[21] written during the first months of 1969
and directed by Arrabal himself (Théâtre de l'Épée de Bois, Paris,
September 1969). This is the play which was directly inspired by
his experience in jail, and which the political prisoners had asked
him to write: 'When I was freed from Carabanchel jail, the
prisoners asked me with great dignity to speak out, to reveal the
truth about the Franquist jails. That is why I wrote...*et ils passèrent
des menottes aux fleurs* which is not a play, but a cry', a cry for
freedom, a cry against oppression, a cry of anger and anguish at
man's bestial behaviour towards man. Arrabal insists that...*et ils
passèrent des menottes aux fleurs* is neither 'art' nor 'theatre', but a
testimony to the resilience of the prisoners and a projection 'of their
mad dreams, their distorted visions, their memories overflowing
with pain and hope'. To write this play, he did not rely on his
inspiration and his personal experiences alone; instead he incorpor-
ated factual information gathered inside the prison, as well as
documentary evidence concerning atrocities committed during and
after the Spanish Civil War.

Amiel, Katar and Pronos are long-term political prisoners and
the play consists of a succession of imaginary scenes, fantastic,
dreamlike, nightmarish, in which the men act out their obsessions:
erotic dreams, dreams of happiness, actual torture scenes, scato-
logical fantasies, blasphemous and religious yearnings, childhood
memories...The three actors, impersonating 'good' and 'bad'
characters as the situations demand, are joined by three actresses
who, too, interpret a whole gamut of different roles. The only part
consistently played by one actor is that of Tosan, who is ostensibly
inspired by Julián Grimau.[22] A faithful mirror of reality, the play
ends in tragedy: no one is released, Tosan is executed. But,
whereas Ybar's execution took place offstage in *Tous les parfums*,
Arrabal transforms Tosan's martyrdom into an elaborate ceremony
with provocative Christian overtones. For his execution Tosan is

placed, naked, on the garrotte and, at the moment of his death, he urinates:

> A woman collects the liquid into a basin. The urine is, in reality, blood. Men and women, singing joyous hymns to freedom and justice, untie Tosan and carry him in procession. They take him to the highest spot in the theatre and link arms around Tosan, who is alive and happy. They sing together the end of repression and the beginning of a new age.[23]

It would be naive to tax Arrabal with naivety. In the reality depicted by the play, the dictator had his way (Franco was still to commit further atrocities before his death in 1975) and flowers were handcuffed. But the theatrical liturgy created by Arrabal for his spectators is staged with the twin ambition to impart information through the senses and to inspire a longing for liberation and happiness in the worst possible circumstances. As Arthur Husk rightly says, in...*et ils passèrent des menottes aux fleurs*, Arrabal displays total control of his obsessions: 'This control allows him to use biographical material without weakening the import of the message he is attempting to communicate. The tight rein he has now on his obsessions makes one feel that the play's attachment to his life and earlier work is not a source of weakness, but of strength.'[24]

In theatrical terms, Arrabal conceived...*et ils passèrent des menottes aux fleurs* as a fully integrated experience: from the moment the spectators reached the theatre to their departure, they were invited to join in a ceremonial game that had been carefully prepared for them. As always, in Arrabal's theatre, the spatial arrangement was of paramount importance and, in this case, the layout of the building itself had been rearranged as shown in the diagram:

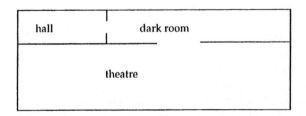

The pre-performance, involving the audience, is carefully described in the stage directions: on arrival, the spectators were met by the stage-manager playing host/MC. Each person was invited to step individually from the brightly lit hall into the black room, where an actor took him, in total darkness, to a 'seat' on the floor or on top of one of the many platforms disseminated through the acting space. All the time, the SM/MC and the actors whispered into the spectator's ear (for example, 'A man will get murdered tonight', 'You are being taken to solitary confinement'..., or almost inaudible, incomprehensible sounds); they comforted them if they were apprehensive or roughed them up a little. Still in darkness, spectators could hear 'strange vocal sounds, a melancholic flute, pygmy music, a woman's sobs' and smell 'rich oriental perfumes'. When the public was assembled ('never more than 100 to 120 people') a voice shouted: 'Open the gate, prisoner Tosan is being taken to the penitentiary.' As the lights came up, the spectator discovered that he was isolated from his companion(s) and that the public was scattered all over the space and on several levels. Arrabal's aim was to break down the actor/spectator opposition: 'The actors invent a game and invite the spectator to join in.' The closeness of actors and spectators was heightened during the performance, when those actors not taking part in a scene sat among spectators, and actresses 'rested their head on the knee of a male spectator'.

This passive 'participation' became direct activity at the end of the performance: after Tosan's resurrection a loudspeaker announced that the play was over and the voice urged the spectators to leave the theatre, but it also suggested that some people might want to stay on 'in order to celebrate "a rite"'. The actors then put a hood over the heads of the remaining spectators before rubbing their hands – 'very gently' – with sand and humming 'some haunting and rhythmic melody', before the loudspeaker encouraged greater physical involvement and proposed some sado-masochist game. When, eventually, the hoods were taken off, 'one of the actors revealed with total sincerity an event of his life which, by its profound tenderness, or sheer horror, or wild eroticism would create such a shock in the audience that at least one spectator would be compelled to speak out.'

The published text (October 1969) states, in an endnote, that the play was currently being performed 'with success and fervour' and that more than half the audience took part in the ritual, 'creating fascinating experiences'. But, in 1978, Arrabal gave a more sober and pessimistic assessment of these improvisations, which never really unlocked the secrets of the spectators' private lives and ob-

sessions. The first ten minutes, recounts Arrabal, went quite satisfactorily, as they were controlled by the anonymous voice of the
loudspeaker. Too well, in fact: having just witnessed a play
denouncing tyranny, the spectators were happy to follow the
Orwellian orders like sheep, whipping and letting themselves be
whipped. But, when told that they were now free to continue 'the
game' on their own, they froze, stood around for a while and
finally applauded the end of the performance: 'Curtain. *Finita la
commedia*. The spectators had not understood a thing.'[25]

...*et ils passèrent des menottes aux fleurs* attracted a great deal of
publicity, even before it was performed, especially from the gutter
press. The reviews were largely negative, although the more
serious writers recognised the importance of the event. The most
positive, intelligent, perceptive article was published by the
Protestant newspaper *Réforme* (18 October 1969), under the
signature of its regular critic, Eric Westphal, the text of which
merits to be quoted at length, as it not only testifies to the special
qualities of this particular play, but encapsulates the essence of
Arrabal's art:

> It is most beautiful, strong, crude, striking. And I should like to
> deal at the outset with the stench of scandal surrounding this
> production. ...To censor this show, that would indeed be putting
> handcuffs on flowers, and he who dared would, in my view,
> cover himself with shame and ridicule. One cannot say what
> Arrabal is saying in the delicate language of Giraudoux. Can one
> speak of horrors, of oppressions, of crimes without graphically
> describing them, without acting them? Torture in Algeria, geno-
> cide in Biafra, napalm in Vietnam and much of what we see in
> our so-called civilized world fills us with indignation, but we
> cannot stomach a realistic, sometimes daring show, which is
> never obscene because it is never gratuitous, on the pretext that
> some people might be shocked? To shock? Yes, of course, it was
> written to shock. And very well written too. [...] Poets do not
> engage in direct violent action. No doubt Arrabal would dearly
> like to assassinate Franco and delete Spanish fascism from the
> European map. ...So, with hands that cannot kill physically, the
> poet strikes a mortal moral blow. This is no less important.

The hypocrites, to whom Westphal makes allusion, did indeed win
the day and the performances had to stop, by order of the courts,

on the pretext that some spectators had been roughly treated during the pre-performance ceremony: Arrabal was personally accused of having bitten the ear of a spectator who complained. The reality is that the Épée de Bois theatre was playing to full houses when...*et ils passèrent des menottes aux fleurs* was closed down.[26]

Arrabal's next play, *Bella Ciao* or *The Thousand Year War* (1972), was also the result of a theatrical experiment. In the wake of May 1968, the authority of the playwright and the director was challenged by actors who wanted a greater say in decision-making and in the elaboration of plays. With Jorge Lavelli, Arrabal therefore proposed to the company of the Théâtre National Populaire (TNP), which had recently commissioned the dramatist to write a play for the following season, that they should attempt a collective creation involving actors, musicians and designers (the technicians were not excluded: they declined to take part at the outset). After the first four days of communal works, all the actors – with one exception – declared that they found the challenge too exhausting, so the piece was devised by four men: Arrabal, Lavelli, the designer (a member of the Communist Party) and an actor (a left-wing militant). The result was an infectious, kaleidoscopic, irreverent romp lampooning all the sacred cows of French and Western society. Another, indirect and unsought-for-result was the closure of the Théâtre National Populaire in Paris.[27]

AUTHOR VS DIRECTOR?

At the time of *Bella Ciao* Arrabal had already a rich experience as the director of his own plays, and in the past twenty years he has become more and more involved in productions. Obviously he sees his creative work as director as the natural continuation of the role of the playwright, since a play does not yield its full meaning, achieve its full impact or attain its final completion until it has been concretely realised on stage. One reason why Arrabal is pursuing his collaboration in the process is *not* because he is unhappy at the work of his directors, unlike Ionesco, who criticises most productions of his plays, or Beckett, who took to directing in order to ensure that his plays should reach the audience exactly as he imagined them.[28] On the contrary, Arrabal has always professed that the director should have complete artistic freedom to do with the author's text what he pleases: 'Once I have written my play, I wish that an amazingly delirious director of genius takes hold of it and without reverence treats it as the *pretext* for his production.' He goes even further: 'I also say to my directors: "You must create something prodigious, even if it means betraying me." Sometimes I get quite a shock, but I always grant total freedom.'[29] In a series of interviews with Alain Schifres, Arrabal analysed at length his attitude towards the scenic enactment of his texts, and never retreated from his position of openness: 'The *mise en scène* must have nothing to do with what I write. For me the process is a relay race, the director getting hold of my scenario and making *something else* of it. He creates wonderful moments and I must watch his work and learn from him for my next play.'[30] In such a conception of the theatrical process, the director becomes a creator on a par with the author: the former writes 'scenically' ('*écriture scénique*'), the latter 'dramatically' ('*écriture dramatiqué*'). Therefore, says Arrabal, if ten directors offer ten different interpretations of one of his plays, he is ready to accept them all. This openness is perfectly in keeping with the principles of 'confusion' as put forward in *Le Panique*. In 'Vers l'éphémère panique',[31] Jodorowsky insists that what distinguishes theatre from the other arts is its essentially ephemeral quality. The aim of theatre is not to create 'works of art', i.e., finished products to last an eternity, but to effect a direct transformation of life: 'Theatre is not an Art, but Knowledge of Life.' A play, or rather a 'spectacular celebration', should be as fluid and as kaleidoscopic as the front page of a daily newspaper showing, side by side, pictures of the Pope and Madonna, Gorbachov and Stallone, together with wildly contrasting headlines: 'everything co-exists, everything asserts its presence'. Furthermore, the characters of a dramatic action are not immutable entities, given once and for all, but they have to be created anew, performance after performance, spontaneously and outrageously. Even if, as David Whitton rightly concludes in his 1981 article, Arrabal is now paying more attention to the written text and concentrates more single-mindedly on the work of the 'speaking actor' as opposed to the spectacular extravaganzas of the 60s and 70s, his willingness to co-operate with directors and to allow them to handle his scripts as blueprints for their productions has helped significantly to liberate the theatre from the tyranny of the written word.

CONCLUSION

In an interview dating from 1976, Arrabal declared:

> I don't know if my plays and my films will still be mentioned in twenty years' time, when I'll be dead; but why is there so much polemic surrounding it? Because I describe a part of ourselves which remains hidden. In the bathroom, there are mirrors; I saw my back and I was frightened: I don't even know my own back! Can you imagine my inside? I can't judge the artistic merit of my theatre. Outside any accepted political or religious norms, I dive into my subconscious, in what you call my phantasms.[32]

The twenty years are almost up; Arrabal is more creative than ever and has no thoughts of dying yet. But we can try and answer his question: is his theatre relevant to us today? The unequivocal answer is yes, but it is also true that fewer of his plays are being performed and that the leading theatres where his major texts were staged in the late 60s and early 70s ignore his new plays. Is it because his writing is less challenging, or that it has become predictable, or that managements are looking for some new form of novelty? I don't think so. The reason for the current disaffection is to be found in the depressing political, cultural and social atmosphere of the late 80s and, I am afraid, such a negative mood is likely to endure for some time to come. But the sad reality of today should not blind us to Arrabal's tremendous achievements as a playwright in the previous decades. His perceived modest standing in the early 90s is a negative reflection on the Thatcherite, selfish and self-centred societies of the Western world.

Jacques Lemarchand, the most respected postwar French drama critic writing for the *Figaro littéraire* (a newspaper which could not be suspected of Maoist sympathies), echoes Westphal's enthusiastic response to ...*et ils passèrent des menottes aux fleurs*, qualifying it as: 'a heartrending call for love in its most simple form and liberty in its purest form'.[33]

For Arrabal's voice to be heard loud and clear once again we must regain a taste for that kind of love and that kind of freedom, for – as Westphal says – these are the crucial things in life. And all that is most crucial in life is to be found in Arrabal's plays.

NOTES

1. Christine Fouche, in *Réforme*, 18 March 1972, reviewing *Bella Ciao*.
2. *Artaud on Theatre*, ed. by Claude Schumacher (London: Methuen, 1988), p. 92.
3. Ibid, p. 101.
4. Interview in the *New York Herald Tribune*, 28 May 1976.
5. See especially, *Baal Babylone*, *Viva la muerte* and *The Two Executioners*.
6. See, for instance, *The Cambridge Guide to World Theatre* (Cambridge University Press, 1988).
7. See Danièle de Ruyter-Tognotti, *De la prison à l'exil* (Paris: Nizet, 1986).
8. See Claude Schumacher, 'The Theatre of the Absurd', in *Encyclopedia of Literature and Criticism*, ed. Martin Coyle et al. (London: Routledge, 1990), pp. 464-74.
9. Given Arrabal's professed admiration for Lewis Carroll, many critics have pointed out the similarity between Zapo/Zépo and Tweedledum/Tweedledee. To place too great a stress on the influence of Carroll on Arrabal, however, could lead to misunderstandings. Arrabal's intent is deadly (or rather vitally) serious.
10. All quotations refer either to Arrabal, *Plays*, volumes 1 to 4 (London: Calder and Boyars, 1962–75) or to Arrabal, *Théâtre*, vols I-XVI (Paris: Christian Bourgois, 1968–) unless otherwise stated.
11. Fernando Arrabal, *Baal Babylone*, an autobiographical novel, develops the theme of guilt and analyses the different and contradictory emotions experienced by the growing boy.
12. In the list of characters Arrabal writes: 'I don't know their names.'
13. Angel Berenguer, *L'Exil et la cérémonie* (Paris: Union générale d'édition, 1977) p. 228: "The society which engulfs Maurice is totally artificial, as artificial as the religion, the peace and the harmony which François offers her son.'
14. It is interesting to compare this ending with that of Václav Havel's first *Vaněk Plays*. *Audience* also ends on a note of ambiguity, whereas the other Vaněk plays unquestioningly hand over the 'moral high ground' to the heroic dissident, and ridicule the other characters.
15. Quoted in Françoise Raymond-Mundschau, *Arrabal*, Classiques du XXe siècle (Paris: Éditions universitaires, 1972) p. 23.
16. See Fernando Arrabal, *Le Panique*, Union générale d'éditions, 18 October 1973, 'L'Homme panique', pp. 37–53.
17. For a detailed description of the production, see *Les Voies de la création théâtrales*, vol. 1 (Paris: CNRS, 1970) pp. 311-40; and David Whitton, *Stage Directors in Modern France* (Manchester University Press, 1987) pp. 163-70.
18. Quoted in Raymond-Mundschau, *Arrabal*, p. 72.

19.   Arrabal's cat, Cleopatra, was nicknamed Patra! Arrabal later said: 'I
      do think that my intention was to write Patria, but my hand traced
      Patra...I'll never know.' The confusion was used to mock Spanish
      justice. Quoted in Raymond-Mundschau, *Arrabal*, p. 27.

20.   Arrabal had long maintained that he didn't want any children. But
      when his daughter Lelia Paloma Ofelia was born, on 14 January
      1970, he became a doting father. His son, born on 15 July 1972, was
      named Samuel: 'Beckett, among other qualities, radiates wonderful
      tenderness and provides extraordinary spiritual nourishment. My
      son is called Samuel to honour him. I should like him to resemble
      [Beckett].'

21.   The title comes from Lorca's poem 'Poeta en Nueva York': 'los
      interminables trenes de sangre/y los trenes de rosa maniatadas' (in
      Lorca, *Obras completas* (Madrid, 1969) p. 515).

22.   Julián Grimau was a Spanish Communist party leader at the time of
      the Civil War. He was arrested on 7 November 1961 and tortured in
      prison. His trial, for alleged crimes committed as a Republican
      Officer between 1936 and 1939, opened on 18 April 1963. Franco's
      cabinet decided the following day that Grimau should be
      condemned to death, and to 'thirty years imprisonment'. He was
      executed, on Franco's express orders, early on 20 April 1963, despite
      universal protest from the Vatican to the Kremlin. In *Tous les parfums
      d'Arabie*, the Grimau character is called Ybar.

23.   Arrabal again directed the play himself in New York, at the Mercer
      Arts Center (21 April 1972). The production was highly successful. In
      that version the optimistic ending was cut and the spectators were
      left with the image of Falidia washing herself in Tosan's blood.

24.   Arthur Husk, 'The Flight from Childhood', unpublished MA dis-
      sertation, University of Glasgow, 1975, p. 68.

25.   See Albert Chesneau and Angel Berenguer, *Plaidoyer pour une
      différence – Entretiens avec Arrabal* (Presses Universitaires de
      Grenoble, 1978) p. 39.

26.   The Belgian production had a very successful run in Brussel in 1971,
      but was censored by the Belgian courts when it transferred to Ghent.

27.   The survival of the TNP had already been threatened in 1968, when
      it started rehearsing Gatti's *The Passion of General Franco*. The play
      was banned by 'de Gaulle's government and this led to Georges
      Wilson's resignation as director in 1972 and the closure of the TNP at
      the Palais de Chaillot.

28.   See Gordon Armstrong, '"A Less Conscious Art": Samuel Beckett
      and Scenic Art in the Eighties', in *40 years of mise en scène*, edited by
      C. Schumacher (Dundee: Lochee Publications, 1986) pp. 111–25.
      Armstrong discusses a controversial production of *Endgame* in
      Cambridge, Mass. (1984), which Beckett attempted to close down. A
      few months before his death Beckett succeeded in preventing the
      Comédie-Française from going ahead with their latest production of
      Fin de partie. Eventually, but against the wish of the director, who
      removed his name from the programme, the play was seen in Paris,

for a very short time, without its 'offensive' pink scenery or the specially written musical score.

29. Arrabal, in an interview with Odette Aslan (21 June 1966) quoted in David Whitton, 'Écriture dramatique et écriture scénique', *Theatre Research International*, vol. VI, no. 2 (Spring 1981) p. 133. My discussion owes much to David Whitton's work.

30. Alain Schifres, *Entretiens avec Arrabal* (Paris, 1969) p. 78 (quoted in Whitton, op. cit.).

31. Arrabal, *Le Panique*, pp. 74–92.

32. Interview published in *Les quatre saisons du théâtre et de la musique*, 25 June 1976.

33. *Le Figaro littéraire*, 20 October 1969.

10

Artaud and Genet's
The Maids
Like Father, Like Son?

GARY DAY

At least two commentators have claimed that Antonin Artaud was an important influence on Jean Genet. Ronald Harwood says this influence was 'enormous'[1] while John Russell Taylor classifies Genet as a 'follower'[2] of Artaud. Such views represent the received wisdom and, like all received wisdom, it needs to be questioned. The purpose of this essay is to examine the influence of Artaud on Genet with reference to *The Maids*,[3] and then to consider examples of other approaches to the play before finally problematising the whole question of 'influence' as a way of making sense of a text, especially when that text is a play.

Artaud's most influential text was *The Theatre and Its Double*.[4] It is a collection of essays which criticises the state of French theatre and proposes a new theatre, the Theatre of Cruelty. What Artaud disliked about his contemporary theatre was its emphasis on entertainment and its unwillingness to challenge the social and political order. He felt that it avoided danger and had too much respect for the past. It was a descriptive, narrative theatre, primarily concerned with defining character and with resolving its emotional and psychological conflicts. At times, Artaud referred to this theatre as psychological theatre, and he objected to psychology on the grounds that it made the unknown known, which resulted, though he does not explain how, in a loss of 'energy' (*TD* 'No More Masterpieces', p. 58), a characteristically loose term in a text brimful of poetry and gnomic utterances.

In addition to being 'psychological', French theatre was also representational, and its plots of 'money...social climbing [and] the pangs of love unspoilt by altruism (*TD*, 'No More Masterpieces', p. 58) were derided by Artaud as 'ridiculous imitation[s] of real life' (*TD*, 'On the Balinese Theatre', p. 42), since they turned the audience into mere 'Peeping Toms' (*TD*, 'Theatre and Cruelty', p. 84). His main objection, however, was to the dominance of dialogue. He called this a 'dictatorship of words' (*TD*, 'Production and Metaphysics', p. 29) which pushed what he considered to be the truly theatrical elements, such as symbols, mimicry, mime and gestures, into the background. In Artaud's view, the script had to go, since it was implicated not just in the repression of everything that was properly theatrical, but also in some 'dark prodigious reality' (*TD*, 'On the Balinese Theatre', p. 43), the nature of which again remains unexplained. Words, he felt, were incapable of expressing strong or true feelings and it was for this reason that he preferred allegories or images, since by disguising what they were meant to reveal they brought more enlightenment to the mind. In this respect, Artaud's was an expressive, rather than representative, theatre.

The name he gave to this expressive theatre was the Theatre of Cruelty. As Artaud was at pains to point out, this had nothing to do with the cruelty individuals inflict on one another; on the contrary, it was intended to show 'the far more terrible, essential cruelty objects can practise on us. We are not free, and the sky can still fall in on our heads. And above all else, theatre is made to teach us this' (*TD*, 'No More Masterpieces', p. 10). It seems that the message of theatre is that man is in bondage to the inanimate world, which contrasts strongly with another statement, that theatre should confront us 'with all our potential' (*TD*, 'Theatre and Cruelty', p. 66). This sort of inconsistency is not untypical of Artaud, and is indicative of his desire to move beyond rationality and so put himself, and us, in touch with vital forces and energies. In his theatre there is a 'reduced role given to understanding' (*TD*, 'Theatre and Cruelty', p. 66); and, while this may in some ways be welcome, in that it is an appeal to the senses and emotions as well as to the intellect, it is also dangerous, for it can lead to the worshipping of those vague but powerful forces which Artaud wanted his theatre to communicate and his audience to experience. Put like this, it is not too difficult to see his theatre as a form of fascist art which 'exalts mindlessness [and] glamourises death'[5] especially when he gives vent to such sentiments as 'Violent...action is like lyricism' (*TD*, 'No More Masterpieces', p. 62).

If one meaning of cruelty relates to objects, another has to do with control; in Artaud's own words, 'cruelty means strictness, diligence, unrelenting decisiveness, irreversible and absolute determination' (*TD*, 'Letters of Cruelty', p. 79). Exactly what this determination and decisiveness are to be exercised on is not clear, but it seems reasonable to assume that it has to do with every aspect of a performance, since what Artaud admired in Balinese theatre was the 'loving, unerring attention to detail', the order and 'the deliberate accuracy directing everything, through which everything happens' (*TD*, 'On the Balinese Theatre', p. 46). Once more there seems to be a contradiction between this statement, with its emphasis on control, and a view of theatre as releasing 'our repressed subconscious' (*TD*, 'Theatre and the Plague', p. 19) and liberating 'powers' which are most definitely 'dark' (*TD*, 'Theatre and the Plague', p. 21).

A third meaning of cruelty refers to creation, and here it has two aspects. The first is that it is 'a hungering after life' and the second is that it is 'a cruel need for creation', which has to be obeyed (*TD*, 'Letters of Cruelty', p. 80). Cruelty is thus both a desire and a command, something that is both within and without the self, and, as such, it overcomes the subject/object division, which has been one of the enduring problems of Western philosophy. Artaud is able to straddle this divide by altering the usual meaning of cruelty, and what he does in criticism is paralleled by what he is trying to do in the theatre, which is to liberate the sign, the sign being understood as every aspect of a production.

One of Artaud's main aims was to restore to theatre a sense of religious or mystical meaning, and one way of achieving this was by 'a return to ancient Primal Myths' (*TD*, 'The Theatre of Cruelty – Second Manifesto', p. 82). Through the poetry of stage language, that is, such things as gestures, postures, ritualistic costumes, master and puppets, all of which should overlap and interconnect, a kind of metaphysics is created which reveals the 'identity of the abstract and concrete' (*TD*, 'On the Balinese Theatre', p. 41). What Artaud means by this is that audiences become aware of the connection, or even unity, between themselves and the primal forces of nature. This is impressed upon them by the fact that the action of an Artaud play – which incidentally deals with universal cosmic themes, change, fate, creation, growth and chaos – takes place around them; the audience is in the centre and the 'play' is performed all around them in a space which admits no division between stage and auditorium. With this staging, together with the combined effect of its poetic devices, Artaud hoped to 'directly affect...the anatomy' (*TD*, 'No More Masterpieces', p. 61) of the audience. The language he uses to describe this process is, however, somewhat suspect – he calls it, on one occasion, a 'tangible laceration' (*TD*, 'Theatre and Cruelty', p. 65). Whether the audience is a body to be scarred by a sadistic dramaturge, or whether it needs such violence for the message to get through, is a question that is never really answered, but it does again raise doubts about the ultimate direction of Artaud's work.

Once the audience is conscious of the primal forces of nature which, it should be stressed, are dark, and cannot be imagined 'aside from a mood of slaughter, torture and bloodshed' (*TD*, 'Theatre and the Plague', p. 21), it is then in a position to 'command...certain predominant powers, certain ideas governing everything; and since ideas, when they are effective generate their own energy, rediscover within [the audience's self] that energy which in the last analysis creates order and increases the value of life' (*TD*, 'No More Masterpieces', p. 60). To Artaud then, theatre is about release, a feeling of energy or even rapture which may then lead to the creation of a new order. This points to the revolutionary potential of Artaud's theatre, which is underlined by his view of stage poetry as anarchic, since it 'questions all object relationships or those between meaning and form. It [stage poetry] is also anarchic to the extent its occurrence is the result of disturbances leading us nearer to chaos' (*TD*, 'Production and Metaphysics', p. 32). Artaud's theatre is somewhere between chaos and a new order. In fact it is doubtful if we can talk about a new order, since Artaud talks mainly about *restoring* theatre to its proper state. Ultimately this means a return to its origins and, as such, betrays Artaud's romanticism. As his language makes clear, he has no real understanding of post-war France; in traditional fashion he rails against its materialism without having any real knowledge of its true material conditions. His writing is prescriptive and hyperbolic, rendering it incapable of producing a clear logical analysis either of theatre or of society. It is also full of contradictions, the most striking of which is between the obsessive desire for control and the longing to release those dark forces which Western society has, in his opinion, so long suppressed. Finding the West bankrupt, he turns to the East and proposes a theatre of ritual and ceremony, completely failing to realise that such a theatre is dependent on a certain stage of economic, political and social development which is not present in the West. Ritual and ceremony also assume shared values, and are closely akin to magic, again making them inappropriate forms for a sceptical society made up of competition.

Despite the criticisms that can be made against Artaud, there is no doubt that his ideas have had an impact on theatre practice. Certainly he was right to criticise the state of pre-war French theatre, and there is nothing wrong with his aim of appealing to the whole person or his desire to involve the audience. The Left is always going to be nervous about such approaches because it is uncomfortable both with pleasure and with the notion of a whole person, neither of which, as far as it is concerned, can exist in a capitalist society where everyone is alienated. Because of this theoretical straitjacket, supported by psychoanalysis, with its view of the divided subject, the Left tends to interpret moves towards regenerating the community and stimulating the emotions as a form of fascist aesthetics. Unfortunately Artaud's language would seem to support their case, but it is important to remember that Artaud was trying to find an alternative to what he considered to be the moral and intellectual bankruptcy of post-war French society. The violence of his imagery is indicative of how radically he felt that society should be overhauled, and it also acts as a metaphor for a society and theatre built around more significant issues. His ideas were an expression not of bloodlust but of 'the value of life', which was intended, unlike fascism, to steer us away from 'chaos famine bloodshed, war and epidemics' (*TD*, 'No More Masterpieces', p. 60).

Turning now to Artaud's influence on Genet, the first thing to say is that it is overrated, at least where *The Maids* is concerned. Artaud's main idea, that 'theatre's production potential is wholly related to staging viewed as a language of movement in space' (*TD*, 'Production and Metaphysics', p. 34), has no bearing whatsoever on Genet's play. In fact, most of the techniques which Artaud suggests would constitute his Theatre of Cruelty cannot be found in *The Maids*. It does not call for the kind of acting area Artaud recommended, nor is it replete with shouts, groans, apparitions, surprises, symbolic gestures, masks, puppets, incantations, rare musical notes, movement exactly choreographed (as if for a dance), objects of strange proportion, or hieratic costumes. Neither is there any eye rolling, pouting lips, twitching muscles or anything else an actor may use to create the massive impersonality which Artaud so admired in Balinese Theatre. Nor is it possible to find in *The Maids* that fusion of sight and sound, intellect with sensibility, which again Artaud found in Eastern theatre. Nor is *The Maids* an example of a return to primal myths; and, while it may be possible to argue that it deals with a universal theme, here the master–servant relationship, so does any good play. Indeed, Artaud's theory may be at its weakest when talking about the subjects of his theatre, for, in one form or another, they have always been part of theatre – a farce is about chaos, though not in the same way as *King Lear*, so it is not a particularly discriminating term to use when prescribing subjects for a new kind of drama.

As has been noted, Artaud's chief objection to theatre was its subordination to the script, and for this reason alone *The Maids* cannot be considered a candidate for the Theatre of Cruelty. Genet's script is crucial for delineating the psychology of Madame and her maids and, to that extent, it is part of Western theatre, to which Artaud objected on the grounds that 'words are used solely to express psychological conflicts peculiar to man and his position in everyday existence' (*TD*, 'Oriental and Western Theatre', p. 65) Indeed, these words so exactly describe *The Maids* that it can almost be seen as a paradigm of everything Artaud loathed, rather than as exemplum of his ideas. Artaud believed that 'theatre's space is physical and plastic' (*TD*, 'Oriental and Western theatre', p. 52), not psychological, but *The Maids* suggests that theatre is a matter of mind rather than a radical innovation in the use of space.

If Genet's play is so different from how Artaud imagined a Theatre of Cruelty, how is it that so many critics have thought otherwise? Perhaps one answer lies in the actions of Solange and Claire, whose behaviour towards both their mistress and each other may be described as 'cruel'. 'I hate her! I loathe her!' (*M*, p. 80), says Solange of Madame and, earlier in the play, she is delighted by the idea of dismembering her: 'Let's sing! ... we'll cut her to bits by the light of the moon' (*M*, p. 65). Both maids, who incidentally are sisters, are also interested in crime.

MADAME: Do you go to trials? You?
SOLANGE: I read the crime news.

(*M*, p. 67)

When Madame expresses similar astonishment at Claire's knowledge of jurisprudence, Claire replies, comically 'I read *True Detective*. I know those things' (*M*, p. 73). This cruelty and interest in crime may be one reason why Genet is seen as a follower of Artaud.

However, there may be some misunderstanding here, for, as we have seen, cruelty in Artaud's sense of the term, has nothing whatsoever to do with cruel behaviour. We are on safer ground with Genet's interest in crime, for Artaud believed that his theatre 'must present everything in love, crime, war and madness'. Furthermore, he wanted to centre his shows 'around famous personalities, [and] horrible crimes' (*TD*, 'Theatre and Cruelty', p. 65), and in this connection it is interesting to note that *The Maids* may very well have been based on the celebrated case of the murderous Papin sisters.[6]

Crime functions, in Artaud, like most of his 'subjects', to effect a kind of release which allows the audience to examine not just the outer world but their own inner one as well – to be facetious for a moment, it's a sort of thinking person's purge. Crime, in Genet, also produces a feeling of liberation:

> CLAIRE: We've read the story of Princess Albanarez who caused the death of her lover and her husband. ...As she stood before the corpses, she saw only death and, off in the distance, the fleet image of herself being carried by the wind. (*M*, p. 62)

In addition to this mystical release, crime offers a practical one, for to kill Madame would be to free the sisters from servitude. Earlier in the play Solange declares that 'I wanted to make up for the poverty of my grief by the splendour of my crime' (*M*, p. 57). Here crime is not just a compensation, it is also something dazzling and magnificent that Solange believes will elevate her: 'The famous criminal...I'm not a maid. I have a noble soul' (*M*, p. 95) and turn her into an object of desire. 'The hangman's by my side!...He's trying to kiss me' (*M*, p. 94). This dazzling, magnificent conception of crime corresponds to Artaud's idea of grand subjects which not only reflect the unrest of the times but also tower above the utilitarian and technological considerations of contemporary society, putting us in touch with fundamental emotions. Moreover, Artaud values a theatre which intoxicates, restoring us to that sense of rapture we have lost, and this intoxication is to be found in Claire's remarks: 'We must be joyous. And sing. Let's sing. ...Laugh!' (p. 65), as well as in Solange's 'We are beautiful, joyous, drunk and free!' (*M*, p. 100).

There is some justification, then, for seeing Genet's conception of crime as being influenced by Artaud. Crime, in *The Maids*, is surrounded by the ritual of Claire dressing up as Madame and Solange dressing up as Claire, and thus they act our their fantasies and frustrations but never quite reach the goal of their little drama, which is to kill Madame; as Solange says: 'The same thing happens every time. And it's all your fault, you're never ready. I can't finish you off' (*M*, p. 46). Ritual was important to Artaud, for he believed that it put an audience's sensibility into a more refined state of perception; but this is not the case with Solange and Claire, who use ritual as a rehearsal for real life, but they so confuse the two that they can no more kill Madame in one than in the other. Their conflation of ritual and reality is not something Artaud would approve of, for he makes a clear distinction between the two (*TD*, 'On the Balinese Theatre', p. 42).

If Solange and Claire do not have their sensibility enhanced, neither do the audience, the play remains a puzzle, an intellectual one too, which distances them even further from those forces Artaud wanted them to perceive. It is not enough, therefore, for Genet to use – even if he consciously did, Artaud's conception of crime, without also using the entire stage language which would make crime signify in an Artaudian way.

Another area where Artaud's influence maybe felt is in the attention Genet pays to gesture. For Artaud, gestures teach us 'the metaphysical identity of abstract and concrete' (*TD*, 'On the Balinese Theatre', p. 35), they bring out a truth that is otherwise hidden from us; they also, though he does not really explain how, 'keep us from chaos'. For Artaud, then, gestures are connected with revelation, true being and order, but this is not the case with Genet. In *The Maids* the gesture seems to be the only reality. Solange says she has made 'the gestures a servant must make' (*M*, p. 92), implying that, even though she is a servant, she has only been playing at being a servant; her 'real being', if she has one, is elsewhere and remains unexpressed. In Genet, therefore, the gesture points toward acting. What the audience is continually reminded of in this play, through the physical gestures as well as through the repetition of the word itself, is that what they are watching is indeed a play; gesture is both real and artificial, breaking down the distinction between those two terms, causing the same kind of confusion as there is between ritual and reality. Gesture, in *The Maids*, seems to have significance only within the paranoid psychology of the individual characters, 'The slightest gesture makes you feel like a murderer trying to slip away by the service stairway' says Claire to Solange (*M*, p. 51). The gesture has no objective, no public meaning. Furthermore, it is linked to crime, for, just as crime is a compensation for the constraints of servitude, so is gesture, elevated to drama, a compensation for a failure to act to change that situation:

SOLANGE: She gets away and you just stand there!
CLAIRE: What do you want to do? Make a scene ...
SOLANGE: Let's get on with it.

(*M*, p. 81)

Paradoxically, acting becomes a compensation for not acting. Gesture, organised into drama or fantasy, is also like crime in that it offers release or liberation. Both the sisters and Madame dream of accompanying or being accompanied by the loved one who is a criminal figure. Claire says to Solange that 'if I have to leave for Devil's Island, you'll come with me. ...We shall be that eternal couple, Solange, the two of us, the eternal couple of the criminal and the saint' (*M*, p. 63), while Madame says that she would follow Monsieur 'to Devil's Island, to Siberia' (*M*, p. 67). In both instances crime becomes the basis of a new role, more abstract and absolute ('criminal and saint') than Solange or Claire, individualised by their names but not knowing how to play who they are.

Gesture in *The Maids*, then, has little in common with Artaud's use of the term, though both writers show an interest in it *per se*. However, there may be some common ground between them when it is remembered that Artaud reviled representational theatre, favouring an expressive one,[7] and gesture certainly functions in an expressive, non-representational way in Genet. However, to see Artaud's influence at work on Genet here may be rather misleading, for Artaud's thinking itself is a product of Symbolism and Surrealism, as indeed is Genet's, since both inherited the same cultural background. Artaud ultimately differs from the Surrealists in suggesting that symbols should have a public, as well as private, dimension, whereas Genet shows the irreducible privacy of the gesture or symbol, and in that sense he is Surrealism's true inheritor. Despite this difference, it is interesting to note that both Artaud and Genet, in favouring a non-representational theatre, signal their lack of interest in society as it is. Artaud looks to renew it from the East and Genet from its own deviant groups. In the thirties, when Artaud was writing, societies were renewed by fascism, and, after the war, it was the turn of consumerism to obliterate those differences which Artaud found in the Balinese and Genet in his criminals and gays. The monolithic society they bemoaned and sought to change continues the same.

It should by now be fairly clear that Artaud's influence on Genet is, to say the least, problematic. It would be easier to make out a case for saying that Aristotle was more of an influence that Artaud, in that *The Maids* shows a unity of place and time, if not action, which, with its opening of the role-play between Claire and Solange, has more in common with the Elizabethan subplot, or even dumbshow, since it compresses, albeit with speech, most of the major themes and actions of the play. Aristotle's theory of catharsis is not entirely irrelevant either, for there is a sense of release at the end of the play, evident in Solange's 'we are beautiful, joyous, drunk and free!' (*M*, p. 100). However, Aristotle looked for this sense of release in the audience, and it is simply not possible to say whether this is their experience at the end of this play. In addition, Aristotle said audiences were purged, perhaps by and perhaps of, the emotions of pity and terror, but these emotions are not really relevant to *The Maids*. Furthermore, Aristotle said that this effect came about through our identification with the characters, but it is impossible to identify with characters in *The Maids* since, to a large extent, it is character which is in question. More joy may be had from seeing whether Aristotle's theory of catharsis surfaces in Artaud, as indeed it does when he writes that seeing something in a theatre so affects spectators that they are incapable of imitating what they have seen once they are outside the theatre (see 'No More Masterpieces', p. 62). This roughly corresponds to Aristotle's notion that tragedy purges us of destructive emotions and is therefore a force for good.

Of course it is possible to pursue this matter of who influenced whom further but, ultimately, that is not the point. Perhaps what we should really be asking is why is it important to understand one writer as being influenced by another? Why should we look at the history of drama, or, for that matter, literature, in such a light? What other approaches does this exclude? One approach is philosophical, for it is possible to use Hegel's model of the master–slave relationship as a way into *The Maids*.[8] This is not to say that the relationship between the maids and Madame is an illustration of Hegel's thesis, merely that there are some similarities which may increase our understanding of it. The master–slave relationship can be understood in two ways: as a relationship between two people in the evolution of self-consciousness, or as the development of self-consciousness within one person with consciousness taking the part of the master and unconsciousness the part of the slave. For Hegel, self-consciousness only exists when it is recognised as such by another self-consciousness. Self-consciousness begins when it is confronted by another self-consciousness and sees in that self-consciousness a quality of being that it has itself, yet which it is not completely aware of. Thus the first self-consciousness is not conscious, because it has not constituted the other self-consciousness as a self-consciousness, and because it has unwittingly projected onto that other self-consciousness its own qualities. Another way of saying this is that self-consciousness has discovered itself in another being and has therefore found itself as another being, which, of course, suggests that there is an 'otherness' in the heart of self-consciousness. In order to become truly self-conscious, it must destroy this otherness in the heart of itself, and it does this by constituting the other self-consciousness as a self-consciousness that is other than its own self.

It is not easy to relate this process to *The Maids* in any systematic way. To begin with we need to distinguish between Solange and Claire acting out their relationship with Madame, and their actual relationship with her. The basic difference between the two is that, in the former, Solange is able to rebel against her mistress and say what she thinks of her:

SOLANGE: Yes, my proud beauty. You think you can always do just as you like. You think you can deprive me forever of the beauty of the sty, that you can choose your perfumes and powders, your nail polish and silk and velvet and lace and deprive me of them?...Solange says: to hell with you!.

(*M*, p. 44)

whereas in the latter she's grateful and deferential: 'Oh! Madame... never....Madame is "too kind"' (*M*, p. 71). However, fantasy and reality do overlap, for, just as Solange attempts to control Claire, the fantasy Madame, so she endeavours to guide and advise the real Madame: 'Madame mustn't get such ideas into her head. You must rest' (*M*, p. 68). There are other blurred boundaries too, and, together, they suggest that Madame's existence in the play, even when she is on stage, is in fact no more than the maids' mental projection. If this is the case, then she is not encountered as a self-consciousness who can confer recognition on the self-consciousness of Claire and Solange. Indeed, Madame is presented by Genet as being little more than a collection of clothes and jewellery, a costume rather than a consciousness. As a result she cannot, as Madame, authenticate Claire and Solange as maids. 'I want', says Solange at one point, 'to be a real maid' (*M*, p. 82). It is because they are not maids that they are dissatisfied; they are not dissatisfied because they are maids. Because of this situation, they are condemned to see in Madame their own deepest desires, without actually being conscious that that is what they are doing. As Madame, Claire asserts that 'Monsieur will be led from prison to prison, perhaps even to Devil's Island, where I, his mistress, mad with grief, shall follow him' (*M*, p. 39) and, as herself, she declares to Solange that 'if I have to leave for Devil's Island, you'll come with me'. In both cases there is a yearning to escape into degradation through crime. Because the maids see themselves in Madame without recognising themselves as such, they cannot be constituted as self-consciousness; a problem aggravated by the fact that, since Madame herself is encountered more as an object than a self-consciousness, she cannot underwrite Claire and Solange's existence. Consequently, the maids have no full self-consciousness nor, it follows, knowledge of themselves, and that perhaps explains their inconsistencies, repetitions and fractured, often illogical, conversations.

Even if Madame were a self-consciousness it would be doubtful whether either she or her maids would achieve that state of self-possession which is implied in Hegel's view of full self-consciousness. The reason for this is that certain *social* requirements are needed for the complete development of self-consciousness, and they are freedom, work and discipline, the latter referring to how the self must submit to certain external rules. Hegel argues that these can only be found in the right measure in a free society, but that if the social order is one of domination and submission, as it is in *The Maids*, then the experience of self-consciousness is divided between the master and the slave. This takes the form of the self being aware of its divided nature, experiencing one part of itself as changing and the other as unchanging. Certainly the sisters have an unchanging part, which Claire identifies as 'the eternal couple of the criminal and the saint' (*M*, p. 63), and their changing part has to do with their constant role-swapping, 'it's my turn to be Madame' (*M*, p. 81) which constitutes both their fantasy and their reality. Madame, too, has a dual view of herself: first of all as Madame, with all her changing moods, and then as the loyal, steadfast lover of Monsieur. Given their internal divisions, neither Madame nor the maids can recognise one another as a fully developed self-consciousness. Hegel suggests a number of ways of compensating for this condition, and the one that most approximates to Claire and Solange is a withdrawal inwards, which corresponds to the sisters' almost psychotic – in the clinical sense of that term – world. It is important to note, in this context, how Solange incorporates Claire, through her death. 'I call upon you to represent me', Claire says to Solange (*M*, p. 97). In this way, Claire dies but remains alive; it is the ultimate movement inwards.

Indeed, a case can be made for saying that what happens in *The Maids* is an internalisation of an external conflict, and that that conflict only partly concerns Madame, for it takes place mainly between the two sisters. 'I hate you', says Claire to Solange (*M*, p. 55). It is difficult to pinpoint all the causes of this conflict, but one lies in the sisters being so alike: 'I can't stand our being so alike', says Solange (*M*, p. 60), and Claire adds 'I'm sick of seeing my image thrown back at me by a mirror, like a bad smell. You're my bad smell' (*M*, p. 61). One way of avoiding this sameness is for one of them to pretend she is Madame, and thus the sisters' play is a response not so much to their relationship with Madame as to the mirror image they have of each other. Their relationship is a constant struggle for mastery and, even though it is Claire who dies, she is in the dominant position, ordering Solange to command her to drink the poisoned tea.

CLAIRE: (*holding her by the wrists*) You bitch! Repeat. Madame must have her tea.
SOLANGE: Madame will have her tea.

(*M*, p. 98)

There are two possible resolutions to this problem. The first has already been mentioned, which is to become that eternal couple, the saint an the criminal; this offers an escape, from the facticity of being, into the absolute. The second is to contain the other within the self, 'I myself am both the thief and his slavish shadow', cries Solange (*M*, p. 88). The thief is obviously the criminal of the eternal couple, but the 'slavish shadow' is more ambiguous. It could refer to the saint, since the saint, by being associated with the criminal, is his shadow; but shadow also refers to darkness, which is the dwelling place of maids and servants generally, and it is described as dangerous (*M*, p. 45). However we choose to interpret this, though, one thing is a clear: Solange's cry represents a desire to be double, and this can only be achieved by incorporating the other, Claire, who is double to the extent that she is the same as Solange. To mention the double echoes the title of Artaud's work *The Theatre and its Double*, but he never quite makes clear what this mysterious double is; actor, costume, or audience, it could be any or all of these or something else entirely. Solange's incorporation of Claire also resolves the relationship with Madame, for Claire does not die as Claire but as Madame, and in the guise of Madame she takes upon herself all the new and imagined slights that the maids have suffered. To that extent she is also a sacrificial figure: her death allows Solange to be Madame, so that the 'real' one will no longer be able to humiliate her. Literally, at the end of the play, acting is equated with death and theatre is consumed in the moment it is performed.

If the relationship between Madame and her maids benefits from a Hegelian approach, so would the relationship between the maids benefit from a psychoanalytic one.[9] The fact that they see in one another a mirror image encourages the critic to examine their relationship in terms of Lacan's account of the mirror stage. This is an attempt to answer the question as to why the paranoid attacks himself in the image of another. Lacan's view is that he projects onto another something unacceptable in himself, and, according to Freud, what that unacceptable thing is, is homosexuality. Here it is important to remember that Genet was a homosexual and that the parts of *The Maids* are to be played by men. *The Maids* would seem to offer support for such a view, not just because of the mirror-like relationship between Claire and Solange, but also because of their paranoia, 'Listen, we're being spied on', says Claire (*M*, p. 83), and Solange adds, 'It's God who's listening to us' (*M*, p. 84); and because of the erotic way in which they perceive each other: Claire says to Solange that she has lovely hair (*M*, p. 64), while Solange tells Claire that she has a lovely throat (*M*, p. 85). If *The Maids* is about paranoia and therefore homosexuality, it is important not to forget the mechanism of paranoia: projection – for that, in a sense, is what constitutes the theatrical experience. Literally, the actor has to project him/herself into the character and then project that character to an audience. The audience, too, have to project themselves into what is happening on stage. So it is clear that projection is an essential part of theatre, which, because of this, is always, potentially, paranoia.

Artaud's strictures on theatre as psychology would discourage both a philosophical and psychoanalytic approach to Genet's *The Maids*, despite the fact that the play deals with a repressed force, which is what Artaud expects theatre to do. Hegel's master–slave relationship is essentially dramatic, as is the mirror stage with all its ramifications. Both philosophy and psychoanalysis not only offer readings of the play: they, as part of the culture, may also be seen as an influence upon it; an influence, moreover, incompatible with the views of Artaud. What still remains to be explained is why critics persist in explaining one author in terms of another. Perhaps there is something patriarchal about it; an influence being tantamount to a form of paternity, which names an legitimises a work. It is a search for origins and therefore stability, but what happens in the process is that the work loses some of its power; by being placed in a tradition, continuity and hierarchy are stressed at the expense of the real nature of the work. This is especially true of drama, which for too long has been regarded as a sub-species of literature. By being assimilated into literature, drama is seen as something written rather than something that is performed. This has the effect of turning drama into an antiseptic activity for a cultural elite who, by approaching it as a text within literary history, rob it of its power to disturb them.

The radical potential of Genet's *The Maids* lies not in its being influenced by Artaud (which in any case is questionable) but in its excessive concern with role-playing; the maids are sisters, mother and daughter, lovers, would-be murderers and a host of other things as well. These multiple roles challenge conventional ideas of character, nowhere more so than in Solange's long speeches at the end which, among other things, point forward to the breakdown of Cartesian rationalism found in Lucky's speech in Samuel Beckett's *Waiting for Godot*. The ceaseless changing of roles suggests a kind of freedom; we live in a society where we move, almost unconsciously, from one role to another; *The Maids* celebrates that fact and shows how we can manipulate it. However, the radical potential of the script is curtailed by its being framed within a realistic set, and by the fact that it is tied to private obsessions, which makes the play inward rather than outward-looking. This, however, is to see *The Maids* as a text, but it is not a text in the same way that a novel is; this is a text that has to be performed and it is through its productions that *The Maids* names itself again and again, each time as something different, not at all like the dutiful son that critics would like it to be.

NOTES

1. R. Harwood, *All the World's a Stage* (London: Methuen, 1984) p. 287.
2. J. Russell Taylor, *Dictionary of the Theatre* (London and New York: Penguin, 1984) p. 113.
3. J. Genet, *The Maids and Deathwatch*, trans. B. Frechtman (London and Boston: Faber and Faber, 1989). All quotations are from this edition, with page references given in the main body of the essay as '(M, p.)'.
4. A. Artaud, *The Theatre and its Double*, trans. V. Corti (London: John Calder, 1985). All quotations from Artaud are from this edition, with the name of the essay and page references given in the main body of the text as '(TD, title, p.)'.
5. S. Sontag 'Fascinating Fascism', in *A Susan Sontag Reader* (London and New York: Penguin, 1987) pp. 305–25 and p. 316.
6. See B. Benvenuto and R. Kennedy, *The Works of Jacques Lacan* (London: Free Association Books, 1986) p. 33.
7. Although Artaud rejected a representational theatre, it is important to remember that he was talking about a particular kind of representational theatre. Ultimately, his view that theatre should reconcile us to the universe implies some form of representation, as indeed does his view that theatre should reveal repressed forces and energies. This is not, as it at first seems, a theory of expression, which has to do with the unique and personal, for the forces and energies he is talking about are profoundly impersonal.
8. For a useful introduction to Hegel's theories, see R. Norman, *Hegel's Phenomenology: A Philosophical Introduction* (Brighton: Sussex University Press, 1976).
9. For a more detailed view of these ideas, together with Hegel's 'influence' on Lacan, see W. Ver Eecke, 'Hegel as Lacan's Source for Necessity in Psychoanalytic Theory', in J. H. Smith and W. Kerrigan (eds), *Interpreting Lacan* (New York: Vail Ballou Press, 1983) pp. 113–39.

11

Weiss/Brook: *Marat/Sade*

GRAHAM HOLDERNESS

Ask even a relatively well-informed person in Britain to name several works by Peter Weiss, and the list is likely to stop at one play: *Marat/Sade* – or, to give it its full title, *The Persecution and Assassination of Marat as Performed by the Theatre Group of the Asylum of Charenton under the Direction of the Marquis de Sade* (*Die Verfolgung und Ermordung des Jean Paul Marat, dargestellet durch die Schauspielgruppe des Hospizes zu Charenton unter Anleitung des Herrn de Sade*, 1964). Weiss's voluminous writing as a whole, which includes prose narrative as well as theatrical work, is virtually unknown in this country. Where, in the British theatrical repertoire, or even in general theatrical knowledge, are plays such as *The Insurance* (*Die Versicherung*, 1952), *Night with Guests* (*Nacht mit Gästen*, 1963), *The Investigation* (*Die Ermittlung*, 1965), *Song of the Lusitanian Bogey* (*Gesang vom lusitanischen Popanz*, 1967), *How Mr Mockinpott was Relieved of his Sufferings* (*Wie dem Herrn Mockinpott das Leiden ausgetrieben wurde*, 1968), *Trotsky in Exile* (*Trotzki im Exil*, 1970), or even the better-known *Vietnam Discourse* of 1968?

The full title of the latter play provides some measure of illumination as to the reasons for this highly selective mediation of a major German dramatist into British culture: *Diskurs über die Vorgeschichte und den Verlauf des lang andauernden Befreiungskrieges in Viet Nam als Beispiel für die Notwendigkeit des bewaffneten Kampfes der Unterdrückten gegen ihre Unterdrücker sowie über die Versuche der Vereinigten Staaten non Amerika die Grundlagen der Revolution zu vernichten* (*Discourse about the early history and the progress of the long-lasting war of liberation in Vietnam as an example of the necessity of armed struggle by the oppressed against their oppressors, and about the attempt by the United States of America to annihilate the bases of revolution*). It is not simply that in Britain there is a general aversion to long titles. The assertively didactic and polemical signalling involved here betokens a political theatre of a kind virtually

nonexistent in Britain, even during the historical period (1950–70)
of Weiss's major work: a political drama which is overtly committed, stridently ideological, aggressively rhetorical in its
strategies of uncompromising insistence on principles of political
morality. British political drama has, by contrast, tended to aim at a
far greater degree of persuasiveness, objectivity, working from the
concrete analysis of specific historical situations towards a socialist
affirmation, rather than starting from a standpoint of declamatory
political conviction.

This is not to suggest any disrespect towards British political
theatre, which has had to develop in its own way by negotiating
the stresses and obstacles of a particular cultural history: it is,
rather, an attempt to identify the particularity of Weiss's type of
political drama, and to suggest reasons for its failure to penetrate
British theatrical culture, apart from the single exceptional
inruption symptomatised by Peter Brook's well-known production
of *Marat/Sade* with the Royal Shakespeare Company, which opened
at the Aldwych theatre in 1964. The relationship involved here
between dramatic and performance texts, between a European
political drama and its reproduction by a British theatrical institution, is a profoundly interesting one. I will argue in this essay that
Brook's production was in some ways a strategic appropriation of a
play initially designed to hew closer to Marxism, and to the
dramaturgy of Brecht, than to the theories of Artaud and the
theatrical techniques of the 'Theatre of Cruelty', which formed the
basis for the British production. In order to make this argument I
will look at the play-text itself; at Weiss's own reactions to its
various productions; and at the kind of theatrical interpretation
which mediated the play to British audiences in Brook's RSC
production.

The play consists of an imagined performance of a play about
the assassination of French revolutionary hero Jean-Paul Marat,
who was stabbed in his bath by Charlotte Corday in 1793. The play
is represented as the work, in terms both of writing and
production, of the Marquis de Sade, who did write and present
plays during his internment at the Asylum of Charenton. This
inner play is thus performed by inmates, assisted and controlled
by the asylum staff, and continually watched by de Sade as an on-
stage spectator. The play scarcely has a linear narrative as such,
though at the outset a 'herald' offers a premonitory plot-synopsis,
stating that Charlotte Corday will come twice to Marat's door

before making her third and fatal visit. The play is divided into episodic scenes, which progress through a range of non-linear theatrical devices: formal debate, political songs, direct didactic addresses to the audience, mime and pageant. The philosophical dialogue between the enlightenment convictions of the revolutionary Marat, and de Sade's settled belief in the perversity and depravity of humanity, occupies a central position; but other voices are also heard. There are the voices of the fanatical priest, Roux, and the revolutionary zealot, Charlotte Corday. There is a continual defence of the status quo from Coulmier, the director of the asylum, who keeps protesting against de Sade's retention of censored cuts, and threatening to stop the play. There is the ironic commentary of the Herald; a Brechtian chorus; and there are the voices of the inmates themselves, who play parts, perform the songs and enact scenes and illustrations of what is being uttered by the main characters.

These techniques – non-linear narrative, episodic construction, satirical songs, mime, pageant, didactic debate and direct address to the audience – clearly typify the strong influence on Weiss's drama of Brecht. And in many ways the play seems a classic Brechtian drama, presenting political violence and human extremity through a philosophical language and a self-reflexive theatrical medium; and presenting a dialectical opposition of political ideas which remains unresolved in the play, but is offered for possible resolution in the lives of the audience. At the play's conclusion, Marat rises from death to deliver his final word of revolutionary faith:

> As a corpse I'm not much use to you
> but all the things I taught were true
> and others now will carry on
> the fight that I Marat begun
> until one day the hour will strike
> when men will share and share alike.
>
> (Weiss, *Marat/Sade*, p. 106)

– to be followed by a definitive statement of de Sade's scepticism:

> So for me the last word can never be spoken
> I am left with a question that is always open.
>
> (Weiss, *Marat/Sade*, p. 107)

The play is a historical drama in a double sense: it invokes the history of the French Revolution through the philosophical convictions of Marat and the narrative of his murder; but it also takes its basic historical setting from the real conditions at Charenton in the early decades of the nineteenth century (de Sade was in residence there from 1801 until his death in 1814), where Coulmier, the progressive director of the psychiatric hospital ('lunatic asylum'), arranged theatrical performances by the patients as part of a programme of therapeutic activities. The doubling of historical periods establishes a usefully synoptic and synchronic view of the Revolution, with the initial popular insurrections, the consolidation of popular government, the Terror and the rise of Napoleon, all available for simultaneous cross-reference and comparison. The main purpose, however, was simply to place in dramatic juxtaposition the two historical characters who did not, in history, thus encounter one another: Weiss wrote in his 'Author's Note on the Historical Background to the Play':[1]

> Sade's encounter with Marat, which is the subject of the play, is entirely imaginary, based only on the single fact that it was Sade who spoke the memorial address at Marat's funeral. Even in this speech the real attitude towards Marat is questionable, since he made the speech primarily to save his own skin; at that time his position was in danger, his name on the list of those marked out for the guillotine.
>
> What interests me in bringing together Sade and Marat is the conflict between an individualism carried to extreme lengths and the idea of a political and social upheaval.

That philosophical dialogue between contradictory political positions, a binary opposition of extreme individualism and revolutionary collectivism, is the basic dramatic structure of the play. Its theatrical structure is governed by the imagined setting of a performance by inmates of an asylum, so that, while de Sade and Coulmier are represented as historical characters, the other participants in the drama are presented by the patients. These two characteristics of *Marat/Sade* – a dramatic structure based on a dialectical opposition of unreconciled contraries, and a theatrical framework locating the action in an 'asylum' – were the starting points of the British production. Weiss's own conception of both these key points, however, differs significantly from Peter Brook's interpretation of them.

Weiss's conception of the dialectic between the two historical characters and their opposed political philosophies was a Marxist dialectic, conceiving of history as a struggle between contradictory forces, which yet has some real outcome; a struggle which involves the participant in political judgements and a responsibility of commitment. The Marxist dialectic does not contemplate eternal oppositions of unreconcilable contraries, but identifies historical forces struggling for mastery, and seeks both to explain and to direct the issue of their struggle. It is a common intellectual strategy for this historical-materialist dialectic to be translated into a completely different theoretical structure, in which the existence of contradictions is held to prove the futility or impossibility of political action. In this liberal-humanist philosophical paradigm the contemplation of a struggle between individual and collectivist political theories would point not towards the necessity of commitment and action, but towards a resigned quietism that sees both sides of every question – and acts accordingly.

Furthermore, Weiss's decision to set the play in the context of the Charenton asylum can be understood in quite different ways. Weiss's description of the asylum seems at some distance from the haunted madhouse of the RSC's production:

> Charenton (to follow J. L. Casper's description in his *Charakteristik der französischen Medizen*, published in 1822 in Leipzig) was an institution which catered for all whose behaviour had made them socially impossible, whether they were lunatics or not. Here were locked up 'perpetrators of crime whose handling in open court would not be in the public interest, as well as others who had been arrested for serious misdemeanours or who had allowed themselves to be used as the evil tools of high intrigues'.   (Weiss, 'Author's Note', *Marat/Sade*, p. 112)

An emphasis on extreme insanity, such as that manifested in the RSC production, is therefore not necessarily called for by Weiss's description of the asylum, which appears there rather as a mixture of psychiatric hospital, penal institution and internment centre for political dissidents and transgressors of the social law – 'a hiding-place for the moral rejects of civilised society' (Weiss, quoting Casper, 'Author's Note', *Marat/Sade*, p. 112). Weiss's design seems to have been to locate the action in a highly symbolic representation of the proletariat, an intensified gathering of the 'wretched and oppressed of the earth', rather than to place the political debates in a context of apparently universal insanity, where the very idea of positive political commitment or effective political action tends to appear ridiculous and grotesque, and where all idealism and morality become subverted by a malevolently ironic sense of the absurdity of things.

It would be misleading to suggest that Weiss's attitude towards the politico-historical dialectic embodied in the play was a matter of settled conviction and *a priori* faith, with de Sade's perverse individualism merely set up as an instance of 'false consciousness', to be routinely discredited by Marat's proto-Marxist affirmations of revolutionary will. The ambivalence towards historical development manifested by de Sade in the play was, to an extent, an expression of Weiss's own doubts: radical political uncertainties encountered in the contemplation of historical tragedy. '*Marat/Sade* is full of doubts, my doubts', Weiss remarked in 1965.[2] Such doubts were never a matter of indecisiveness about the correctness or validity of Marat's point of view, with which Weiss, from the outset, acknowledged a basic sympathy: but rather about the status and effectivity of that revolutionary philosophy in the context of a society which could be conceived as irrational and uncontrollable in its self-destructive energy. There is, therefore, real ambivalence in the discursive space between Marat and de Sade, since a rationalist dialectic could hardly survive in an irrational universe; and de Sade's principled individualism might therefore, paradoxically, appear to be a rational response to the nature of the world.

The most significant theoretical product of the play in terms of Weiss's own convictions was, however, that it led him to a resolution of doubt and ambivalence in a formal embracing of socialism:

> In the two possible choices remaining to me today I see only in the socialist ordered society the possibility of removing the existing disproportions in the world...my work can only be fruitful if it stands in direct relation to those forces which signify for me the positive strength of this world.

This evolution of commitment led Weiss to rework the text of *Marat/Sade*, which went through no fewer than five versions between 1963 and 1965, when the above statement was written. The dramatist's preference for Marat's position was evidently signified, to his own better satisfaction, in a production by the Volkstheater, directed by Hans Anselm Perten: this version he called 'the best of them all, the only interpretation grasping Marat's true heroic revolutionary mould' (quoted in Hilton, *Peter Weiss*, p. 43). In this staging the crowd could be seen uniting with a sense of political purpose, where in earlier productions – and certainly in Peter Brook's – the crowd was clearly an assembly of lunatics, reflecting in their insanity the irrationality of nature and society (see Hilton, *Peter Weiss*, p. 42).

Peter Brook's 1964 production of *Marat/Sade* had its roots in the 'Theatre of Cruelty' experiment conducted by Brook and Charles Marowitz in 1963–4. A small company was assembled to conduct a series of exploratory workshops dedicated to the discovery of a new theatrical language, freed from the constraints of narrative and the conventions of naturalism. The working title of the experiment was taken from the theoretical writings of Antonin Artaud.[3] In January 1964, the company performed, at the Lamda (London Academy of Music and Dramatic Art) theatre, an 'open workshop' featuring a surrealist sketch by Artaud, and Charles Marowitz's collage *Hamlet*. When, a few months later, Brook received the manuscript of Weiss's *Marat/Sade*, he perceived the play as exemplifying an Artaudian irrationalist theatre: 'he was immensely excited to find a complex of people, sounds, and action, in which words were an essential element but not, except for notation, a separable one'.[4] According to J. C. Trewin, Brook found in the play a fascinating conjuncture of opposed theatrical tendencies, rational and irrationalist, Brechtian and Artaudian, a drama of empathy and a drama of alienation: 'the two opposing tendencies, Artaudian (demanding the spectator's complete and intense involvement) and Brechtian (insisting on the spectator's alienation), must come together in performance' (Trewin, *Peter Brook*, p. 145).

In practice it was the Artaudian influence that characterised the performance, destabilising the rationalist dialectic of Weiss's 'epic' theatre by emphasising the madness of the asylum's inmates as the basic theatrical language of the play. Each actor rehearsed a detailed study of a chosen form of insanity. Brook took advice from psychiatrists and visited psychiatric institutions. The company studied paintings and filmic representations of insane subjects, and read articles on mental illness. Brook worked with the cast on

perfecting this irrational theatrical language before the script came
into collective consideration. The actors were encouraged to 'dig
out the madman' in themselves, to discover personal expressions of
insanity. 'We were all convinced', said a young Glenda Jackson,
'that we were going looney' (Trewin, *Peter Brook*, p. 145).

The collective display of madness proved, in performance,
profoundly disturbing for the theatre audience. Brook's objective
was to secure a theatrical discourse which would, in formal terms,
juxtapose and synthesise a broad variety of styles – 'Everything is
put in its place by its neighbour – the serious by the comic, the
noble by the popular, the literary by the crude, the intellectual by
the physical: the abstraction is vivified by the stage image, the
violence illuminated by the cool flow of thought' – and in
hermeneutic terms would produce in the spectator a response of
total participation – everything about this play is designed to crack
the spectator on the jaw, then douse him with ice-cold water, then
force him to assess intelligently what has happened to him, then
give him a kick in the balls, then bring him back to his senses
again'.[5] One is forced to enquire what measure of intelligent
appraisal could be expected of a spectator who has been cracked
on the jaw, doused with cold-water and kicked in the balls. In
performance, the dramatic effect of this production became a very
un-Brechtian overwhelming of the senses, with an Artaudian
theatrical discourse of panic and violence; a species of 'total theatre'
which obliterated Peter Weiss's carefully balanced dialectic of
reason and emotion, sanity and madness, political conviction and
cynical perversity.

> Dramatically, the play was a debate. ...But what most people
> remembered, shuddering, was the visual impact...the chalky
> clothing, the writhing limbs, the hysteria, the grimacing, the
> lolling heads, the whirr and thud of the guillotine, the buckets of
> blood, the schizoids and cretins, eroto-maniacs and manic-
> depressives, the faces peering from the hidden baths. ...Then the
> end, for Brook saw that the close of a production crowned all: the
> moment when the entire company, advancing towards the edge
> of the stage, fell to fighting, and to smashing up the bath-house.
> On a signal, all went quiet. The audience applauded, whereupon
> the cast replied with the sudden irony of a slow hand-clap. 'If we
> had conventional curtain-calls' said Brook, 'the audience would
> emerge relieved, and that's the last thing we want'. An Aldwych

audience, shocked and battered, never emerged relieved. (Trewin, *Peter Brook*, p. 147).

Neither is it probable that any 'shocked and battered' member of the audience could have drawn from this production the conclusions to which Peter Weiss's experience of writing the play pointed him – that of a resolution of the historical and political dialectic in a commitment to socialism.

In October 1965 Brook collaborated with David Jones on a 'public reading', given by the RSC at the Aldwych, of Peter Weiss's documentary piece, *The Investigation*. Based on the Frankfurt War Crimes trials of 1964, *The Investigation* deals with the enormity of the Holocaust entirely in terms of documentary evidence, the testimony of witnesses at the trials, newspaper reports, statistical evidence. Such realities, Weiss recognised, could have their own kind of artistic power: 'In the demand for truth only the most intimate personal statements were valid. Diaries, case histories, reports from prisons deprived novels of their force.[6] *The Investigation* could, of course, have found a theatrical form very similar to *Marat/Sade*: instead, it stands at the opposite extreme, a purely rationalist theatre insisting on a rational comprehension of irrational violence and political insanity. If those 'shocked and battered' spectators of *Marat/Sade* returned, they left performances of *The Investigation* in an extremely modified temper:

> I had not known a quieter audience, either in the theatre or as it came into the hush of early morning London. (Trewin, *Peter Brook*, p. 150).

The Investigation was premiered in 17 theatres throughout Europe on that evening of 19 October 1965. One of the productions was directed by Erwin Piscator, who celebrated Weiss's piece as a restoration of the German political theatre: 'a serious attempt to restore to the theatre within the larger supraregional framework its position as a moral institution' (quoted in Hilton, *Peter Weiss*, p. 47). In Britain, the awed silence of that October audience has been preserved: unlike *Marat/Sade*, *The Investigation* has virtually disappeared from the map of British theatrical history.

NOTES

1. Peter Weiss, 'Author's Note on the Historical Background to the Play', *The Persecution and Assassination of Marat as Performed by the Inmates of the Asylum of Charenton under the Direction of the Marquis de Sade*, English version by Geoffrey Skelton, verse adaptation by Adrian Mitchell (London: Calder and Boyars, 1965) p. 112.
2. Peter Weiss, quoted from *Encore*, vol. 12 (1965), in Ian Hilton, *Peter Weiss: A Search for Affinities* (London: Oswald Wolff, 1970) pp. 42–3.
3. Antonin Artaud, *The Theatre and its Double*, trans. Victor Corti (London: Calder and Boyars, 1970).
4. J. C. Trewin, *Peter Brook: A Biography* (London: Macdonald, 1971) pp. 144–5.
5. Peter Brook, 'Introduction' to Weiss, *Marat/Sade*, p. 6.
6. Peter Weiss, *Leavetaking and Vanishing Point* (London: Calder and Boyars, 1964) p. 270.

12

Time, Identity and Being
The World of Václav Havel

PETER MAJER

In his first speech to the Federal Assembly in Prague (25 January 1990), playwright Václav Havel, in his new role as President of the Republic of Czechoslovakia, focused on the phenomenon of time:

> In my offices in the Prague Castle, I did not find one single clock. To me, that has a symbolic meaning: for long years, there was no reason to look at clocks, because time had stood still. History had come to a halt, not only in the Prague Castle but in the whole country. So much faster does it roll forward now that we have at long last freed ourselves from the paralysing strait-jacket of the totalitarian system. Time has speeded up.[1]

As Guillaume Apollinaire notes, in his poem, 'La Zone', 'les aiguilles de l'horloge du quartier juif vont à rebours'. The clock in the Prague Jewish quarter, at the Jewish Town Hall tower, moves backward, as if symbolising – poetically as well as historically – the absurd movement of time: no longer forward, no longer even static, but really moving back. Czech history has moved back a number of times. The dormant and petrified beauty of Prague, a city described by Franz Kafka as the mother with claws, with its backward-moving clock, with its legends of slumbering knights who would return 'when the time is right', made the theme of Time a central feature of Czech philosophical thinking, traceable in the writings of Comenius, Bernard Bolzano, T. G. Masaryk and, more recently, Jan Patočka.[2]

The dramas of president–philosopher Václav Havel contain many elements which relate directly or indirectly to Time, which in Havel's interpretation is primarily an existential category, in the same sense as viewed by Albert Camus, Jean-Paul Sartre, or Martin

Heidegger. But to Havel, Time is quite a specific entity. It is more tangible and man-related than Heidegger's Time, which has always a metaphysical, abstract dimension, and relates to existence itself, as expressed in the very title of Heidegger's major philosophical work *Sein und Zeit* (Being and Time), published in 1927.

Heidegger's concept of Time, as interpreted by Jan Patočka (in whose clandestine seminars Havel took part when he wasn't serving a prison term), helped Havel survive some depressing times of isolation. In isolation, be it physical or psychological, time slows down. The very private and inward-looking existence forced upon people by a totalitarian regime which inspires fear of meaningful action and interaction, lest the meaning they produce turns out to be subversive, are the stuff from which Havel weaves his slow-moving but inwardly intense drama. He represents a conflict of the individual struggling with events and human relationships stuck in a time warp. His characters struggle to escape from a cobweb of meaningless events which move predictably and tediously in a closed circle. Their struggle seems equally meaningless to those for whom suspended time has become the only tangible reality, in which they know only how to function, and survive. In Havel's plays, individuals struggle with a world which is grinding to a halt, and that threatens to blur any difference between people and to bring human existence to a fossilised end.

This bleak picture is most poignantly illustrated in Havel's play *The Mountain Hotel* (1976),[3] whose characters meander in circles, repeating phrases which betray nothing of their individuality or any personal thoughts, and which gradually become interchangeable to a point where personal identity no longer matters and communication becomes impossible. No one listens to anyone and no one expects to be listened to. As if they were all a single character, a hydra-like monster speaking through several mouths, they say the same things, becoming a symbol of uniform repetitive thinking. Any yet, at one point, out of the blue and almost out of character, one of the mouths (Drasar) says:

Isn't it time to break the barriers between us? To take off our conventional masks and open up to one another just a little? We may not realise it but time flies, life is short and your sojourn here flows like water – and before you notice, some of you begin to leave, and those who stay behind feel remorse – unfortunately too late – how little they were able to say to those who are now irretrievably gone, how little they were able to let them know that – in spite of everything – they cared and felt something deeper for them –[4]

Milan Uhde, the playwright and now the Czech Minister of Culture, describes the characters in this play. They are

not people with a past, a present, or an identity, with attributes and relationships. They are sloughing all of these off and one wonders if they ever wore them. The only thing that covers them now are their names. Their actions, their status, careers, destinies, feelings, dreams, dialogues, amours, flirtations, peel off their personalities like a label off a bottle. The labels are interchangeable, the content evaporates. Void is all that remains.[5]

This is a reflection of a deformed social reality as Havel perceives it, a society which extols empty slogans and makes them into yardsticks with which to measure non-existence, often masquerading under the banner of bizarre ideological façades.

In this kind of world, one might as well be in prison. Havel was offered a choice between prison and exile. As if to discover for himself the meaning of life separated from time, to clarify, as he calles it, the 'naked values', timeless and eternal, which would give human existence a meaning in any circumstances, any conditions, Havel chose prison. In his letters from prison to his wife, Havel writes:

I think a great deal about the meaning I should give to the prison years which I am facing. Last time, I wrote about the possibility that it might lead – if I manage it well – to an overall psychological and mental reconstruction of myself. Why do I believe that? In recent years, I have lived rather an odd, unnatural, exclusive existence, as if in a glasshouse. That is going to change now. I shall be one of many small and powerless ants. I shall in a sense be returning to the old times, thrown into the world in a similar way I was when I worked as a lab assistant, as a stage-hand, or when I was a soldier or a student. I shall be a mere number, I shall be one of many and no one will expect anything of me or take any special notice of me. For some people outside, I shall probably be an 'institution', but I shall know nothing about it, I shall live in a different world with different problems. This return to the earlier existential situation – a situation in which I thrived best and in which I also created most – might help me with this inner reconstitution which I spoke about last time (losing my stiffness and lack of self-confidence, stop seeing myself through the eyes of others who expect something from me, give up my nervousness, self-doubt, etc.) One of the specific things I might do is to start writing more for the theatre again – as an observer of 'the theatre of the world'...[6]

Serving time in prison and attempting to reconstruct Time internally helped Havel focus on the deformations of time existing in the world outside. For Havel as a playwright, the static cobweb of Czech totalitarian tedium was the framework within which drama was created by the two clashing concepts of time, with a predictable end: whatever happens, whatever action an individual might take, round in circles he goes. For Havel as a philosopher and politician, the unpredictable and exciting events of November 1989 provided the explosion through which compressed time burst out with speed and confusion, and which required a playwright to take charge. Too many suppressed dramas were now writing themselves out and needed to be harnessed. And an observer cannot escape the impression that, just as Havel the playwright once struggled to speed time up, Havel the statesman may now be struggling, if not to slow time down, then at least to channel the millions of accelerated personal dramas into a coherent dramatic shape.

Focus and purpose, which Havel has been trying to give his confused nation, are to him not merely a philosophical concept, but a specific entity linked to a restoration of individual identity lost in years of meaningless, mechanised, uniform patter and prescribed action. Years in which people could lose their sense of identity to a point when they could end up visiting themselves, like Pludek in *The Garden Party* (1963).[7]

The threat to identity is real in any political system, so much more so in a totalitarian one. Havel's *The Garden Party* has two absurd organisations, whose job is to ensure loss of identity: the liquidation department and the commencing service. Between them, they make people blend into each other and gradually liquidate them by making them indistinguishable. Uniformity is the ideal, exceptions are out. When the play's protagonist, Pludek, becomes director of both institutions, even the institutions themselves blend into each other and become indistinguishable. Their activities are an

Orwellian pretence, a cover-up of some mysterious activity which is the opposite of what the institutions claim to stand for.

Similarly, *The Memorandum* (1965) takes us to an unspecified office where scientists are mere officials and administrators pretending to be engaged in scientific experiments, exchanging repetitive meaningless banalities. Havel further foregrounds this pseudo-reality of pretence and camouflage by their concern with an artificial language – 'Ptydepe', which destroys universal human values by depriving people of the ability of communicate anything sensible, and by stripping words of their meaning.[8]

In most of his plays, Havel deals with the issue of 'The Inner Lie' and the possibility of dismantling it, be it a self-deception or deception about the world. However, many of his characters simply refuse to find out anything about themselves, to identify who they are. In *The Garden Party*, Hugo Pludek's father, when asked who exactly he is, replies with dismay: 'I? Who am I? Look. I don't like such one-sided questions. I really don't!'[9]

In their search for identity Havel's heroes get entangled in situations of existential conflict with established social structures. They need to defend their identity, if for no other reason, then at least to come to terms with, and to be able to survive in, a totalitarian society. Those who do not defend their identity often end up like the protagonists of *The Increased Difficulty of Concentration* (1968),[10] where a conflict occurs when two sets of 'scientists' meet and make each other's work impossible. They are mainly clerks or bureaucrats or scientists from a variety of ephemeral institutes and establishments, who carry out their activity with enthusiasm but without any results. Everything degenerates into personal and sexual relationships between secretaries and bosses, superiors and their staff.

Havel returns to the atmosphere of pseudo-science of his earlier plays in his more recent work, *Temptation* (1985).[11] *Temptation* presents a renowned scientist, Dr Foustka, tempted by the devil. Foustka is one of those scientists engaged in unspecified work for an institution with unspecified purpose. His job is to protect and supervise the 'scientificality of science' and guard it against any infiltration by unscientific irrationality. But Foustka dabbles in the esoteric, the occult and the magical, so his encounter with the devil is only a matter of time, and to fall into the devil's claws means never to be able to get out again. The devil, here, functions as a system from which there is no escape. Foustka's identity has to be defended in conflicts with his boss and colleagues, in an atmosphere of fears and anxiety, seeping through from outside.

The Faustian theme, which Havel knew as early as 1977 (at the inception of Charter 77), had by then acquired a specific Czech significance. In the Czech predicament of that time, the inept and comic devils were personified by interrogators and supervisors. In order not to lose himself, not to betray those he represented or ideals he believed to be true, Havel, like his protagonist, Foustka, had to strive for personal integrity or, in Heidegger's terms, authenticity, truthfulness, and loyalty to one's true self. He had to struggle to preserve his identity in the face of the devil, in the face of temptation by evil. Evil was seen as loss of identity, through collaboration with, or connivance at, the dehumanising machinery of totalitarianism, and was to be fought. Pressure to conform in return for relative comfort had to be resisted. All these became issues of everyday existence, not only for characters in dramas, but also for individuals in Czech society.

In this situation, drama becomes a way of expressing and defining models of existential conflicts resembling simulated situations in experimental psychology. An illustration of a psychological premise in specific human situations is often carried ad absurdum.

The absurdity of totalitarian politics is parodied in Havel's play *Conspirators* (1970),[12] where general prosecutor Dykl describes the new candidate for the dictator's job, Colonel Moher, with these words: 'Let me be frank. His awful self-confidence scares me. He considers all his decisions automatically correct, however many proofs one may present of his errors. Or take his dreadful implacability. I am an old veteran but I must say that when he described how severely he was going to deal with the students, he scared the daylights out of me. Imagine a situation when practically all power is concentrated in his hands.' Major Ofir replies: 'His measures are, admittedly, often somewhat harsh. But what matters is that his goals are beneficial.' Dykl: 'Forgive me, Major, but history will not judge our intentions but only and solely our deeds. We may repeat a hundred times that we are building a new and more humane world. But what will all this mean when the imprints of our blood-stained hands cry out from every single stone of our glorious edifice.'[13]

Havel makes a direct attempt to decode and identify the absurd features of totalitarian pseudo-government in *The Beggars' Opera*

(1975),[14] linking it with criminality which does not stop short of murder. The city chief in the play is, at the same time, chief of all gangsters. Whoever leads a gang must also report to the police, and the chief of police runs the entire criminal network. He does, to be sure, solve some crimes and prosecute some criminals, but does not forget to use this to enrich himself and strengthen his personal power.

Such a deformed society induces a crisis of awareness of the meaning and purpose of life and the world, and leads to a dissipation of human identity. Man goes on living merely as a robot. Havel's dramas, in his own view, carry the dissipation of identity into 'a dismemberment of the dramatic character, suspension of time and absence of a coherent story on which an identity of a character could assert itself. Time loses its human dimension, comes to a halt or runs around in a circle.'[15] Events do not connect or relate to each other any more, and are not heading towards a solution or conclusion. Man, instead of being their creator, becomes their powerless victim. In the dismemberment of the storyline into disconnected elements which do not match, traditional drama, as a sequence of time, disappears. It becomes, as it has in Havel's plays, a psychodrama – a conflict of psychological states rather than real characters.

Havel's early plays, such as *The Garden Party*, *The Memorandum*, and *The Increased Difficulty of Concentration*, can be seen as an updated illustration of Existentialist philosophy, a philosophy of a man on the run. Havel's Existentialism, however, is returning to humanism steeped in a passionate desire to make sense out of absurdity. The running man will soon have nowhere left to run, he has to seek certainty within himself by reclaiming and accepting responsibility for his actions, and even for events which he might have thought were not of his own doing. Hence the often repeated claim, in his addresses to his fellow citizens: 'We all have our share of responsibility. All of us carry totalitarianism within ourselves.'[16]

With the Soviet invasion, in 1968, and Jan Palach's death a few months later, the political climate changed drastically. For Havel, it meant that he could no longer maintain his ironic distance. He wanted to scream rather than laugh. If, in his earlier plays, he had been ironically modelling the totalitarian machine, he was now becoming vitally interested in the destiny of the human individual crushed under its wheels.[17]

The philosophy of integrity and responsibility is what informs his later plays and what gives them the shape of Socratean dialogues. In the '*Vaněk Plays*',[18] Havel introduces the protagonist, who serves as a catalyst, bringing to the surface and exposing the existential dilemmas of his environment. Often silent and self-doubting, Vaněk is a kind of a modern Socratic character leading his co-players, but also readers and viewers, to clarify the nature of their 'presence in the world'. By his very presence, Vaněk challenges basic ethical categories of human responsibility and integrity.

Havel's meticulously constructed plays are not always easy to decode, and the level of abstraction often makes identification and empathy with individual characters impossible. The Vaněk plays - '*The Audience*' in particular – enjoyed international success, perhaps mainly because they clearly drew on Havel's personal experience, presenting real and tangible situations and characters.

Prison may have damaged Havel's health, but it did, as he acknowledges, wake him up from understandable lethargy and laziness to systematic and serious philosophical work. Having experienced, in prison, the Sartrean 'Hell is being with others', he could no longer satisfy himself with Sartre's intellectual 'roads to freedom', but had to reach for concrete tangible freedom, for himself and his nation, for which he felt responsible.

Havel used his prison time to search for his inner self, identity, individuality. In a letter to Olga, no. 13, he writes:

> You may find it odd that prison of all places should serve me for a self-reconstitution, but I truly believe that cut off for a longer period of time from all ties which I myself turned into limitations, I could gain inner freedom and a new sovereignty. This is not, of course, merely a revision of my view of the world, my aim is a better fulfilment of the tasks imposed on me by the world – as I see it. I do not want to change myself but be myself in a better way. This may resemble somewhat the hopes with which Dostoyevsky's heroes go to prison – but in my case, it is not so pathetic, so absurd, or so religious...[19]

Largo Desolato (1984)[20] bears the mark of Havel's experience of life in prison and of interrogations leading to it. Its main character is a man who falls victim to fabricated accusations, an intellectual whose identity is destroyed by the whims of officialdom, by a power system which wears him down and makes him not just its victim but also its co-creator. However steadfastly the hero, philosopher Kopřiva, may hold to his intellectual integrity, he remains unable to maintain human relationships.

Havel is not just a playwright dealing with philosophical questions, but a philosopher in his own right. His plays, which started as jolly and absurd comedies, Ionesco style, gradually turned into modern Socratean philosophical dialogues. In them, however, wisdom is not imparted by a teacher to a student, but discovered in the course of a lonely character's conflict with a world whose reality does not match its established description.

To Havel, the appearance of absurd drama – which has also been referred to as 'anti-drama' – is a result of living under stress, with no obvious way out. Remove the stress and drama is set in motion anew, returning to its classic story shape. With no way out, Havel searches for a way in – a rediscovery of his identity which would no longer depend for its creation on external circumstances but could start creating itself from its own resources. From the discovery of a higher, timeless and self-generating dimension of Being, which Havel believes is present in man's inner self in any circumstances, comes that which removes the stress of absurdity. The rediscovery of a man's intrinsic higher identity is, to Havel's philosophical thinking, absolutely essential for any serious and systematic creative work. It is that which brings about the integration of the dissipated elements of man – and thus generates meaningful action.

One of the principal philosophical problems for Havel is probably the very concept of Being, which was the pivotal issue with all existentialists, Heidegger in particular. But Heidegger, or other existentialists, never presented a precise definition of the concept of Being. Havel felt a need to define it. While Heidegger's approach is focusing on the awareness of death, on 'Sein zum Tode' (Being towards Death), Havel affirms life as the absolute horizon and parameter of Being, including the human individual. Being as a philosophical issue is very much present in his later letters from prison. Havel writes :

> The orientation of Being as a state of the spirit can also be interpreted as faith: a man oriented towards Being has profound faith in life, the world, morality, a purpose of things and of himself: his attitude to life is accompanied by hope, awe, humility and spontaneous respect for its mystery.[21]

Havel is not only trying to define this concept in the context of awareness, consciousness, thinking, but also as a reflection of the spirit. He writes, 'What exactly is spirit, a reflection of consciousness? I would say that this dimension of "self" can be seen as a certain "duplication" of Being.'[22]

The awareness of Being, which, for Havel, may be given any name including God, is a gradual integrative process, completing man inwardly and enabling him to reach self-realisation. It is an essential need of any man to aspire to his inner integrity, an ability to find within himself the very essence of Being, and identify with it.

Havel's entire work,[23] dramatic, philosophical and political, is permeated with a desire to set things right, to rectify the absurdity of the world he lives in. To free the individual from lies, from meaningless phrases, from enforced pretence. He struggles against all that is shallow, vague and false in human relations. His quest is to help create a society in which individuals will again desire to understand each other, tolerate each other's shortcomings and forgive each other's mistakes and lapses. He refuses to be the judge of his persecutors because he knows that they, as tiny screws in a dehumanised machine, did not know any better.

His life as a writer, philosopher and statesman is an attempt to realise the utopian vision of a world where, in the words of a 1989 revolution poster, 'truth and love shall triumph over lie and hate'.

NOTES

1. Václav Havel, *Projevy* (Prague: Vyšehrad, 1990) p. 24.
2. Jan Patočka (1907–77), outstanding Czech philosopher and interpreter of Hegel, Husserl and Heidegger. Patočka died after police interrogation as a main spokesman of the human rights manifesto, Charter 77. For an informative selection of his writing, see Jan Patočka *Philosophy and Selected Writings*, ed. Erazim Kohák (Chicago: University of Chicago Press, 1989).
3. Václav Havel, *Horský hotel*, in *Hry 1970–76* (Toronto: Sixty-eight Publishers, 1977).
4. Ibid., p. 235, own translation.
5. Milan Uhde, *Návštevy a navštívení V. Havla*, in *O divadle* (Prague: Lidové noviny, 1990) p. 231.
6. Václav Havel, *Dopisy Olze* (Brno: Atlantis, 1990) pp. 38–9, own translation; English edition: Václav Havel, *Letters to Olga* (London: Faber and Faber, 1988).

7.   Václav Havel, *Zahradní slavnost*, in *Protokoly* (Prague: Mladá fronta, 1966) pp. 15–65. English edition: *The Garden Party*, translated and adapted by V. Blackwell (London: Cape, 1969). For a detailed discussion of this play, see E. Paul Trensky, *The Garden Party Revisited*, in *Czech Literature since 1956: A Symposium* (New York: Bohemica, 1980) p. 103.

8.   Václav Havel, *Vyrozumění*, in *Protokoly*, op. cit., p. 140. English edition: *The Memorandum*, trans. by V. Blackwell (New York: Grove Press, 1980).

9.   Václav Havel, *Zahradní slavnost*, ibid., p. 63.

10. Václav Havel, *Ztížená možnost soustředení* (Prague: Orbis, 1969). English edition: *The Increased Difficulty of Concentration*, trans. by V. Blackwell (London: Cape, 1972).

11. Václav Havel, *Temptation* (London: Faber and Faber, 1988), trans. G. Theiner. For an interesting discussion of this work see Goetz-Stankiewitz, *Variations of Temptations – V. Havel's Politics of Language*, London: Modern Drama, vol. XXXIII, no. 1 (March 1990) pp. 93–105.

12. Václav Havel, *Spiklenci*, in Havel, *Hry 1970–76*, op. cit.

13. Ibid., p. 38.

14. Václav Havel, *Žebrácká opera*, in Havel, *Hry 1970–76*, op. cit.

15. Václav Havel, *O divadle*, ibid., p. 46.

16. Václav Havel, *Projevy*, ibid., p. 12.

17. Václav Havel, *Dramatici o dramatu*, in *O divadle*, op. cit., pp. 44–6.

18. Václav Havel, *Three Vaněk Plays – Audience, Protest, Unveiling*, trans. by Jan Novák and Věra Blackwell (London: Faber and Faber, 1990).

19. Havel, *Dopisy Olze*, op. cit., p. 31.

20. Václav Havel, *Largo Desolato*, trans. Tom Stoppard (London: Faber and Faber, 1987).

21. Havel, *Dopisy Olze*, op. cit., p. 347.

22. Ibid., p. 321.

23. For a short bio-bibliography of V. Havel, see Václav Havel, *Living in Truth*, ed. J. Vladislav (London: Faber and Faber, 1989) p. 95. See also M. Goetz-Stankiewitz, *The Silenced Theatre* (Toronto: University of Toronto Press, 1979); E. Paul Trensky, *Czech Drama since World War II* (New York: M. E. Sharpe, 1978).

13

The Germans in Britain

ANNA-MARIE TAYLOR

The British influence on German drama may go back at least as far as Lessing. In his descriptions of the pernicious influence of constricting French neo-classicism, Lessing exhorted his compatriots to construct a national drama along the more 'natural' lines of their English counterparts, especially Shakespeare, and many writers seem to have responded positively to his advice.[1] Plays by Schiller, Goethe, Büchner and Brecht resound, both faintly and loudly, with Shakespearian language and references. But the British presence is not exclusively represented by reverence for one writer. On frequent occasions, dramatic models and characters from a whole range of British drama, from authors as diverse as Christopher Marlowe, George Lillo, and John Gay, have shaped, liberated and given rise to German texts. In fact, British dramatic writing, particularly that of Shakespeare, had, by 1933, become so fully absorbed into the literary tradition in Germany that it posed problems to literary critics of the time who wished to emphasise the native dramatic tradition at the expense of foreign models. In the same way that German writers, both living and dead, were subject to strict racial considerations, much literary examination was conducted as to whether Shakespeare was *undeutsch*, or whether his work conformed to the laws of the new Germanic art by displaying a *nordisch* temperament.[2]

After 1945, and most particularly since the mid-1960s, with a younger, post-Hitler generation of writers and directors emerging in the theatre, questions of national temperament have been replaced by more appropriate questions, of dramatic and historical inheritance, in the minds of dramatists and theatre workers in both Germanies. Given the bombastic production methods of earlier directors, and the tendency encouraged in the Third Reich to adulate 'great' dramatists, it is not surprising that Shakespeare's plays, along with the German classical texts of writers such as

183

Schiller, Goethe and Kleist, have been given radical and unsettling stagings in Germany by directors such as Peter Stein and Peter Zadek, Heiner Müller and, more recently, Robert Wilson. Similarly, modern German play-writing, as in Botho Strauss's *Der Park* (1983) and Heiner Müller's *Hamletmaschine* (1977), takes stock of the Shakespearian heritage, and provides disconcertingly contemporary refractions of *A Midsummer Night's Dream* and *Hamlet*.

Despite the destabilising of a Shakespearian tradition, based to a large extent on reverence for the writer's *Genie*, the German theatre's indebtedness to British drama is far from over. In the last decade both Shakespeare and modern British playwrights continued to be well in evidence in the West German theatre repertoire. Thus, in the theatre season 1980/1, drawing on 125 public theatres[3] there were 30 Shakespeare productions, with *As You Like It* and *Hamlet* being most prominent. Contemporary British writers who featured in this particular season included Alan Ayckbourn, Edward Bond, Barry Keefe, Harold Pinter, Stephen Poliakoff and David Edgar. As perhaps might be expected, Peter Shaffer's *Amadeus* was the most widely performed new British play. Apart from Shakespeare and post-war dramatists, productions of G. B. Shaw, Oscar Wilde, R. B. Sheridan and Ben Jonson (amongst others) could have been seen throughout the Federal Republic. The naturalisation of British drama was perhaps most keenly seen in the programming of plays around Christmas time. Theatre-goers in Pförzheim and Aachen could have enjoyed the seasonal delights of Alan Ayckbourn's *Das Festkommittee*, whilst in Ulm an adaptation of Dickens' *Oliver Twist* was the mid-Winter show.

By the end of the 1980s the classics of Wilde, Jonson, Shakespeare et al. had remained well in evidence, and new British writing was still very prominent, even though indigenous contemporary playwrights, such as Thomas Bernhard, Tankred Dorst, Heiner Müller and Botho Strauss, were now staged more often in the main houses of West German theatres, rather than, as in the previous decade, in workshop and studio theatres.[4] The names may have varied from year to year (in the late eighties Caryl Churchill, Michael Frayn, Trevor Griffiths, David Hare and Willie Russell supplanted Barrie Keefe and Mike Leigh, joining the ever-present Bond, Pinter and Ayckbourn), but theatre-goers in a large West German city had as much opportunity of seeing professional productions of modern British drama as their equivalents in, let us say, Newcastle or Plymouth. Similarly, Shakespeare remained as popular as ever, with an actual increase in the number of productions – over 40 in the 1987/88 season, and over 50 planned for 1988/89.[5] Such a total compared very favourably with Britain, where the main theatres,[6] in 1989, offered just under 50 new Shakespearian productions, of which 11 were by the Royal Shakespeare Company. The central position of British drama in the repertoire was further seen by the way that, during every season, nearly all the main West German theatres had at least one British play on offer, with some, as in the case of the prestigious Freie Volksbühne in Berlin and Schauspielhaus in Bochum, presenting two or three British dramas.

The long and complex history of Shakespeare appreciation and staging in Germany has been researched quite thoroughly else-where,[7] and is becoming increasingly well-known to English readers. Work has commenced, as well, on the reception of more recent British and Irish playwrights in Germany.[8] What is less well-known, and what I should like to concern myself with in this essay, is the other side of this theatrical relationship. By drawing on the repertoires of British theatres over the last decade, and on the critical reception of individual productions, I should like to invest-igate the extent to which German-language playwrights have been performed, and the ways in which these playwrights have been viewed in British during the past ten years.

In contrast to the many productions of British plays in West Germany, there were proportionately fewer German dramas per-formed in Britain. Even if we allow for discrepancies between the state of the theatres in Britain and the FRG, such as the number of stages, amount of subsidy and number of productions each season, which were exceeded in every case in West Germany, the number of productions was still small. In 1989, for example, only five large playhouses staged German plays (Derby Playhouse, Liverpool Playhouse, Lyric Hammersmith, Sheffield Crucible, and Royal National Theatre), with a handful of smaller theatres and compan-ies providing a few more performances. Admittedly, this was a fallow year, but it was not untypical of others during the 1980s. Much more than in the Federal Republic, the choice of foreign texts seemed to be dependent on individual enthusiasm and taste rather than on institutional and audience expectations. Thus, in the pattern of settlement of German drama in the 1980s, certain theatres proved themselves good hosts, largely through the efforts of individual Germanophiles. For example, the association of translator and director, Robert David MacDonald, with Glasgow

Citizen's Theatre, has ensured the theatre of the strongest German component in the repertoire of a large subsidised stage, with 13 productions in the 1980s[9] including a world première of Rolf Hochhuth's play about modern-day political assassination, *Judith*. Indeed, MacDonald's services to German drama in Britain were rewarded by the rare distinction of the Goethe Medal, conferred by the Goethe Institut in 1984.[10] The Citizen's efforts to publicise German drama, and the theatre of mainland Europe, is, of course, not merely a question of MacDonald's, and artistic director Giles Havergal's, personal preferences. By turning away from English models of production and play-writing, and by looking Eastwards rather than to the South East, the theatrical practices of Berlin and Moscow have been made more prominent than those of Stratford and the South Bank, in a way which is nationalistically appropriate. Similarly, the Traverse Theatre in Edinburgh[11] is characterised by a strong European presence in its repertoire, enlisting translator Antony Vivis, on a number of occasions, to translate contemporary German plays by Manfred Karge, Franz Xaver Kroetz and Fitzgerald Kusz into Scots idiom for East Coast audiences.

Despite these laudable examples by the Citizen's and the Traverse to assimilate German drama, many other theatres have been less eager to schedule German plays, although some individual theatres, such as the Haymarket Studio in Leicester and London's Old Vic, and a number of small clubs and touring venues, such as the Almeida and the Orange Tree Theatre in London, have regularly initiated and welcomed productions over the last ten years. Most important of these, in recent years, has been London's Gate Theatre, which has defined its identity by staging little-known European texts, in particular German plays, and by introducing more 'European' modes of playing to the theatre audience. Of course, the British theatre has been just as reluctant, maybe even more reluctant, to stage French or Spanish or (with the exception of Dario Fo) Italian drama. However, what needs to be examined is why, despite the fact that Germany's theatrical practices, above all those of Brecht, have been of crucial importance to the development of post war political and instructional theatre in Britain, no interest in German drama as a whole has developed in the British theatre.

Rather in the manner that certain pioneering jazz musicians' work has both consciously and unconsciously shaped the style of later players, Brecht's influence on several post-war British theatre practitioners has been extensive and pervasive. Like the influence of Louis Armstrong on all younger trumpeters, or of Charlie Parker on everyone who has picked up an alto sax since 1945,[12] Brecht's dominant presence in the British theatre has been both direct and indirect, both credited and unacknowledged. And rather in the way that later musicians might be hesitant to pin down, or even be unaware of, formative influences, there has been, in the last decade, a reluctance by playwrights and practitioners to relate their work directly to Brecht's examples. Indeed, there has been a tendency to deny any affinity with his work and his didactic drama, as in Howard Barker's polemic, *Arguments for a Theatre*. Despite this reticence and downright rejection, it is still possible to establish some sort of Brechtian legacy in the professional British theatre over the last 30 years or so (i.e., since the first visit of the Berliner Ensemble in 1956). Lines of descent and patterns of kinship may be difficult to trace, but there is a demonstrable relationship between Brechtian practice and the demotic impulses which informed Joan Littlewood's Theatre Workshop and John McGrath's 7:84 companies, and which animated the work of shorter-lived touring groups such as Red Ladder and Broadside Mobile Theatre Company in the 1970s. Furthermore, as Michael Coveney states, there was an affinity between the organisation and playing style of the Berliner Ensemble and what became established in British theatre:

the example of the Berliner Ensemble is at the root of our own post-War theatre. Their first momentous visit here in the mid-1950s informed the aesthetic of the Royal Court and the ensemble principle behind the formation of the Royal Shakespeare Company.[13]

Added to this, it is possible to establish some kind of lineage between Brecht's practices and the experiments in democratic play-making, and in defamiliarising techniques of character presentation, exploited by groups such as the Joint Stock Theatre Company and Women's Theatre Group. These concerns for popular, politically informed theatre-making, coupled with a desire to go beyond consistent realism, were also present, of course, in other practitioners of the Left in Britain, Germany and the Soviet Union.[14] However, there seems little doubt that the visits of the Berliner Ensemble in 1956,[15] and the much cited 'Road to Damascus'-like conversion of critics like Kenneth Tynan, who publicised Brechtian playing in as enthusiastic a fashion as Lessing had praised Shakespeare two hundred years earlier, aided the dissemination of these ideas. Brecht's adoption into British theatre culture was also helped by a fruitful period in Anglo-German literary relations during the late 1950s and 1960s, characterised by John Willett's and Michael Hamburger's work, resulting in a large number of translations from German literature, which brought about a growing acquaintanceship with Brecht's plays and theories, and modern German writing in general.[16]

As far as play-writing is concerned, the form of the Brechtian *Lehrstück* has imprinted itself firmly on the work of 'Theatre in Education' practitioners, and there are without doubt a good number of post-war plays which, in their discursive and dynamic treatment of historical events and social relationships, must claim some kind of kinship with Brecht. Examples which immediately spring to mind include John Arden's *Sergeant Musgrave's Dance* (1959) and *The Workhouse Donkey* (1963), Trevor Griffiths's *The Party* (1973), David Hare's *Fanshen* (1975), Caryl Churchill's *Vinegar Tom* (1976) and *A Light Shining in Buckinghamshire* (1976), David Edgar's *Maydays* (1983) and Howard Brenton's and David Hare's *Pravda* (1985). More recently, it can be argued that the most powerful theatrical responses in 1990 to events in eastern Europe all bear some vestigial family resemblance to Brecht's work. David Edgar's discursive *The Shape of the Table*, Howard Brenton and Tariq Ali's epic, if supposedly 'Meyerholdian', *Moscow Gold*, and the inter-polated episodes of Caryl Churchill's more surreal play about Romanian conditions, *Mad Forest*, seem to grow from Brecht's model of political drama, with Edgar's portrayal of political changes and historical movement around a committee-table show-ing perhaps the most familiarity.

Brecht's plays themselves have been absorbed into the main-stream as well. As Klaus Schulz remarked in 1977:

I believe that it is now possible to see a parallel between what happened to the work of Shakespeare in Germany in the early nineteenth-century and what is happening to Brecht's work in relation to Britain now. Shakespeare, on the one hand, was 'germanized', while Brecht, on the other, appears well on the way to being 'anglicized'.[17]

Such 'anglicisation' has continued, and can be seen in the way that Brecht's later plays have been taken up by the education system. Presumably because of the musical element, exotic locations, folk-tale motifs and large casts, they are regularly performed as school plays and by youth theatre companies. Similarly, Brecht's 'mature' plays, such as *The Caucasian Chalk Circle* and *The Good Person of Szechwan*, are firmly embedded in the 'A' Level German curriculum and university Drama and German canons as texts to be examined. Here Brecht's *oeuvre* is often treated as not being subversive, recalcitrant nor socialist, as his works have been accorded the status of 'classic' texts, a feature which has also been deeply imbedded in the production methods of his plays. Progressive, liberal interpretations predominate, rather than Marxist ones. The solutions to the dilemmas presented in Brecht's plays are represented as more befitting a Germanic *Sozialmarktwirtschaft* or Western liberal democracy. Such 'capitalism with a conscience' was seen in Deborah Warner's 1989 production of *The Good Person of Szechwan* at the National Theatre, where parallels were made between the urban dispossessed of waterloo and the homeless and hungry of Brecht's China; and more overtly in a production of *The Threepenny Opera* I saw at the Bristol Old Vic in the early 1970s, where, at the end, the cast came out into the auditorium to appeal on behalf of local charities. However, the transmutation of Brecht's plays into 'timeless' classics, that paradoxically promote the values of a progressive late capitalism, was not always the case in the eighties. More decidedly socialist productions included the National Theatre's forthright and overtly didactic touring production of *The Mother*, in 1986, and Manchester Contact Theatre's 1986 version of the same play, which related it directly to the miners' strike; and the hard-hitting and controversial Brecht adaptation, *Fears and Miseries of the Third Term*, at the Liverpool Playhouse, of 1989, which inspired the wrath of local Conservative councillors. These proved to be very different theatrical experiences from the well-meaning liberalism of many Brecht productions, or the entertainment of West End Brecht, the 1987 *Rise and Fall of Arturo Ui*, which was a vehicle for comedian Griff Rhys Jones.

As far as the British theatre repertoire in the 1980s was concerned, the choice of Brecht texts was remarkably varied. The national companies favoured the 'later, greater' works such as *Life of Galileo* and *Mother Courage*,[18] with, not astonishingly, the smaller houses and venues staging lesser-known works such as *Puntila and*

his Manservant Matti, Man Equals Man and *Conversations in Exile.*
Most memorable (at least for the journalists sent to review it and
the Edinburgh fire officer who had to close it down) was the 1986
experimental version of *Baal* by Yugoslavia's Theatre of Scipion
Nasica, which was viewed by its audience through holes in the
floor of the stage at Edinburgh's George Heriot's School. The
seemingly favourable, if somewhat varied, climate of Brecht
assimilation was reflected in the theatrical notices of productions
of Brecht's plays in the press from 1980 to 1990. Taking a sample of
150 reviews, from national newspapers and journals, of professional productions of well-known plays such as *Mother Courage* and
rarely performed ones such as *Edward the Second,* covering most
major London and larger provincial openings, I discovered that
half the reviews in my sample (75) were positive about play and
performance; 47 were wholly negative, whilst the remaining
reviews were ambivalent or inconsistent – either they were non-
committal, or they praised the play and criticised the production
(or vice versa).

The positive reviews outweighed the negative ones, but what
was striking, when reading how Brecht's work had been received
over ten years, was the overwhelming force of the vituperatively
hostile critics. Brecht's work, despite its 'classic' status in many
quarters, still appeared to present serious problems to a group of
theatre critics – problems not just of a political nature, but, given
their interrelatedness, also of form, tone and intention. As might be
expected, many, but not all, of the damning assessments were from
critics working for newspapers of the Right. There were honorable
exceptions – John Barber of the *Daily Telegraph*, for example, proved
to be a singularly sympathetic and open-minded critic – but the
voices in the dominant organs of the press were regularly hostile.
Given the prevailing political climate of the last decade, Brecht-
baiting on account of his perceived political line and dramatic
tedium was acceptable sport, as is clear from such statements as:

So far so good, but comrade Brecht is unable to leave us to draw
any conclusions of our own from his characters and their
behaviour, insisting instead on haranguing us in simplistic
propaganda.[19]

Unfortunately our didactic playwright clears his throat half an
hour from the end and the simple-minded Marxist message is

rammed home at tedious length, which explains why the play is revived infrequently.[20]

Devoutly Marxist, old Bertolt never lets dull facts gets in the way of an argument.[21]

...it may be the fault of Brecht, who, it becomes clearer, disguised a baleful misanthropy as political conviction. No wonder his unyielding image of humanity as cowardly, devious and brutal because obsessed by self-interest could only be countered by advocating a system now rejected by most of its victims.[22]

...brandishing his obsessive middle-class guilt about the plight of put-upon tarts, about the wickedness of money, about the foulness of Establishment behaviour.[23]

Chief Brecht derider was Milton Shulman, long-serving critic of the *Evening Standard*. In a corrosive and belligerent fashion, Shulman individuated himself as a critic by opposing the decent and measured 'Oxbridge liberalism'[24] of critics such as Michael Coveney and Michael Billington. Whilst Coveney and Billington were internationalist and tolerant, Shulman presented himself as an extirpator of all things pretentious and recondite in the theatre, works often of overseas origin. Whilst his colleagues' copy was balanced and fair-minded. Shulman's was often hasty and partisan in its judgements. In the same immoderate terms in which Shulman dismissed the Bucharest Bulandra Theatre's *Hamlet*:

...at the Lyttelton last night I fear it was a dramatic feast to be enjoyed chiefly by Romanian speakers. Undoubtedly there will be pseuds in the audience who will claim that it is possible to be elevated by Shakespeare spoken in gibberish.[25]

Brecht's work was continually derided.

Brecht's claim that the Tutor reveals the origins of 'German misery' neglected to add that audiences are also likely to catch the disease.[26]

In 1943 B. B. laid his heavy ideological hand on this uncommitted character. ...It was a deed that only robbed Schweyk of his

timeless appeal as an apolitical figure who survived by opportunism alone, but also squeezed most of the fun out of the
character.[27]

Since I have for decades been disenchanted by the communist
lobby and the intellectuals' bandwagon that have enshrined
Brecht's reputation somewhere between Shakespeare and Ibsen, I
must declare my resistance to his appeal.[28]

Apart from castigating the unacceptability of the playwright's
political line, the Brechtophobes in Britain in the last ten years also
carried on an established practice of denigrating Brecht and his
works because of their supposedly simplistic world-view and
wearisome lack of humour. The 'negative' critics' responses to
plays and productions were characterised by such statements as:

Brecht was never one of nature's humorists. Dedicated Marxists
may find heavy jibes against capitalism mildly funny but on the
whole his comic touch is as subtle as a guillotine.[29]

That Brecht, on the strength of his life and oeuvre, had little sense
of humour would be irrelevant to his work as a committed
playwright if he hadn't, as he saw it, written comedies.[30]

This supposed lack of humorous content, or the presence of a
humour which defies translation into Anglo-Saxon idiom, caused
difficulties for some critics, as did the familiar criticisms of Brecht's
plays, that his characters lack depth and that his plays are intellectually undemanding, if not at times simple-minded:

...tendentious in his handling of historical fact, solemn and
childish in his moralising, and a purveyor of grey, globular
dialogue.[31]

The boredom of 'the dreary Teuton's'[32] plays in performance was
described in heart-felt terms:

'...The darkness is lifting, at last comes the day,' one feels that
one has also endured a long night and rejoices with them...
ponderous teutonic Marxist tale.[33]

At the close, one feels that the action has taken place not at the height of the Thirty Years War but for the whole length of the Hundred Years War.[34]

In a production by Philip Prowse which has already been attacked for not being Brechtian enough – i.e. bleached, austere and boring.[35]

The penalty shoot-out was bad enough, but there was worse. I also suffered Bertolt Brecht.[36]

In line with political events in Eastern Europe, by 1990 an elegaic note began to distinguish some reviews:

...it represents Brecht as he best deserves to be remembered; as a poet of all the inconsistent life that hypocrites and governments perenially try to censor.[37]

It will be a great pity if poor old Brecht goes totally out of the window now that Germany is being united and the revolution has come about not quite in the way that he might have hoped. I shall continue to regard his plays with respect and to believe that he had a sense of humour.[38]

However, in contrast, there remained the obdurately unreceptive critics who, in their gleeful and self-congratulatory columns, were happy to 'rejoice that history has blown to ribbons the political credentials of the absurdly overrated communist playwright Bertold Brecht',[39] who were prepared to 'rejoice, for I thought I would never again have to sit through one of those confused, clumsy and excruciatingly boring plays with which Brecht attempted to instil into his audiences a proper appreciation of the joys of communism'.[40]

When we turn to productions of German drama written before the majority of Brecht's plays were written, we find a fairly similar pattern of critical response. Here, a more 'neutral' and measured reaction was apparent, with, however, some generalisations about German drama, and Germans, breaking through. As with Brecht in performance, I took a sample of reviews over the decade – in this case 200 to reflect the rather larger number of texts in the repertoire.

Again, the reviews covered most major productions in London, the larger repertory theatres and some smaller club theatres. Here there were proportionately more ambivalent reviews (40) and positive reviews (114), and fewer (46) negative reviews. Of these negative reviews, the blame for the failure of the production was ascribed much more to the production methods (particularly attempts to impose 'modernity' on the text by uprooting it from its historical context), than to the dramatist, as in the case of Brecht in the British theatre. Here, the label of 'classic' appeared to have had a peculiarly talismanic power to protect German-language authors from the onslaughts of London-based newspaper critics.

An altogether more comfortable, more conciliatory and less hectoring tone is apparent in the reviews as a whole. The relative absence of German drama in the British repertoire was bemoaned, and, unlike the staging of little-known Brecht plays, which were often dismissed for their lack of theatrical worth, the playing of lesser-known texts such as Georg Kaiser's *From Morning to Midnight* and Arthur Schnitzler's *Intermezzo* was welcomed. Although German drama was not prominent over the decade as a whole, the 1980s were significant for the number of premieres of dramas long unperformed. Amongst others, the 1980s saw for the first time Lessing's *Miss Sara Sampson* (1755), Goethe's *Faust Part Two* (1832), Hebbel's *Maria Magdalena* (1844), and various plays by Arthur Schnitzler. The unfamiliarity of these plays posed fewer difficulties for critics than the supposed intractability and vulgar Marxism of Brecht's works. Here, critical shorthand and journalistic cliché proved helpful to the reviewers in locating unfamiliar plays and dramatists within cultural and theatrical contexts. The several Schnitzler and Wedekind productions were given historical validity by reference to *fin de siècle*, Mittel Europa and Freud's Vienna, whilst Lessing's, Goethe's, Kleist's and Schiller's plays were frequently located inside and outside German Romanticism, Prussian militarism and the *Aufklärung*. Also of benefit to the critics were comparisons with other European dramatists. Hence, parallels were made between Büchner and Shakespeare and Brecht, Wedekind and Strindberg, Goethe and Dante, and even Kaiser and Villiers de L'Isle-Adam.[41]

Alongside the sketching in of an assumed cultural background, critics were also more obviously relaxed with what they understood to be the moral universes of the various dramatists than they had been with Brecht's views of 'social being' (*das soziale Sein*). By replacing questions of political and economic choice with issues of moral speculation and human motivation, these productions were made more accessible. Therefore Büchner's *Danton's Death* was said to present 'perennial truths about the implacable nature of revolution and its effects on the soul of man',[42] and this desire to find a universality, or at least pan-Europeanism, of meaning informed many discussions of dramas such as Kleist's *Prince Friedrich of Homburg*, Goethe's *Faust* and Schiller's *Mary Stuart*. Conversely, some critics also located certain plays as not travelling over the North Sea too well, remaining stubbornly within their German or Austrian cultural contexts, either because of their required style of playing, or because of the specificity of their subject matter or historical background. Several reviewers felt this to be the case with Hebbel's *Maria Magdalena*, Kraus's *The Last Days of Mankind*, Kleist's *Prince Friedrich of Homburg* and Wedekind's *Lulu* plays.[43] More particularly, certain features of German drama were brought to the reader's attention, such as 'symbolism as turgid as swirling waters',[44] 'windy fulminations',[45] 'odd moods of abstraction',[46] and 'teutonic marching song',[47] which possibly reinforced received impressions of German drama as over-long, over-earnest and justifiably over-looked. However, as indicated earlier, what was noteworthy with the 'classic' productions was the infrequency of such pronouncements.

When we turn to German drama written after Brecht's death, magical powers no longer seem to protect the texts. Between 1980 and 1990 there were far fewer modern plays performed and reviewed than classical works or Brecht plays. An analysis of 100 reviews discovered 52 positive reports of the proceedings, 24 negative reviews and 24 ambivalent assessments. Of the plays as a whole, it seemed as if dramatists such as Dürrenmatt and Frisch, who had been well received two decades earlier, were no longer in fashion, and 'new' writers played in Britain were limited to a small number of names and translations. Manfred Karge was made prominent by the Traverse Theatre's interest in him, as were Franz Xaver Kroetz and Ernst Jandl. Botho Strauss's plays were performed in a variety of places, ranging from large theatres such as the Crucible in Sheffield and London's Old Vic, to the Almeida, and the Vaudeville Theatre in the West End. As mentioned before, the Citizen's in Glasgow staged Hochhuth's *Judith*, as well as *The Representative*. Otherwise, contact with contemporary German theatre was a haphazard affair, with works performed in likely and unlikely venues, such as Peter Stein's *The Hairy Ape* and Peter Handke's *The Long Way Round* at the National Theatre, and Pina Bausch's Wuppertaler Tanztheater at Sadlers Wells, Heiner Müller at Croydon Warehouse and Berlin's radical 'Theatre in Education' troupe, Grips Theatre, at the Shaw Theatre.

Best received of the group of contemporary German dramatists was Franz Xaver Kroetz, and plays performed included *Through the Leaves, The Nest* and *Request Concert*. Here, cultural equivalents like Edward Bond and Harold Pinter could be found, and the style of Kroetz's writing, with its uncompromising realism, coupled with his characters' submerged yearning for a better life, was not unfamiliar to critics coming from British writers such as Jim Cartwright and, of an earlier generation, John Osborne and Arnold Wesker. The thoroughness of Kroetz's delineation of the brutality and hopelessness of lower-middle and working-class German· life unsettled some reviewers, but on the whole the 'luminous realism'[46] of his work, and its potential for performance, were highly rated.

Less successful, according to the critics, was the work of Manfred Karge, East German-born author of *Man to Man* and *The Conquest of the South Pole*. Both of these plays, like several productions of Kroetz plays, opened at the Traverse Theatre and were later transferred to the Royal Court in London. Although well reviewed in Scotland, these two plays seem to have been subjected to critical deflation in London. *Man to Man*, a one-woman piece based on the true story of a woman who had to take on a male identity to find employment during the German Depression, was given the same unsympathetic assessment meted out to Brecht. Karge's inexorable deconstruction of Ella/Max Gericke's personality, and the author's attempt to create parallels between her/his annihilation and reconstruction and the fate of the various Germanies this century, were regarded as 'pretentious' by certain unsympathetic critics:

> ...a peculiarly depressing load of old pseudo-Brechtian rubbish. ...The vileness of the world would be marginally less without Herr Karge's *Man to Man*.[47]

> The author is German writer, Manfred Karge, self-confessed disciple of that old Teutonic playwright, Bertolt Brecht.[48]

Karge's *The Conquest of the South Pole*, which deals with the fantastical 'transfiguration of hopeless existence'[49] by a group of unemployed young men, who act out Amundsen's expedition to the Antarctic, met with a similar division of opinion, and was similarly brought into line by the London critics for its possibly over-rated acclaim in Edinburgh. Again, Karge's metaphorical use of the theatre, and the fragmented narrative, which at times resorts to an unsettling use of the third person, were perceived as problems in its transposition to the British stage.

Even greater difficulties for British reviewers were caused by Botho Strauss's plays and Pina Bausch's Dance Theatre. Here, there was a veritable chasm between the Ancients and the Moderns. In the case of Bausch, great enthusiasm was occasionally expressed at the Wuppertaler Tanztheater's attempts to exploit all aspects of performance, to revitalise the relationship between *Tanz* and *Theater*:

> ...seldom have I emerged from such a session so moved, exhilarated and eager for more.[50]

Elsewhere, this production brought out familiar complaints about the undue and 'excruciatingly boring'[51] length and the failure of the two shows, *1980* and *Kontakthof* to yield obvious meanings. The 'unbearably slow pace of the enterprise'[52] elicited further complaints, and, whilst some critics recognised that Bausch's 'disjointed, allusive, illogical, sometimes outrageous, frequently harshly funny'[53] work could be valid despite its lack of obvious linear narrative and harmony, others were less tolerant:

> ...as if some plodding, methodical and efficient researcher had carefully tabulated what was involved in avant garde theatre and had assembled it for one performance without really understanding anything.[54]

Contemporary critics tend to rely on plot synopsis when discussing modern drama or unfamiliar 'classic' texts, and both Bausch and West German writer Botho Strauss proved singularly resistant to such an approach. Strauss's plays dispense with conventional plotting, and 'are characterised neither by dramatic conflicts nor by a linear development'.[55] Added to this lack of narrative expectation, 'Strauss's theatre is no longer a theatre of consciousness but a kind of *seance* with literary traditions and mythological situations into which present-day characters are introduced as types.'[56] Such self-conscious abstraction, and both playful and earnest manipulation of literary tradition, did not endear themselves to many reviewers (nor audiences) when it came to *Great and Small, The Park* and *The Tourist Guide*. Again there was no critical consensus. Some critics extended a warm welcome to his 'most striking, original and entertaining new play in London'[57] and 'not oppressively Teutonic'[58] work, with others left extremely uncertain as to its dramatic worth:

> What should have been a major event is, in fact, a bit of a yawn punctuated by giggles. Can it really be simply trendy rubbish?[59]

Even with legitimate theatrical comparisons, ranging from Beckett and Ionesco to Strindberg, Chekhov, and the Neo-Expressionists liberally cited, critics such as Shulman professed bafflement:

> Do not ask me what it means. That way madness lies.[60]

I had, in my own enthusiasm for German dramas, envisaged Anglo-German literary relations in the theatre to behave rather like the exchange systems of some islands in Melanesia. Here, as in the Kula system,[61] gifts are elaborately and continuously exchanged between islands. In such a way, I felt, Anglo-German theatrical exchanges were beginning to develop, with two centuries of German appropriation of British drama being reciprocated by the adoption of Brecht, and other modern German dramatists, by the British theatre. But modern Britain is no Trobriand Island, and, when I looked more closely at recent patterns of performance in the British theatre, it became clear that there were still considerable obstacles in the way of German drama being accepted readily into the repertoire.

From what I have stated so far, it may look as if I am laying the blame for this slow acceptance entirely with the notepads of London's theatre critics. It is certainly difficult to assess whether the hostile attitude to German drama expressed by some critics was a symptom of a more complex breakdown in cross-cultural literary relations, or whether the critics (given their visibility in column-inches and in the auditorium) were a more direct cause in the tardiness in acceptance. To establish any answers here would require a much more complex survey than the limited one I have undertaken, and would have to examine much wider avenues of cross-cultural exchange. These other areas of investigation would include the publishing industry, questions of translations (the translator is often overlooked to the extent of invisibility, with the commercial pressure of letting a famous name, such as Howard Brenton or Tom Stoppard, 'adapt' a literal translation), the pressures of arts funding and sponsorship, and the fluctuating interaction of Anglo-German literary relations over a much longer period.

However, what I can conclude is that repertoire and critics do appear to provide a valid 'Ort der Verständigung' (site of understanding),[62] for repertoires and reviews over a decade indicate how a group of dramas or dramatists have been valued and perceived. Of course there are problems in relying on an ephemeral form of writing, not least in the way that quite a good deal of dramatic activity in the provinces went unrecorded by the London-centric critics. What emerges from the decade as a whole is a reluctance by larger theatres to stage German drama, and an obstinate reluctance, on the part of a small but verbally forceful group of critics, to discuss certain German plays in anything but a combative fashion. Jim Hiley sums up 'the critic's job' as follows. Apart from recording their responses as openly as possible, critics even 'see themselves as cultural guardians...audiences are to be protected from anything too outrageous and unsettling. Much contemporary criticism betrays a subtextual anxiety about what will be acceptable to an imagined public who are bright but vulnerable.'[63] Such 'cultural guardian-ism' can be seen in the attempts by certain theatre critics, over the last decade, to protect the theatre-going public from the excesses of German drama. The reader was warned off from the supposedly inaccessible or overtly political texts of writers such as Brecht, Strauss, Karge, Kaiser and Kleist. These works may or may not have displayed what Charles Powell's memorandum for the chequers 'Think Tank' in 1990 felt the German character presented: *'in alphabetical order, angst, aggressiveness, bullying, egotism, inferiority complex, sentimentality'*,[64] but, according to some critical voices, they were deemed gloomy, lacking in humour, over-arty, tedious and tendentious.

As elsewhere, the events in Eastern Europe in the Winter of 1989–90 took the British theatre much by surprise, as is clear from the 'catching-up' exercise evident in 1990, with a much increased number of German plays in production. It will take at least another ten years to establish whether this *Wende* (turning-point) in the

British theatre is mere modishness or a more significant development in literary relations with Germany.

NOTES

1. G. E. Lessing, 'Briefe die neueste Literatur betreffend', no. 17, 16
    February 1759, in *Kritik und Dramaturgie* (Leipzig: Reclam, 1969)
    pp. 37–40.
2. See, for example, Hermann Wanderscheck, *Deutsche Literatur der
    Gegenwart* (Berlin, 1938) in Joseph Wulf, *Theater und Film im Dritten
    Reich* (Frankfurt am Main: Ullstein, 1983) pp. 251–2.
3. 'Theater Heute' (Seelze and Zurich: Orell Füssli and Friedrich
    Verlag), offered in its 'Jahrbücher' 1980–1988, listings of repertoires
    from all FRD theatres.
4. Ursula Schregel, in *Neue Deutsche Stücke im Spielplan am Beispiel von
    Franz Xaver Kroetz* (Berlin: Spiess, 1980), discusses how new West
    German plays were often directed by relative unknowns in studio
    theatres.
5. Ibid., pp. 365–86. Schregel confirms this pattern for the previous
    decade. There were 537 Shakespeare productions from 1970–8, with
    a peak of 84 in the season 1970–1. There were exactly the same
    number of Brecht productions in 1970–8. Of modern British and Irish
    authors, Beckett and Pinter predominated (226 and 128 productions),
    with James Saunders (90), Brendan Behan (59), and Joe Orton (50).
6. Information from David Lemmon, *British Theatre Yearbook* (London:
    Croom Helm, 1990).
7. For example, a recent study is Simon Williams, *Shakespeare on the
    German Stage: 1586–1914* (Cambridge: Cambridge University Press,
    1990).
8. As in P. Stapelberg, *Sean O'Casey und das deutschsprachige Theater
    (1948–1974): Empirische Untersuchungen zu den Mechanismen der
    Rezeption eines anglo-irischen Dramatikers* (Frankfurt am Main: Lang,
    1979), which deals most thoroughly with the critical reception of one
    dramatist.
9. Michael Coveney, *The Citz* (London: Hern, 1990) contains a useful
    appendix of productions from 1969 to 1990.
10. Cordelia Oliver, *Robert David MacDonald and German Drama*
    (Glasgow: Third Eye Centre, 1984) contains the honorary lecture
    given on the occasion of MacDonald being awarded the Goethe
    prize.
11. Joyce McMillan, *The Traverse Theatre Story* (London: Methuen, 1988)
    details all productions from 1962 to 1987.
12. I am grateful to Ian A. Bell, English Dept, UCW, Aberystwyth, for
    helping me locate an analogy with jazz.

13. Michael Coveney, *Financial Times*, 29 August 1984.
14. The workers' theatre movement is well documented in Raphael Samuel, Ewan MacColl and Stuart Cosgrove, *Theatres of the Left, 1880–1935* (London: Routledge and Kegan Paul, 1985).
15. Maro Germanou, 'Brecht and the English Theatre', in *Brecht in Perspective*, ed. Graham Bartram and Anthony Waine (Harlow: Longman, 1982) pp. 208–24, offers a succinct but detailed account of Brecht in Britain up to 1981.
16. Ute Kreuter, *Übersetzung und Literaturkritik: Aspekte der zeit-genössischer deutsch-sprachiger Literatur in Grossbritannien 1960–81* (Frankfurt and New York: Lang, 1985), documents the 'Golden Age' in literary translation very effectively.
17. Klaus Schulz, 'Foreword', in *Bertolt Brecht in Britain*, ed. Nicholas Jacobs and Predence Ohlsen (London: Irat/TQ, 1977).
18. The National Theatre, despite being castigated by some reviewers for its unadventurous scheduling policy, did perform a number of not so well known German texts in the 1980s, including Kleist's *Prince Friedrich of Homburg*, Franz Werfel's *Jacobowsky and the Colonel* and Arthur Schnitzler's *Dalliance*.
19. Robin Ray, *Punch*, 22 April 1987.
20. Giles Gordon, *Punch*, 6 March 1985.
21. Kenneth Hurren, *Mail on Sunday*, 8 November 1984.
22. Martin Hoyle, *Financial Times*, 8 May 1990.
23. Christopher Grier, *Scotsman*, 30 August 1984.
24. As John Elsom points out in *Post-war British Theatre Criticism* (London: Routledge and Kegan Paul, 1981).
25. Milton Shulman, *Evening Standard*, 21 September 1990.
26. Milton Shulman, *Evening Standard*, 16 March 1988.
27. Milton Shulman, *Evening Standard*, 24 September 1982.
28. Milton Shulman, *Evening Standard*, 5 July 1990.
29. Milton Shulman, *Evening Standard*, 17 March 1983.
30. Giles Gordon, *Spectator*, 17 March 1983.
31. Christopher Edwards, *Spectator*, 17 November 1984.
32. Kenneth Hurren, *Mail on Sunday*, 8 July 1990.
33. Francis King, *Sunday Telegraph*, September 1983.
34. Francis King, *Sunday Telegraph*, 11 November 1984.
35. Michael Coveney, *Observer*, 13 May 1990.
36. Kenneth Hurren, *Mail on Sunday*, 8 July 1990.
37. Meredith Oakes, *Independent*, 6 September 1990.
38. Malcolm Rutherford, *Financial Times*, 5 June 1990.
39. Christopher Edwards, *Spectator*, 14 July 1990.
40. Charles Osborne, *Daily Telegraph*, 6 July 1990.
41. Michael Billington's cultural location for Kaiser's *Flight to Venice*.
42. Michael Billington, *Guardian*, 28 July 1982.
43. For example, Lee Breuer's American Repertory Company's glitzy modern *Lulu*, brought to the Edinburgh Festival in 1982, was savaged by the critics on these grounds.
44. Clive Hirschhorn, *Sunday Express*, 26 November 1983.
45. Francis King, *Sunday Telegraph*, 23 April 1982.

46.   Irving Wardle, *Independent on Sunday*, 6 May 1990.
47.   Charles Osborne, *Daily Telegraph*, 8 January 1988.
48.   Kenneth Hurren, *Mail on Sunday*, 10 January 1988.
49.   Paul Taylor, *Independent*, 24 November 1988.
50.   Mary Clarke, *Guardian*, 15 September 1982.
51.   Edward Thorpe, *Evening Standard*, 15 September 1982.
52.   Peter Williams, *Observer*, 20 September 1982.
53.   Clement Crisp, *Financial Times*, 15 September 1982.
54.   Nicholas Dromgoole, *Sunday Telegraph*, 20 September 1982.
55.   Irmela Schneider, 'Myth and Mythology in the Drama of Botho Strauss', in *A Radical Stage: Theatre in Germany in the 1970s and 1980s*, ed. W. G. Sebald (New York: St Martin's Press, p. 35).
56.   Ibid., p. 35.
57.   Michael Billington, *Guardian*, August 1983.
58.   Michael Coveney, *Financial Times*, September 1983.
59.   Robin Thorber, *Guardian*, January 1988.
60.   Milton Shulman, *Evening Standard*, September 1983.
61.   Ruth Benedict, *Patterns of Culture* (London: Routledge, 1963) pp. 111–13.
62.   See Introduction to Kreuter, *Übersetzung und Literaturkritik*, pp. 13–22.
63.   Jim Hiley, *Listener*, 25 January 1990.
64.   Charles Powell, *Guardian*, 16 July 1990.

14

The Theatre of Dario Fo and Franca Rame

Laughing all the Way to the Revolution

ANGELA MONTGOMERY

Dario Fo is one of the most prolific and best-loved contemporary European playwrights. To speak of his work in terms of 'text' is to misunderstand his living art, to speak of it excluding Franca Rame is impossible. As a team, they have worked tirelessly at mounting their scathing, and often hilarious, satires of Italian society and politics. These plays, which are true theatrical events, are aimed at raising the proletariat's awareness of the suppression of popular culture by the ruling classes, and the necessity of dismantling bourgeois society. In this aim, and often in method, they take their inspiration from the medieval 'giullare' (a travelling jester), who sought to combat the ruling class with the potent weapon of laughter. Their work has always been directly linked to the class struggle, in particular the problems of the rights of workers, students, prisoners and women.

Dario Fo's theatre is a theatre of situation, and as the situations Fo chooses to represent are those of immediate political and social relevance, these are the events which have shaped the development of his work. To consider his work is to consider also its social, political and historical context; it is essentially dialectical. The form and content of Fo's theatre has acted as a kind of barometer of the times. It is impossible to consider Fo and Rame's theatre separately from their lives and their political work. I would therefore like to give a summary of their activities over the years, highlighting particular plays as space does not allow a discussion of their entire and considerable output.

Fo was born into a working-class family in the north of Italy, his father was a railway worker and his mother came from a peasant family. He moved to Milan in 1940 to study Art. His studies were interrupted by the war, during which he helped the Resistance, and by a nervous breakdown in 1950. As a form of therapy, Fo immersed himself in a favourite activity: writing and performing. This therapy became the work of his life, and he remains one of the most outstanding writers and stage performers of our time.

Franca Rame, unlike Fo, is a 'figlia d'arte' ('dau~hter of art'). She was born into a famous travelling theatrical family and has acted since she was eight years old. The methods used by her family, of dramatising local histories as they travelled, combined with Rame's irreproachable theatrical instinct, have been major contributing factors in Fo's work. They met during a summer Revue in Milan in 1951, and married in 1954.

We might be tempted to say that Fo's theatre falls into two periods – before and after 1968. Some of the most outstanding events of the post-war years were the revolutionary struggles of students and workers which, following the riots in the University of California, Berkeley, in 1964, reached their violent climax in May 1968 in France, and in the hot autumn of 1969 in Italy. While the repercussions of this movement were only slightly felt in Great Britain, they had enormous impact in Italy, and are still frequently referred to. It was an unprecedented expression of solidarity against the oppressive ruling regime, and it united factory workers, students and intellectuals in the class struggle. It was the expression of the emergence of a new generation. Following the false promises of the economic boom of the early sixties, the desires of workers and students coincided in their demands for greater working rights and a more informal culture, one which was not dominated purely by the interests of the bosses.

It was following these events that Fo and Rame revolutionised their way of doing theatre. Up until then they had performed their political satires in conventional commercial theatres. Fo had already caused a stir in 1953 with his play *Un dito nell'occhio* (A Finger in the Eye, 1953), written together with Franco Parenti and Giustino Durano. For Italy this was a completely new kind of review. A potted history of the world, it was an innovation in both its format and its political comment. This was followed by a similarly intentioned *Sani da legare* (Sane to be Locked Up, 1954), which was mercilessly censured. This led to the end of the collaboration between Fo, Durano and Parenti. After some work in cinema, Fo and Rame formed the 'Compagnia Fo–Rame' in 1958. Indeed, the years between 1959 and 1967 are referred to as Fo's bourgeois period. These years saw the production of the plays *Gli arcangeli non giocano a flipper* (Archangels Don't Play Pin-ball, 1959), *Aveva due pistole con gli occhi bianco e nero* (He had two pistols with white and black eyes, 1960), *Chi ruba un piede e fortunato in amore* (Steal a foot and you'll be lucky in love, 1961), *Isabella, tre cavalli e un cacciaballe* (Isabella, Three Horses and a Conman, 1963), *Settimo: ruba un po meno* (Seventh Commandment: steal a bit less, 1964), *La colpa e sempre del diavolo* (It's Always the Devil's Fault, 1965), *Ci ragiono e canto* (I think things out and I sing, 1966), and *La Signora è da buttare* (The Lady's for Dumping, 1967).

GLI ARCANGELI NON GIOCANO A FLIPPER
(Archangels Don't Play Pin-ball)

This was Fo's first major success with the bourgeois audiences, and, although it is a sparkling comedy, it is not without social comment. The play opens with some young good-for-nothings playing a practical joke on one of their gang, Lungo, in which they convince him that he has married a beautiful young woman, Angela. The ceremony turns out to be a fake, and the woman a prostitute. There follows a complicated series of events, at the end of which Lungo wakes up to discover it has all been a dream. Lungo is devastated, as he thinks he has lost his Angela. He accuses the archangels of playing pin-ball with him for sport. However, the dream has been a prediction: the marriage scene repeats itself, but this time Lungo is able to command the situation and wins the hand of Angela.

The play contains many elements of traditional farce and comedy, including dream sequences, mistaken identity, plays within plays and commedia dell arte-type 'lazzi' (physical gags), for example, when the doctor listens to Lungo's chest and the gang repeats the gesture in a line, all ears to chest; the hilarious scene in the Ministry in Rome, where Lungo is faced with a series of booths and closing shutters when he tries to make a claim for his pension, but he eventually manages to trap the clerks under their shutters with their rubber stamps round their necks, and create a kind of stamping machine for his documents. Unfortunately he ends up classified as a dog. There then follows the comic spectacle of Lungo impersonating a dog in a kennel, and performing tricks for a retired circus magician who buys him as a stray. The recurrent theme of mistaken identities continues when Lungo impersonates a Minister, a scene in which there is much burlesque losing of trousers. Although this play is a 'bourgeois' comedy, it is important for its early signs of political orientation. The character, Lungo, describes himself as a 'giullare' of the coffee bars. It is, therefore, his role in the play not just to amuse but to highlight social injustices. Thus, the central comic sequences in the Ministry in Rome, and in the dog kennels, are biting satires on a crippling and inhuman bureaucracy and the indignity of having a padrone (boss), but served up in a way palatable for a bourgeois audience.

Fo and Franca Rame also appeared on State television, in 1962, in a very popular musical show, Canzonissimo. This brought them into open conflict with the reactionary State: their contract was prematurely terminated as they would not accept the censorship of the politically controversial nature of their material.

Throughout this period, Fo had been developing his own peculiar brand of explosive satire, which found its voice more and more in the grotesque expression of the domination and exploitation of the proletariat by the ruling classes, and in its references to popular culture. His theatre became increasingly 'political'. This was particularly evident in *Ci ragiono e canto*, an important moment in the political development of Fo's work: a show which dealt with the enormous wealth of popular culture by using its songs, with a reinvention of their origins, of their profound links – materialistic – with gestuality, with work.[1]

By 1969, however, Fo and Rame felt they had become the 'buffoni della borghesia' (clowns of the bourgeoisie): the bourgeoisie was willing to accept their heavy satire as long as it took place within its own structures, i.e. in the commercial theatres. They therefore decided to abandon commercial theatre completely. As Franca Rame puts it:

> We had realised that, despite the hostility of a few, obtuse reactionaries, the high bourgeoisie reacted to our spankings almost with pleasure. Masochists? No, without realising it, we were helping their digestion. Our whipping boosted their blood circulation, like some good birching after a refreshing sauna. In other words, we had become the minstrels of a fat and intelligent bourgeoisie. This bourgeoisie did not mind our criticism, no mat-

ter how pitiless it had become through our use of satire and grotesque technique, but only so long as the exposure of their vices occurred exclusively within the structures they controlled.[2]

They decided to put themselves completely at the service of the working class, which meant abandoning the structures of the bourgeoisie for those of the proletariat. Fo went from being an artist who was 'friend of the people' to being an artist at the service of the proletarian revolutionary movement, 'giullare' of the people among the people, in the quartieri, in occupied factories, in squares, in covered markets, in schools.[3]

However, according to Rame it is a mistake to consider the events of 1968 as being the real turn-about in their work, or the moment at which they changed from doing traditional theatre to doing political theatre:

> In fact, our true turning-point, the point that really mattered, we took at the very beginning of our journey, 22 years ago, when with Parenti, Durano and Lecoq, we staged for the first time *The Finger in the Eye*. Those were the days of Sceipa and his subculture, of Pacelli (the pope) with his civic committees, the days of total censorship. Police superintendents, ministers, bishops and cops understood it immediately: we were a company of communists and we were making 'red propaganda'.[4]

To operate in this new phase of their work, the theatre group Associazone Nuova Scena was formed. This company put on shows within the theatrical circuit of the PCI (Italian Communist Party) and the ARCI (Cultural and Recreational Division of the PCI). The group developed a new way of presenting the plays and breaking down the fourth wall, involving the audience directly: the shows were followed by a debate in which the public commented and contributed to the final version of the script. There was also a general debate on political issues. This method of composition is essential, as it avoids completely the danger of writing popularist theatre; Fo and Rame's theatre does not condescend to the people, it comes from the people. This period includes the plays: *Grande pantomima con bandiere e pupazzi piccoli, grandi e medi* (Grand Pantomime with flags and small, big and medium-sized puppets, 1968); *Mistero Buffo* (Comical mystery), (1969); *Legami pure che tanto spacco tutto lo stesso* (Tie me up, do, I'll still smash everything, 1969);

L'operaio conosce 300 parole, il padrone 1,000, per questo lui e il padrone (The worker knows 300 words, the boss 1000, that's why he's the boss, 1969). With *Mistero Buffo*, Fo continues his research into the origins of popular culture, and, with *Il padrone* and *Legami*, the PCI is criticised for not being sufficiently revolutionary. This criticism gave rise to friction which led to a schism between the Nuova Scena and the PCI and ARCI.

MISTERO BUFFO

The monologue, for Fo, is of fundamental importance in a theatre which takes its inspiration from the popular theatre of 'fabulatori' (fable tellers). His theatre is naturally 'epic', as it contains this quality of story-telling. *Mistero Buffo* is a series of monologues and dialogues topped and tailed by speeches directed to the audience. This work represents a moment of crucial importance in Fo's 'recupero' (recovery) of the medieval, which he describes as 'un salto mortale a rovescio' (a death-defying leap backwards).[5] Recovering the method and the means of making theatre used by the 'giullare' allows him to practise theatre as a totality, 'superando la visione esclusivamente letterario del testo' (overcoming an exclusively literary vision of the text).[6] It is also a way of shaking the audience out of their role as pure spectators: they have to actively use their imagination. Moreover, it has assisted him in discovering a centuries-long 'mystification'; that culture always originates from the ruling classes and never from the people. As an illustration of this mystification, *Mistero Buffo* begins with the debunking of the story 'Rosa fresca aulentissima' as a courtly love poem. Fo reveals that it is in fact a 'giullarata' which has been censored and appropriated by the ruling classes. The surname of the author, when correctly deciphered, reveals the scurrilous name of a giullare. Whereas in school books he is referred to as Cielo (Sky) d'Alcamo, his name is in fact Ciullo (Sicilian dialect for male organ) d'Alcamo. The characters are a tax collector and a serving woman who both pretend to be noble. The central theme of the poem, read in this key, is not courtly love but an abusive law which allowed the nobility and the rich to rape or murder in tranquility; they had only to pay the 'defensa' and they were immediately excused. In this light, the poem becomes an expression of social outrage and a means of raising popular consciousness.

Fo goes on to explain in the introduction the centrality of the Church for the people. It was above all a meeting place, and the religious festivities and enacting of Bible stories provided the opportunity for heavy satire at the expense of the clergy. The 'giullari' risked being burned at the stake for such activities.

The pieces which make up *Mistero Buffo* are religious stories, but, far from reinforcing the oppressive dogmas of the Church, they are cries of social indignation. The piece about Pope Boniface VIII is a caustic satire of this corrupt and vicious Church Leader. Even when the figures are divine, it is always human dignity which is stressed. Thus *'Strage degli innocenti'* (Slaughter of the Innocents) serves as an indictment of the cruelty of war and the cruelty of God, who allowed such human suffering. The fable of the blind man and the cripple is not a glorification of Christ's miraculous powers, but an expression of the indignity of sweating for a boss: 'Non è dignita avere le gambe dritti, avere gli occhi che vedono, dignita è non avere un padrone che ti sottomette' (Dignity is not having straight legs and eyes that see, dignity is not having a boss over you).[7] The story of the birth of the 'Giullare' shows him as a peasant who proudly works his own land but who is forced out by the cruelty of the jealous owner of the valley, who burns the land and rapes his wife. Finally stripped of everything, he is visited by Jesus, who blesses him with the gift of a loose tongue which will allow him to 'schiacciare questi padroni e i preti e tutti quelli che gli stanno intorno: i notai, gli avvocati, ecetera' (to crush the bosses and the priests and all those around them: the notaries, the lawyers etc.) (*Mistero Buffo*, p. 80). The Christ of *Mistero Buffo* is a revolutionary and humanitarian figure. He is a 'povero Cristo', a kind of suffering everyman.

Fo's *Mistero Buffo* is far from an exercise in literary history. These revolutionary 'giullarate' are equally relevant for today, both in their restoration of the dignity of popular culture, and in their message. Indeed, Fo makes constant reference to contemporary events. Thus, in 'La Nascita del Villano' (The Birth of the Peasant), Fo is able to make a comparison with the bosses of today. Just as, in the 'Mistero', the peasant had to have special trousers so that he did not have to waste time going off to urinate, Fo relates the case of a factory in Bologna where the workers were allowed only two minutes and thirty-five seconds to go to the lavatory! The keynote throughout, including the Passion stories, is human suffering, compassion and dignity.

As a result of the schism with the PCI and ARCI, Fo and Rame formed a new group in 1970: 'La Colletiva Teatrale la Comune'. Alongside this was formed 'il circolo "la Comune" di Milano', which produced a series of cultural and political initiatives. This group had a new aim: to create a cultural circuit of the revolutionary Left which would provide an alternative not only to the bourgeois circuit, but also to the revisionist one. Within the revolutionary struggle, culture is of paramount importance:

> For the proletariat 'culture' means 'A conception of the world which is radically alternative to the bourgeois conception of the world', it means consciousness of the true reality of capitalist exploitation, scientific consciousness of the laws which regulate it and the laws of its violent destruction, for the construction of socialism.[8]

MORTE ACCIDENTALE DI UN ANARCHICO
(Accidental Death of an Anarchist)

La Colletiva Teatrale acquired performance space in Via Colletta. Perhaps the most noteable play of this early period of 'La Comune' was 'Morte accidentale di un anarchico', a grotesque farce in two acts. This comedy ostensibly tells the story of an Italian emigrant anarchist who 'fell', in a hysterical fit, from the window of a police station in New York, but, through an artistic 'transference', it actually refers to the 'suicide' of the anarchist Pino Pinelli at the police headquarters in Milan during the inquest into the bombings in Piazza Fontana. Pinelli was accused of being involved in the bombing, which killed 16 people, but Fo and many others believed the charges to be trumped up by the State. It was an indictment of the 'strage di Stato' (massacre by the State), that is, a policy of tension, by the right-wing State against the Italian left-wing, in which many left-wingers lost their lives. The historical moment of the writing and performance of this play is therefore one of extreme tension. The play performs an essential function within the class struggle, that of counter-information. This is a reinterpretation of the information supplied by the ruling classes, from the point of view of the proletariat. The highly provocative satire of this play is served up in an exhilaratingly farcical comedy. The play is set almost entirely in the room in the police headquarters from which the anarchist 'fell'. A madman is being interrogated, as he has been caught impersonating a psychiatrist (one of a series of identities which he habitually assumes). Meanwhile, the police are being investigated regarding the circumstances of the death of the anarchist. The madman, having intercepted a telephone call for the police inspector, and having lifted some documents, manages to pass himself off as the investigating judge come to reopen the inquest on the circumstances of the anarchist's death. Through his 'investigation' he is able to recreate the circumstances of the anarchist's death, whilst thoroughly ridiculing and exposing the inconsistency of the police inspector's version of the facts. The madman, having gained the confidence of the police, is able to suggest that the anarchist was 'persuaded' to jump from the window by the police. The play gives full scope to a range of farcical stage business, using disguises, false limbs, funny walks and slapstick punches and kicks. The energetically farcical tone of the play acutely heightens the deadly seriousness of its insinuations. The licensed fool, in this case the madman in the guise of a judge, is able to voice Fo's case against the State: (a) that the police are guilty of the anarchist's death:

MADMAN: ...first of all you arbitrarily stop a free citizen, then you abuse your authority to detain him beyond legal limits, so you traumatise this poor worker saying you've got proof that he blew up the railway, then you deliberately label him psychotic so he loses his job, seeing as his alibi of playing cards doesn't hold up, and lastly, the final blow: you say his friend and comrade from Rome has confessed himself guilty of the Milan massacre: his friend is a filthy assassin. And so he sadly comments 'it's the end of anarchy', and throws himself off! Are we crazy? At this point we can hardly wonder that a poor wretch has a hysterical fit. No, no, no, I'm sorry, but in my opinion you're guilty, and how! You're completely responsible for the death of the anarchist! You should be immediately charged with instigating suicide![9]

and (b) that the Milan bombing was deliberately engineered to detract attention from the political struggles of the left-wing during the hot autumn:

MADMAN: ... Certainly, you are a journalist and you'd really wallow in a scandal of the kind ... you'd just be a bit uneasy to discover that that massacre of innocent people in the bank served solely to bury the struggles of the hot autumn ... to create the right tension so that the citizens themselves, disgusted and indignant about so much subversive violence, would demand a powerful State!   (Dario Fo, *More accidentale di un anarchico*, p. 93)

The 1970s were troubled for 'La Commune'. They were evicted from their premises in Via Colletta, Franca Rame was raped and beaten by a group of fascists, and Dario Fo was imprisoned in Sardinia. There was also a serious crisis within the group, which led to its disbandment.

However, in spite of enormous practical and personal difficulties, Fo and Rame decided that the work must go on. In response to the coup d'état in Chile in September 1973, they mounted the show '*Guerra di popolo in Cile*' (People's War in Chile). This play had a dual purpose, both as a condemnation of the Christian Democrats in Chile and their role in the overthrow of the 'Unidad Popular', and, by drawing an exact parallel, as an attack on the Italian Christian Democrats, who were considered to be the principal enemy in the struggle of the masses.

The group needed a new base, and so they occupied the disused Palazzino Liberty and obtained over 80,000 subscribers. This also became the base of 'Soccorso Rosso', a group formed by Rame in 1972 to aid prisoners. Their first performance in the new premises was '*Non si paga non si paga*' (Can't pay! Won't pay!), about the appropriation of goods by the working classes during an economic crisis. (It is interesting to note that this play, which deals with civil disobedience, was revived in Britain during the civil protests against the Government's introduction of the Poll Tax in early 1990.) This play is exemplary of Fo and Rame's method of taking the material directly from the people, discussing it, reading and rereading and finally debating the play with the people before putting it on stage. Earlier that year, in June 1974, they had responded in the same immediate way to a tragic event; a bomb exploded during an anti-fascist demonstration by trade unions; nine were killed and ten injured. For 'La Comune' this was a clear example of fascist violence, supported by the bosses and the Christian Democrats. They immediately organised a show in the square in Brescia in order to launch a mass debate. The show consisted of a 'presentation', acting of material already within the repertory, and finally testimonies about the massacre, followed by a debate. This format is essential to the theatre of Fo and Rame. It is a 'spettacolo d'intervento' – an immediate theatrical response to a precise political situation – with interventions by those directly involved, with the precise aim of raising consciousness of the urgency of the class struggle:

> The show was not received as a consolatory moment, of passive and external entertainment. It was a real moment of consciousness, which succeeded in proposing the need to wish 'to know more', to understand together how to get organised, what to do. For this reason, unlike the bourgeois theatres where, once the play has finished and been digested, the public gets up and goes, in the square in Brescia no one gets up.[10]

The late 1970s include the plays *'Il Fanfani Rapito'* (Fanfani Kidnapped, 1978) – a caustic satire on the Christian Democrats; *'La marijuana della mamma è la piu bella'* (Mummy's marijuana is the best, 1976) – about the problem of drugs as a means of exploiting the working classes; *'Tutta Casa, Letto e Chiesa'* (All Home, Bed and Church, 1977) – a series of female monologues on the situation of women in society, written by Fo and Rame; and the monologue, *'Storia di una tigre'* (Story of a Tiger, 1979), inspired by a trip to China and dealing with the importance of taking responsibility for one's action. Fo and Rame also appeared again on national television, causing considerable scandal with their politically explosive material.

The 1980s began with the blocking of a visit to the USA: Fo and Rame were refused visas. They toured with *'Clacson, trombette e pernacchi'* (Hooters, Trumpets and Raspberries, 1980), a daring satire which involves the kidnapping of Gianni Agnelli, the owner of Fiat and one of the richest and most powerful men in Italy. Using the theme of a kidnapping, Fo is able to refer throughout the play to the kidnapping of the politician Aldo Moro and the strong-arm tactics used by the government with the terrorists, which led to the killing of Moro. Stuart Hood suggests that this is Fo's last major political work.[11] The reason for this can be found in the gradual eroding of political commitment in the 1980s, within an increasingly materialistic society. However, Fo and Rame's productivity, commitment and success have continued throughout the eighties. Fo produced another one-man show, *'Fabulazzo osceno'* (Obscene Fable, 1982) and he and Rame give seminars and workshops in the USA, London and Edinburgh. Further shows included *'Quasi per caso una donna: Elisabetta'* (Almost by chance a woman: Elizabeth, 1984); *'Parti Femminili: Una Giornata Qualunque; Coppia Aperta* (Female Parts: A Day like Any Other, Open Couple, 1988), by Fo and Rame; and most recently, *'Il papa e la strega'* (The Pope and the Witch, 1990).

TALKING ABOUT WOMEN: FRANCA RAME'S THEATRE

In an interview with Franca Rame I was surprised to learn that, despite her theatrical heritage, her political activity has always been more important than being on stage.[12] She is a woman who has successfully combined the roles of political activist, artist, wife and mother, and she has done this with extraordinary beauty and elegance. Acting just happens to be part of her working life. It is this all-roundedness which gives her particular authority as an interpreter of women's struggles. As Barbara Schulman puts it: 'Hers is a "popular" approach to feminism, a blend of mime, story-telling, burlesque and stand-up comedy – all traditions rooted in popular theatre – which can be appreciated by the masses, not just the converted'.[13] There is nothing intellectual about Rame's feminism, it is too far rooted in every-day reality. On stage she has an in-finite range of expression, flawless technique and an epic detach-ment which is at times devastating in its effect, as, for example, in the monologue 'Lo Stupro', which, through its very detachment, succeeds in being almost unbearingly moving. As Dario Fo puts it: 'the public is amazed and fascinated because it's clear that they have never seen a woman act with such detachment...without forcing...and at the same time manage to achieve so much involvement'.[14]

It is perhaps true to say that the late 1970s and the 1980s have seen a more marked emphasis in the portrayal of women in Fo and Rame's work, although the role of women has central importance throughout, for example, the earlier role of Antonia in *Tutti Uniti! Tutti Insiemi! Ma scusa, quello non è il padrone?* (All united! All together! Sorry, isn't that the boss?, 1971). Here, the events of the class struggles from 1911– 22, the founding of the Italian Communist

Party and the beginnings of fascism are recounted through the formation of the character of a young and fun-loving woman who, through contact with left-wing activists, becomes politically conscious. It is a role which deals with the dignity of women, the refusal of the physical and moral Catholic subjection (of women) to men.[15] At the beginning of the play Antonia is arrested at a 'subversive' meeting place, which she innocently thought was a place for dancing. When interrogated by the police, she simply repeats what she has heard at the meeting place. This makes her the mouthpiece for some strong accusations against the police, the State, and the war in Libya. Disconcerted by what she has heard, she asks the Carabinieri Captain for assurance. She has been told that 'there is no more justice, that justice only belongs to those who command', and that 'you Carabinieri and all the police are "ever faithful", but only to the interests of the bosses'. She begs the Captain to tell her that it is not true:'... calm me down, tell me that all citizens are respected...that it's not a question of having or not having money...that you're not interested in anybody's wallet.'[16] Antonia falls in love with Norbert (or Saxophone, as she calls him), one of the subversives from the meeting place, and marries him. She progresses in the course of the play to the status of a real revolutionary. After shooting the fascist who killed her husband, she laments that she has 'shot the dog, instead of the owner'. What is needed is:

to destroy all of you, all the one thousand, two thousand, ten thousand of you...bosses, bandits, exploiters! All you ten thousand who live on the shoulders of millions of wretches, pulling them by the necks...and they talk about so many robbers... they're just a joke! Every moment, without even saying hands up, you rob someone...every hour, every minute with guns... every hour you kill someone. When will the ones who've been cheated understand...when will they decide...they just need a shake, by God! And you and all your hangers-on chop! We won't save a single one...chop!   (Dario Fo, *Tutti Uniti, Tutti Insiemi*, p. 165)

However, women's issues really come to the fore in a series of plays in which, for the first time, Franca Rame is also author, including *'Tutta Casa, Letto e Chiesa'* (All Home, Bed and Church, 1971), and *'Parti Femminili'* (Female Parts, 1986), consisting of 'Una

Giornata Qualunque' (A Day like Any Other) and 'Una Coppia Aperta' (An Open Couple), and accompanied by the monologue, 'Lo Stupro' (The Rape).

TUTTA CASA, LETTO E CHIESA (All Home, Bed and Church)

Like *Mistero Buffo*, this is a tour de force for an actor. A series of monologues, it deals with the exploitation and repression of women, and, although these are strident issues, it copes with them with strength, humour and resilience. The first piece, 'Il Risveglio' (Waking Up), is a highly amusing and disturbing account of a normal day in the life of a factory worker. Waking up late, she has to quickly see to her baby before taking it to the creche on the way to work. In her rush she carries out a series of comically confused actions, and then realises she cannot find her key. This gives dramatic licence for her to re-enact the events of the previous evening in order to remember what she did with the key. There follows an action-packed and hilarious description of the tormented life of this woman, which turns out to be little more than survival: her monotonous and gruelling work in the factory, her dual role as exploited worker and full-time wife and mother of a demanding baby and husband, her mental disorientation due to tiredness, the impossibility of a fulfilling sentimental life due to lack of time and energy. In spite of the energetic humour, the text states explicitly the double exploitation of the female worker: 'the multinational boss steals your travelling hours from you and you get mad, but you don't get mad about the hours he steals from me...and apart from working for him I'm also your unpaid servant'.[17] Even the institution of the family is seen as having sinister capitalist ends:

> The family, this blessed family was deliberately invented so that all those like you with their nerves shot from the killing work routine come home to their do-everything wife as if she was a big comfy mattress! We turn you out, good as new, for free, so you can go back to the factory nice and refreshed to produce better for the multinational! (*TCLC*, p. 14)

'Una Donna Sola' (A Woman Alone) deals with sexual harassment. Using the device of speaking to a neighbour over the balcony, the nightmare life of this woman emerges. Her husband, utterly jealous, locks her up in the house all day, where she distracts herself by having music blaring in all the rooms while she gets on with the chores. As in the previous monologue, the words are regularly interspersed with the routine actions of the speaker. She is continually pestered by all the men in her life: her husband, who phones incessantly to know what she is doing, and who beats her; her wheelchair-bound brother-in-law, who, when not watching porno-videos, keeps trying to grope her; a peeping Tom across the way; a dirty phone-caller and a love-sick student. She is clearly regarded merely as a sexual object by all of them, even by her husband, who says he loves her:

> he keeps me locked up at home to protect me…he clouts me round the ear…and then he wants to make love…and he couldn't care less if I want to or not. I always have to be ready, like Nescafe… washed, clean, perfumed, shaved, warm, lithe, willing and silent. …I just have to breathe…and make a little noise now and then so he knows I'm there. But I'm not there at all, with my husband, I can't manage to, I don't feel, you know, that word I can't manage to say, it's not easy: orgasm.   (*TCLC*, p. 29)

The monologue ends violently with the surprise revolt of this woman, who burns and squashes the groping hand of the student in the door, pushes the brother-in-law in the wheelchair down the stairs, shoots the peeping Tom, and awaits the arrival of her husband with gun in hand. Both in this piece and in 'Il Risveglio', the male presence is humiliatingly belittled, in the first instance the inert sleeping husband, and in the second the paralysed brother-in-law, in contrast to the active and dynamic woman.

The second part begins with 'La Mamma Fricchettona' (Fricchettona is a Roman dialect word which describes a woman not restricted by the sexual and social conventions of society). The piece is an indictment of the conventional life of the housewife and mother, as supported by the Catholic Church. Once again, the male presence is insignificant: a priest in a confessional. The protagonist, who resembles a gypsy, has run into the confessional to hide from the police. The life of the woman is revealed through the device of her confessing herself. Her life has been turned upside down by love, first by marrying her husband and so ending up with the responsibility of a house and a baby, and secondly by the love of her son, an extreme left-winger. The son runs away from home, and the mother, desperate to find him, disguises herself as a kind of hippy. She leaves behind all the order of conventional life and begins to frequent the 'drop out' circles in an effort to find her son. This becomes a process of liberation for her, and she realises that 'love is disorder! Life, liberty, imagination, they're all disorder … compared with the order you want to give us, Father!' (*TCLC*, p. 53).

'*Abbiamo Tutte la Stessa Storia*' (We All Tell the Same Story) is a hard-hitting fairy-tale about the exploitation of women which exists even between comrades: 'How is it that if one of us doesn't get straight into a comfortable position, up with the slip, down with the knickers, legs spread wide, then she's a prudish shit, with a complex, brought on by a repressed reactionary–imperialistic–capit-alistic–masonic–Catholic–conformist upbringing?' (*TCLC*, p. 57). The tale is about a little girl who has a rag doll which says terrible swear words and longs to be treated badly so she can feel like a 'real woman'. The doll quickly becomes aware of the sting of this conditioning. The little girl grows up and marries a highly pre-sentable engineer. She thinks she is happy but the doll knows better:

> You're an idiot just like I was with the naughty cat, when I pretended to be happy, because after all I had a man, even if he did beat me up I was always his woman. So this prick of an engineer doesn't beat you, but he leaves you here all day like a dummy and he doesn't say a word to you which is even worse, you shit-head.   (*TCLC*, p. 62)

The figure of the rag doll acts as the inner, unrepressed voice of the woman. By listening to and accepting this inner voice the girl is eventually able to feel free.

The monologue 'Medea' is an impassioned plea against the rules of a male-dominated society in which men 'mature' with age and women 'wither'. Medea realises that the women are victims of laws instigated for the convenience of men. Instead of resigning herself to giving up her place as mother and wife to a younger woman, which would be in keeping with the submissive nature of women, she decides to murder her children so that 'a new woman' may be born.

The theatre of Dario Fo and Franca Rame is not easy to reproduce; the leading roles are indelibly stamped with the virtuosity of Fo and Rame, many of the situations are so Italian that they are almost impossible to translate satisfactorily into another language, the acting style must have the right degree of detachment or it may lapse into over-generalised buffoonery. However, the issues of the plays remain universal, hence their success all over the world. Although the writing at times verges on didacticism, and although the plays now have to respond to an increasingly con-sumerist and apathetic society, the strength, sparkling wit and committed struggle of Fo and Rame continues:

This fight for people's rights (garantismo), which has been written off by some fringes of the movement that have now collapsed and dispersed, this fact of still being present within the class struggle, getting involved in factory occupations, in prob-lems regarding, e.g., heroin (like the groups who collect money and organise in order to save young people from addiction) ... all this work is what saves us from collapse, from the disarray that most intellectuals in Italy are falling into. Were it not for that work, we would collapse in the same way.[18]

NOTES

1. Lanfranco Binni, *Attento Te...! Il teatro politico di Dario Fo* (Verona: Bertani, 1975) pp. 222–3.
2. Franca Rame, in the introduction to Dario Fo's *Can't Pay? Won't Pay!* (London: Methuen, 1987).
3. Binni, *Attento Te...!*, p. 224.
4. Franca Rame, in the introduction to Fo, *Can't Pay? Won't Pay?*
5. Dario Fo, in Luigi Allegri, *Dario Fo: Dialogo provocatorio sul comico, il tragico, la follia e la ragione* (Rome and Bari: Laterza, 1990) p. 133.
6. Dario Fo, in Allegri, *Dario Fo* p. 135.
7. Dario Fo, *Mistero Buffo* (Turin: Einaudi, 1977) p. 40.
8. Binni, *Attento Te...!*, p. 73.
9. Dario Fo, *Morte accidentale di un anarchico* (Turin: Einaudi, 1974) p. 37.
10. Binni, *Attento Te...!*, p. 123.
11. Stuart Hood, in the introduction to Dario Fo's *Can't Pay? Won't Pay!*
12. Interview with Franca Rame, Teatro Quirini, Rome, 26 May 1990.
13. Barbara Schulman, 'It's All Bed, Board and Church', *Plays and Players*, July 1982, p. 33.
14. Dario Fo, in L. Allegri, *Dario Fo*, p. 149.

15. Dario Fo, in L. Binni. *Attento Te...!*, p. 43.
16. Dario Fo, *Tutti Uniti! Tutti Insiemi! Ma scusa, quello non è il padrone?* (Turin: Einaudi, 1977) p. 88.
17. Franca Rame and Dario Fo, *Tutta Casa, Letto e Chiesa* (Verona: Bertani, 1978) p. 14; hereafter cited as '(TCLC, p.)'.
18. Dario Fo, in *Dario Fo and Franca Rame Theatre Workshops at Riverside Studios* (London: Red Notes, 1983) p. 60.

Index